Understanding Migration with Macroeconomics

Eugenia Vella • Jordi Caballé • Joan Llull
Editors

Understanding Migration with Macroeconomics

palgrave
macmillan

Editors
Eugenia Vella
University of Sheffield, Sheffield, UK

MOVE, Barcelona, Spain

Jordi Caballé
Universitat Autònoma de Barcelona
Barcelona, Spain

Barcelona GSE, Barcelona, Spain

Joan Llull
MOVE, Barcelona, Spain

Universitat Autònoma de Barcelona
Barcelona, Spain

Barcelona GSE, Barcelona, Spain

ISBN 978-3-030-40980-7 ISBN 978-3-030-40981-4 (eBook)
https://doi.org/10.1007/978-3-030-40981-4

This Palgrave Macmillan imprint is published by the registered company Springer Nature Switzerland AG.
The registered company address is: Gewerbestrasse 11, 6330 Cham, Switzerland

Contents

Notes on Contributors

Guilherme Bandeira holds a Ph.D. from the European University Institute in Florence and is affiliated with the New South Wales Treasury in Australia. Previously, Guilherme worked as a Staff Economist in the Macro-financial Analysis and Monetary Policy Department of the Bank of Spain. His work has appeared in the *International Journal of Central Banking*.

Emily R. Barker is an Economic and Social Research Council (ESRC) funded Ph.D. student at the University of Sheffield, UK, and an associate fellow of the Higher Education Academy. The title of her Ph.D. thesis is "Essays in the Macroeconomics of Migration".

Ekrame Boubtane is Associate Professor of Economics and Fellow of the Centre for Studies and Research on International Development at University Clermont Auvergne in France. She is also Invited Professor at the Paris School of Economics. Her research interests are in international migration. Her work has appeared in the *Journal of Economic Dynamics and Control* and *Oxford Economic Papers,* among others.

Jordi Caballé is Professor of Economics at Universitat Autònoma de Barcelona, fellow of Fundació Markets Organizations and Votes in Economics (MOVE) and affiliated professor at the Barcelona Graduate School of Economics. He holds a Ph.D. from the University of

Pennsylvania. He has authored more than 35 journal articles, and they have appeared in many journals, including *Econometrica*, *Journal of Political Economy*, and *Review of Economic Studies*.

Andri Chassamboulli is Assistant Professor of Economics at the University of Cyprus. Andri holds a Ph.D. from the University of Maryland. Most of her research is on frictional labour markets and immigration. Her research has appeared in journals such as the *International Economic Review* and *Review of Economic Dynamics*.

Emmanuel Comte is a Senior Research Fellow in the area of Migrations at CIDOB, Barcelona Centre for International Affairs. Emmanuel holds a Ph.D. in the History of Europe and of International Relations from Sorbonne University. Previously, he held positions at the European University Institute, the University of California, Berkeley, and the Vienna School of International Studies. He has recently published *The History of the European Migration Regime: Germany's Strategic Hegemony* (Routledge, 2018).

Hippolyte d'Albis is Senior Researcher at CNRS and Professor at the Paris School of Economics. He specializes in population ageing, generational economics, and international migration. He is an associate editor at the *Journal of the Economics of Ageing*, the *Journal of Demographic Economics*, and *Public Finance Review*. His work has appeared in the *Journal of Economic Theory*, *Journal of Mathematical Economics* and *International Economic Review*, among others.

Anna Kyriazi is a Postdoctoral Researcher at the University of Milan. Previously, she was a Postdoctoral Research Fellow at the Institut Barcelona d'Estudis Internacionals. She holds a Ph.D. in Political and Social Sciences from the European University Institute in Florence. She works on comparative ethnicity and nationalism, migration, and political communication. She has published in *Ethnic and Migration Studies* and *Ethnicities* and with top academic publishers.

Eleni Kyrkopoulou is a Postdoctoral Researcher at Athens University of Economics and Business and a Research Analyst at the National Bank of Greece. Her research interests lie in the areas of Labour Economics, Immigration, Crime, and Education.

Joan Llull is Director of Fundació Markets Organizations and Votes in Economics (MOVE), Associate Professor at Universitat Autònoma de Barcelona, and affiliated Professor at the Barcelona Graduate School of Economic. His work has appeared in the *Review of Economic Studies* and the *Journal of Human Resources*, among others. He holds a Starting Grant from the European Research Council. He has editorial positions at *Economic Journal*, *Review of Economic Studies*, *Labour Economics*, and *SERIES*.

Matija Lozej is a Senior Economist at the Central Bank of Ireland, Irish Economic Analysis, Macroeconomic Modelling. Matija holds a Ph.D. from the University of Amsterdam. He has worked with small open economy and multi-country Dynamic Stochastic General Equilibrium models with labour market and financial frictions. His work has appeared in *NBER International Seminar on Macroeconomics*, *International Journal of Central Banking*, and *Labour Economics*, among others.

Theodore Palivos is Professor of Economics at Athens University of Economics and Business. He has also been on the faculty of Louisiana State University and Tilburg University. His research interests are in the areas of Labour Economics, Macroeconomics, and Public Economics. He has served on several editorial boards and as co-editor of the *Journal of Macroeconomics*. He has authored more than 35 journal articles, and they have appeared in many journals, including *American Economic Review*, *Review of Economic Studies*, *International Economic Review*, and *Journal of Economic Theory*.

Eugenia Vella is an Assistant Professor at the University of Sheffield, UK, and Marie Skłodowska-Curie Fellow in Fundació Markets Organizations and Votes in Economics (MOVE) in Barcelona. Previously, she was Jean Monnet and Max Weber Fellow at the European University Institute in Florence. She holds a Ph.D. from the Athens University of Economics and Business. Her work has appeared in the *Journal of International Economics*, *Journal of Economic Dynamics and Control*, and *Economic Inquiry*, among others.

List of Figures

List of Tables

1

Introduction

Eugenia Vella

The UK Independence Party (UKIP), the Front National party led by Marine Le Pen in France, and the Alternative für Deutschland party in Germany all gained prominence in their respective countries with anti-immigration platforms. Anti-immigration positions have underpinned, among others, the Brexit vote in 2016 in the UK and policies of the Trump administration in the United States. In sending countries, such as Southern and Eastern European countries, emigration has been a public concern, too.

In parallel to this political importance of migration, the economics of migration has developed as a major research field (see e.g. the books by Zimmermann and Bauer 2002; Mueller and Mills 2013; Borjas 2014; Chiswick and Miller 2014; Bansak et al. 2015; Borjas et al., 2019; Borjas and Chiswick 2019). There exists an extensive amount of academic work on the microeconomic aspects of migration. Yet, there is still a shortage

E. Vella (✉)
University of Sheffield, Sheffield, UK

MOVE, Barcelona, Spain
e-mail: e.vella@sheffield.ac.uk

E. Vella et al. (eds.), *Understanding Migration with Macroeconomics*,
https://doi.org/10.1007/978-3-030-40981-4_1

of books specifically dealing with the macroeconomics of migration, even though there are macroeconomic factors that can help to explain why migration has become such a debated and contentious topic. Natives often view immigrants as posing threats to jobs and driving down wages. There is also the view that immigrants are a fiscal drain for the host economy, especially when, unable to secure a job, they benefit from public services without contributing. Natives also have a tendency to perceive unemployed immigrants as indulging in illegal and criminal activities. Conversely, others recognise that immigrants help the host economy grow through a variety of channels: by providing a different set of skills and being complementary to the local labour force, by easing labour supply shortages, and by stimulating aggregate demand in the economy through their demand of goods and services. The fiscal contribution of immigrants is more significant when immigrants are younger than natives, especially of working age, and occupy high-skilled positions.

In the economics of migration, there is already a number of studies with a microeconomic focus. Topics of interest include the effects of migration on wages and employment, both for immigrant and native workers (e.g. Borjas 2003; Ottaviano and Peri 2012; Dustmann et al. 2010), the impact of immigration on public finances (e.g. Borjas 1999; Storesletten 2000; Dustmann and Frattini 2014), on productivity (e.g. Peri 2012), on prices and the composition of demand (e.g. Lach 2007; Cortes 2008), and on house prices (e.g. Saiz 2003; Sá 2014). Yet, the links between migration and macroeconomic aggregates, such as per capita GDP, remain little explored.

This book aims to fill this gap by providing a brief but multifaceted overview of the macroeconomics of migration as a research field. This book is an edited collection of, but not limited to, contributions from participants in a workshop on the macroeconomics of migration that took place at the University of Sheffield in June 2018. The chapters analyse, both empirically and theoretically, the challenges that international migration poses both for sending and receiving countries. They touch upon several current debates related to the labour market effects of migration for natives, taxation and emigration, migration and the informal economy, migration and business cycles, and brain waste. This book thus provides a first step to a comprehensive synthesis of the macroeconomics of migration. In addition, this book aims to connect the macroeconomics of migration with the rest of the field of migration studies. To this end, the last chapter, which is co-authored by a historian and a political scientist, evaluates the new insights that this book offers for the other disciplines in that field, including history, sociology, and political science. This chapter also offers suggestions on the way to enhance further interdisciplinary collaboration between macroeconomics and other disciplines in the field of migration studies. The authors of the volume include both academics from several countries—including the UK, France, Spain, Austria, Greece, and Cyprus—as well as practitioners from the Central Bank of Ireland and the New South Wales Treasury in Australia. Finally, the book targets not only academics, but also practitioners and policymakers who wish to take a closer look at the macroeconomic effects of migration and learn about the current challenges posed by immigration or emigration.

This introductory chapter offers an overview of the recent migration trends by focusing on European countries for two reasons. Firstly, there has been a gradual convergence in labour mobility between Europe and the United States in recent years, reflecting both a fall in interstate migration in the United States and a rise in the role of migration in Europe (Beyer and Smets 2015). Secondly, the literature on Europe so far is less developed than the literature on the United States. This chapter then summarises the state of the art in the macroeconomics of migration up to now, before synthesising the findings of the various chapters included in this volume.

1.1 Recent Migration Trends in European Countries

Based on data from Eurostat, this section highlights three recent migration trends in Europe.[1] First, the share of immigrants increased between 2009 and 2017 in the 15 older European Union (EU) member states, with the exception of peripheral countries. Second, following the unfavourable socioeconomic conditions created by the Great Recession and subsequent debt crisis, many peripheral countries shifted away from being host countries to being sender countries. Third, although immigrants tend to be younger compared to natives, their level of educational attainment relative to that of natives varies among the EU15 countries.

According to the data for 2017 presented in Fig. 1.1, Austria displays the largest share of immigrants (i.e. foreign-born) in its population among the EU15 countries.[2] Nearly 19% of Austria's population are foreign-born, with just under half of them born in the European Economic Area (EEA).[3] In the UK, immigrants amount to around 14% of the population. The share of EEA immigrants in the overall British population equals 5.5%, that is nearly 40% of immigrants. In Greece, 11.6% of the population are immigrants, with a bit less than 30% among them being EEA immigrants. The reason is the proximity of Greece to major emigration countries in the Middle East and North Africa.

Next, Fig. 1.2 shows the percentage change in the share of immigrants in EU15 countries between 2009 and 2017. Finland experienced the fastest increase in the share of immigrants in the overall population, with an increase of 58% in 8 years. The UK experienced the fastest increase concerning EEA immigrants. Their share in the British population

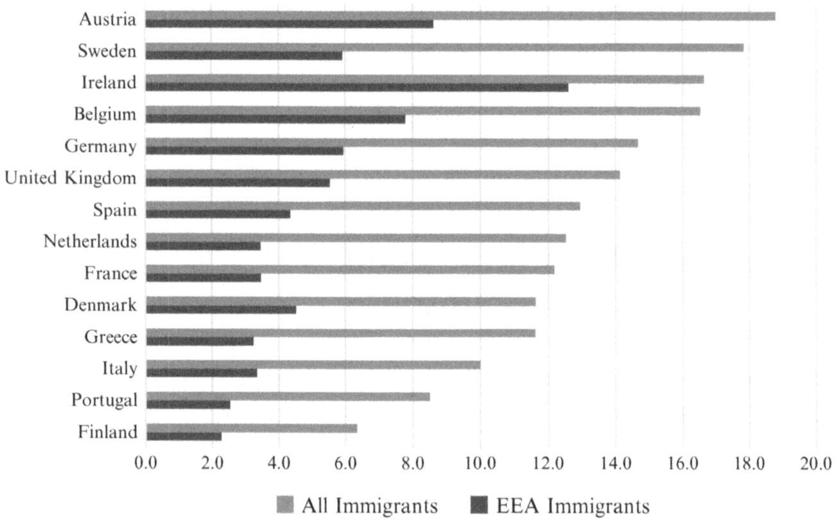

Fig. 1.1 Population share (%) of immigrants in EU15 countries (except for Luxembourg), 2017. (Source: Eurostat)

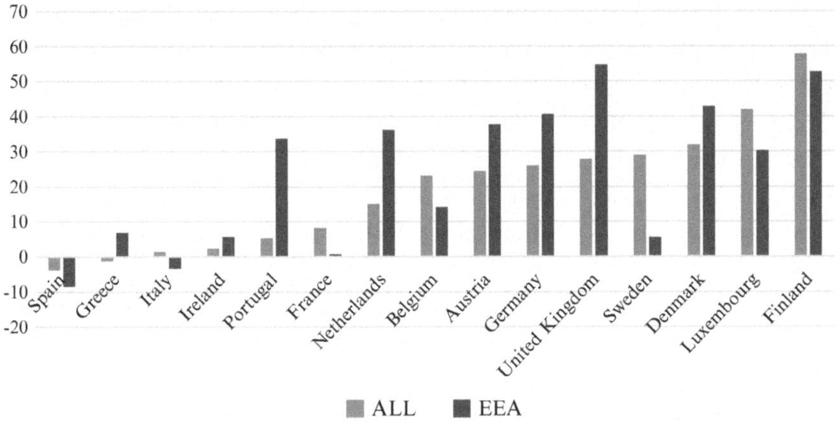

Fig. 1.2 Percentage change in immigrant population share in EU15 countries, 2009–2017. (Source: Eurostat)

climbed from 3.6% in 2009 to 5.5% in 2017. However, following the Brexit vote, this trend started to reverse. Data from the UK's Office for National Statistics (ONS) show that net long-term migration from the EU amounted to only 101,000 in 2017—the lowest figure since 2013. By contrast, Fig. 1.2 shows that Spain and Greece experienced a decrease in the foreign-born share of the population from 2009 to 2017 and other peripheral countries experienced the smallest change in immigrant share. The reason is that, following the Great Recession and subsequent debt crisis, there was a particularly strong surge in unemployment in Europe's peripheral countries, such as Portugal, Italy, Ireland, Greece, and Spain, for example. There was also a policy course of austerity measures, which included taxation, cuts to social benefits, and restrictions to recruiting new public sector employees. In these unfavourable economic conditions, the pattern of migration flows in these countries changed. Those recent hosting countries of immigration experienced a surge in emigration of workers looking for more favourable employment opportunities, often in the so-called core countries of Europe. In Spain and Greece, as a result of the crisis, both natives and recent immigrants were among the emigrants.

Figure 1.3 takes a closer look at the case of peripheral countries. In these countries, immigration outweighed emigration until the crisis, when this trend reversed. By 2011, Ireland, Greece, Portugal, and Spain all experienced higher outflows than inflows. Inflows remained higher than outflows in Italy, but with a significantly decreasing difference. There are at least two factors behind the Italian case. Italy's unemployment rate was not as dramatically affected as the other countries' (see Table 1.1). Also, the Italian government granted significant reductions of the taxable employment income to highly skilled workers in an effort to incentivise the entry and return of such workers. From 2016, immigration outstripped again emigration in Ireland, Greece, and Spain. Besides the recovery after the Great Recession, this recent trend has also to do

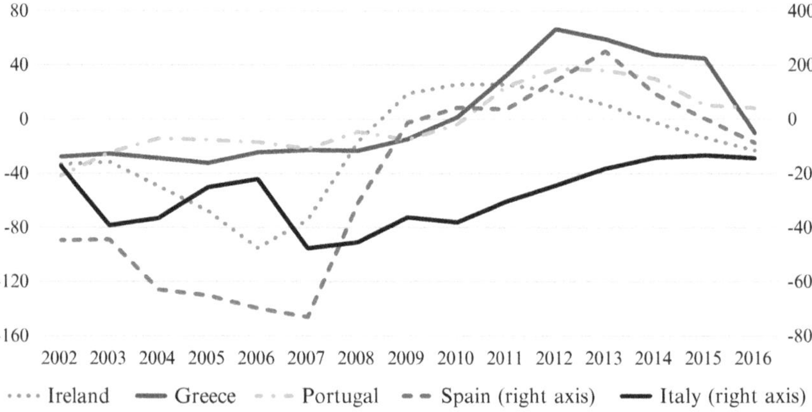

Fig. 1.3 Net migration flows (outflows-inflows) for Europe's peripheral countries in thousands of people, 2002–2016. (Source: Eurostat)

Table 1.1 Unemployment rates in Europe's periphery (% active population), annual averages

	2009	2010	2011	2012	2013	2014	2015	2016
Ireland	12.6	14.6	15.4	15.5	13.8	11.9	10.0	8.4
Greece	9.6	12.7	17.9	24.5	27.5	26.5	24.9	23.6
Spain	17.9	19.9	21.4	24.8	26.1	24.5	22.1	19.6
Italy	7.7	8.4	8.4	10.7	12.1	12.7	11.9	11.7
Portugal	10.7	12.0	12.9	15.8	16.4	14.1	12.6	11.2

Source: Eurostat

with the large surge in immigrants from the Middle East and North Africa. The Mediterranean is the gateway for Europe and, as a result, Spain, Italy, and Greece (along with Cyprus) have been the main recipients of those migrants.

As far as the educational profile of migrants is concerned, Fig. 1.4 compares educational attainment between native-born and foreign-born in 2017. At the EU level, we can see that on average immigrants appear to be less educated than natives. Around 32% of immigrants have not attained more than a level of lower secondary education, compared to 21% of natives. In Greece, Italy, and Spain, immigrants' levels of education are even lower. In a striking contrast, in Portugal and Ireland, immigrants are better educated than natives. In Portugal the level of education of the native population is lower than at the EU level. In Ireland, nearly 52% of immigrants have attained tertiary education. At the EU level, a similar share of immigrants and natives have attained a tertiary level of education. Yet, immigrants are often—at least initially—underemployed. An OECD report has found that overqualification is more prevalent among recent immigrants than settled immigrants (OECD 2017). Finally, migrants are typically younger than natives (Fig. 1.5).

What follows presents additional evidence on immigrants in Germany and the UK—Europe's most important destination countries. Germany is the second largest immigration country in the industrialised world, after the United States. According to Eurostat data for 2017, immigrants represent 14.7% of the country's total population. Using data from Germany's Federal Statistics Office (DESTATIS), Figs. 1.6 and 1.7 show the substantial increase in arrivals of migrants from Europe's periphery including Eastern and Southern countries. These flows resulted from the adverse labour market conditions in these countries in the aftermath of the Great Recession and from the recent enlargement of the EU to some Central and Eastern European countries.

In addition, as a result of the Syrian civil war, Europe experienced large migration flows from that country, in addition to flows from other war-torn countries, including Afghanistan and Iraq. Germany received the greatest number of asylum applications. Table 1.2, using UN Refugee Agency data, shows the evolution of the number of refugees in Germany since 2013. This cohort of refugees enters the German labour market.

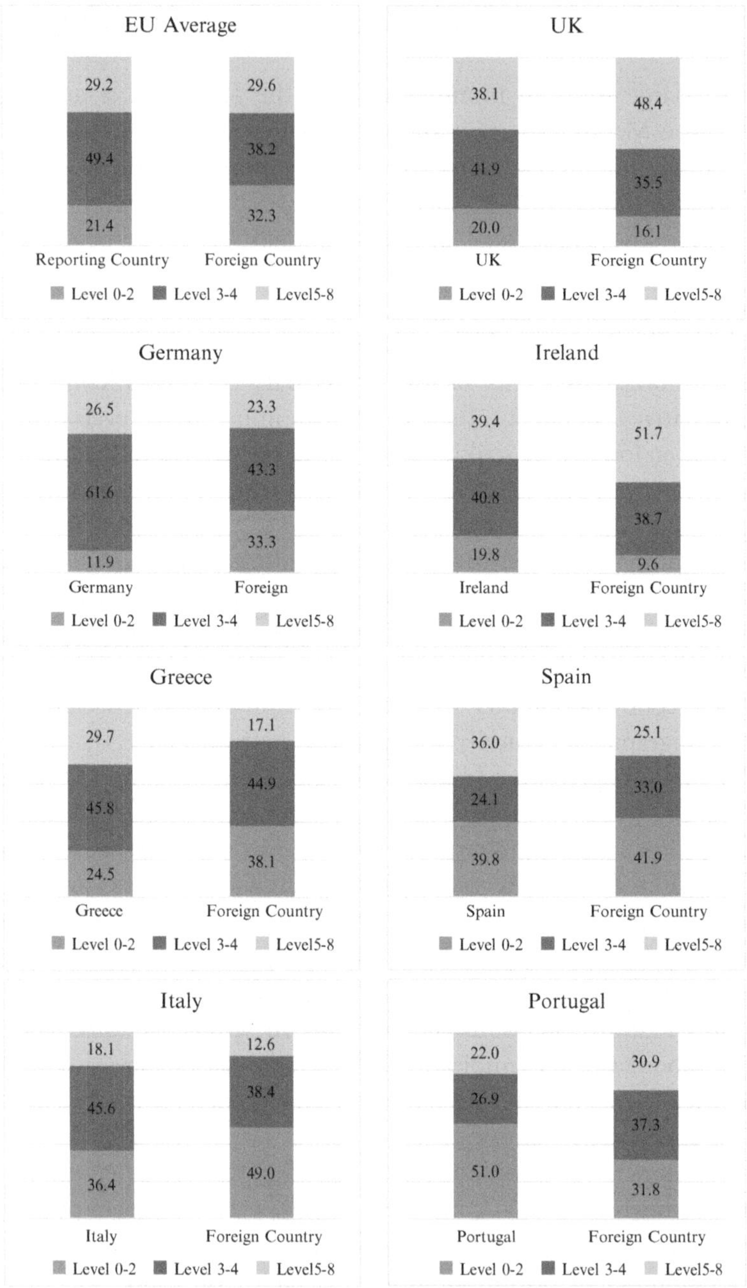

Fig. 1.4 Education attainment by country of birth, 2017. Note: Level 0–2: less than primary, primary and lower secondary education; Level 3–4: upper secondary and post-secondary non-tertiary education; Level 5–8: tertiary education. (Source: Eurostat)

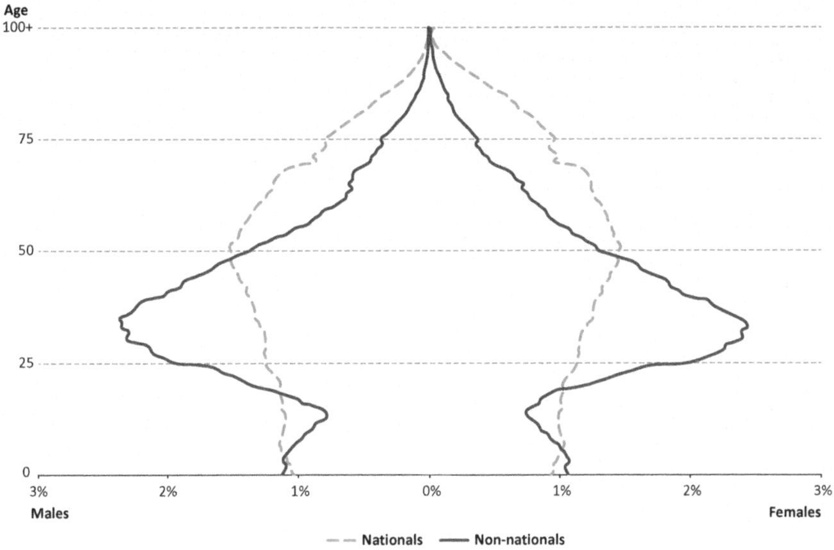

Fig. 1.5 Age structure of the national and non-national populations (%), EU28, 1 January 2016. (Source: Eurostat)

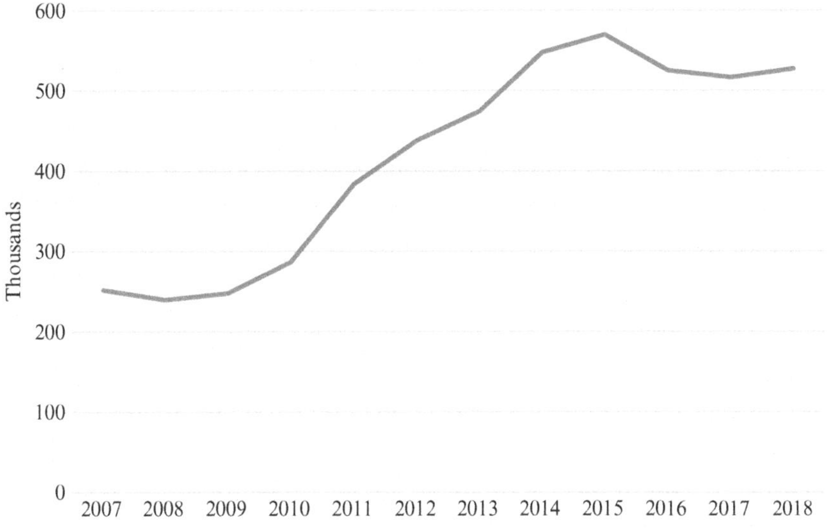

Fig. 1.6 Sum of migration inflows (in thousands) to Germany from Romania, Bulgaria, Poland, Romania, Slovakia, Latvia, Hungary. (Source: Destatis)

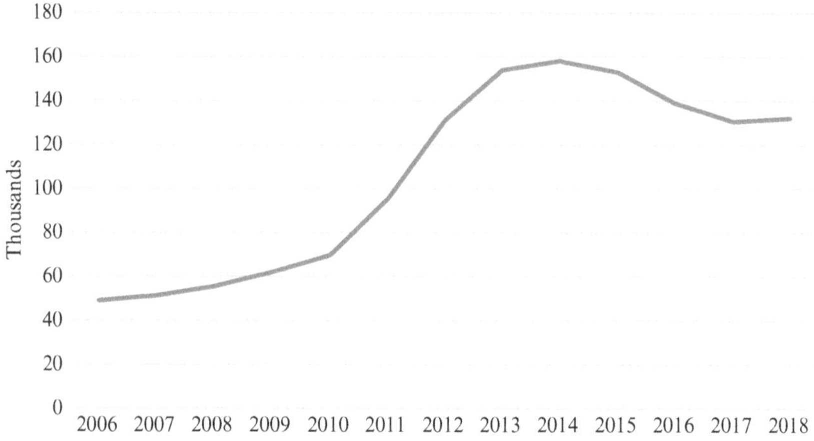

Fig. 1.7 Sum of migration inflows (in thousands) to Germany from Portugal, Ireland, Greece, Spain. (Source: Destatis)

Table 1.2 Number of refugees in Germany

Year	Number of refugees
2013	187,600
2014	217,000
2015	316,100
2016	669,400

Source: UN Refugee Agency (UNHCR)

Figure 1.8 provides evidence that immigrants in Germany are younger than natives. A large proportion of non-nationals are around the 30-year-old age bracket, that is more than 23% of non-nationals are between 25 and 35 years of age, against close to 13% of the national population.

Figure 1.9 breaks down educational attainment in Germany by country of birth and shows that immigrants are less educated than natives. Just below 12% of those born in Germany have attained lower secondary education or less, while the corresponding figures for the EU28 and non-EU28 born are 24% and 38% respectively. Table 1.3 shows a slight increase in educational attainment among foreign-born in Germany between 2008 and 2017. The proportion of those with, at most, lower secondary education has declined and the proportion of those with tertiary education has increased. Although German natives also tend to have

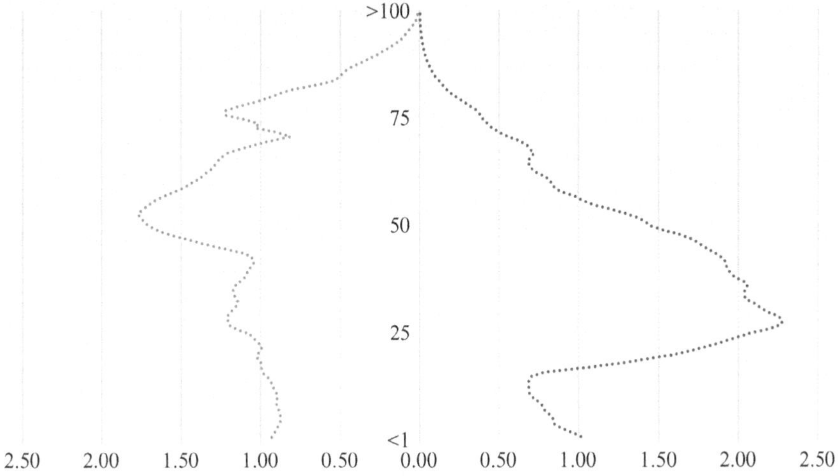

Fig. 1.8 Age structure of the national (left) and non-national (right) populations (%), Germany, 2017. (Source: Eurostat)

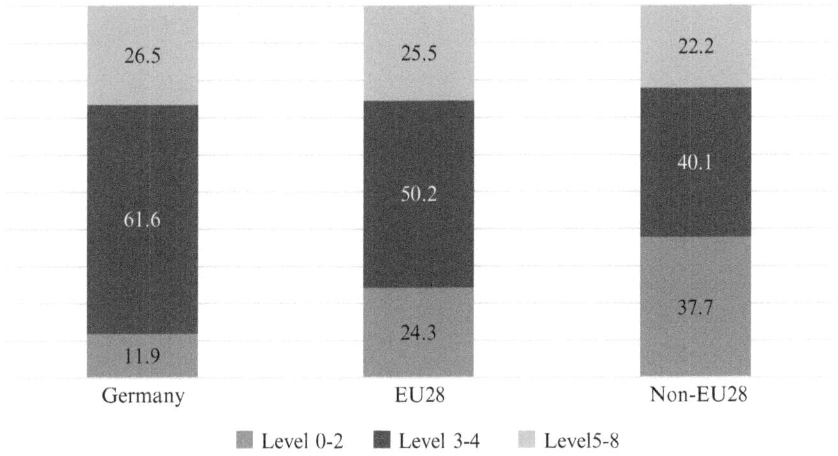

Fig. 1.9 Educational attainment in Germany by country of birth, 2017. Note: Level 0–2: less than primary, primary and lower secondary education; Level 3–4: upper secondary and post-secondary non-tertiary education; Level 5–8: tertiary education. (Source: Eurostat)

Table 1.3 Educational attainment of foreign born (% population), Germany

	2008	2017
Level 0–2	37.6	33.3
Level 3–4	44.4	43.3
Level 5–8	18.0	23.3

Source: Eurostat

Note: Level 0–2: less than primary, primary and lower secondary education; Level 3–4: upper secondary and post-secondary non-tertiary education; Level 5–8: tertiary education

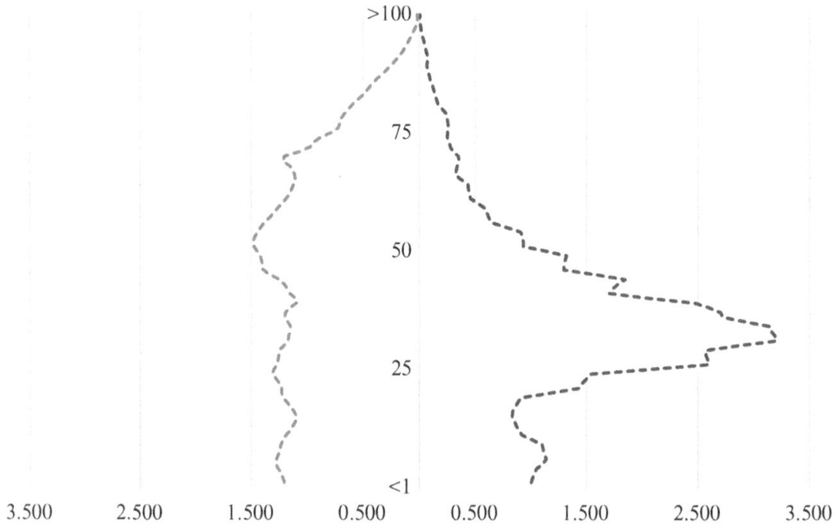

Fig. 1.10 Age structure of the national (left) and non-national (right) populations in the UK, 2017. (Source: Eurostat)

higher educational attainment, the increase is not as significant as in the case of immigrants.

In the UK, the share of immigrants was just above 14% of the population in 2017. Figure 1.10 compares the age structure of nationals (left) and non-nationals (right) in the UK. A larger share of the non-nationals is aged between 25 and 35 than in the national population: 31.5% against 13.2%.

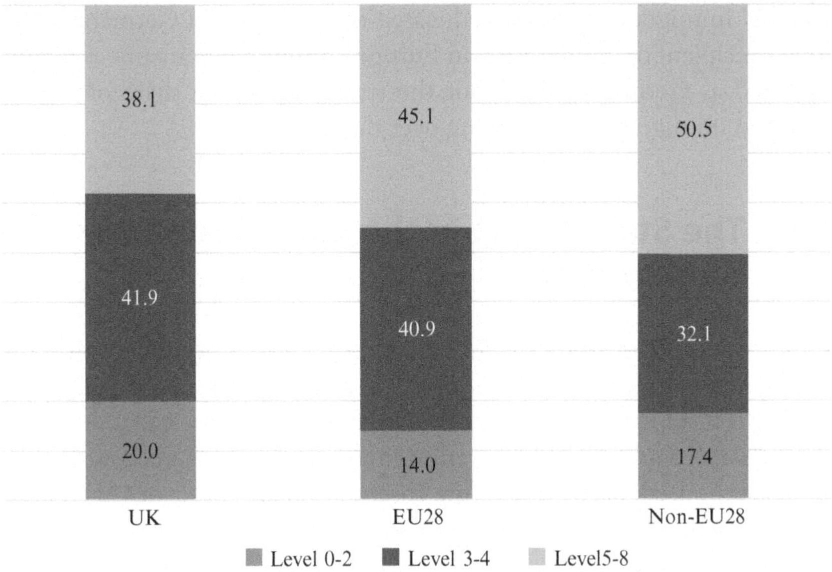

Fig. 1.11 Educational attainment in the UK by country of birth, 2017. Note: Level 0–2: less than primary, primary and lower secondary education; Level 3–4: upper secondary and post-secondary non-tertiary education; Level 5–8: tertiary education. (Source: Eurostat)

Compared to those born in the UK, both EU28 and non-EU28 born are less likely to be categorised among the least educated. Moreover, immigrants are more likely to have attained tertiary-level education (see Fig. 1.11). However, although immigrants have on average attained a greater level of education, this is not correlated with being employed in an appropriate skill-level occupation (Dustmann et al. 2013).

To sum up, among the EU15 countries, the share of immigrants in the population has increased between 2009 and 2017. Due to unfavourable socioeconomic conditions following the Great Recession, this has not happened in certain European peripheral countries, where migration outflows outweighed inflows. In Italy, fiscal policies, in the form of tax cuts, incentivised the retention or the return of high-skilled workers. Immigrants in Europe typically are younger and possess a lower level of education than natives. The UK, Ireland, and Portugal are exceptions as far as educational attainment is concerned. In the UK, both EU and non-EU immigrants are more educated than natives. In Germany—the largest recipient of immigration in Europe—immigrants are not as highly educated as German natives, but the trend is that the share of highly educated immigrants is increasing over time.

1.2 The State of Art in the Macroeconomics of Migration

While a number of studies have analysed the impact of immigration on employment and wages with disaggregate data, a systematic investigation of the effects of immigration on standard macroeconomic variables is still missing. The amount of immigration literature using macroeconometric models is limited, partly due to the absence in many countries of reliable quarterly series for net immigration over a sufficiently long period of time.

Using a Structural Vector Autoregressive (SVAR) estimation, Furlanetto and Robstad (2019) have recently proposed a new identification scheme that enables to disentangle immigration shocks from other macroeconomic shocks. They do so by imposing sign restrictions on a sample of Norwegian quarterly data over the period 1990–2014. Notably, immigration is an endogenous variable in the model and can respond to the state of the economy. The authors find that an exogenous immigration shock lowers unemployment, has a positive effect on prices and on public finances in the medium run, no impact on house prices and household credit, and a negative effect on productivity. Other recent contributions include Kiguchi and Mountford (2019) who provide an analysis based on US annual data. They show that a shock to the working population (coming from immigration but could also be due to domestic factors) results in a temporary reduction in GDP and consumption per capita. D'Albis et al. (2016) use monthly data for France over the period 1994–2008 in a SVAR model where identification of shocks is based on a recursive scheme. The results indicate that immigration responds significantly to France's macroeconomic conditions and increases GDP per capita. Two other analyses focus on New Zealand—a country for which detailed data on immigration flows is available. In the first, McDonald

(2013) studies the effect of an immigration shock on house prices in a SVAR identified with a recursive scheme. He shows that an immigration shock has a strong positive effect on house prices and construction activity, thus boosting aggregate demand even more than aggregate supply. The second study, by Armstrong and McDonald (2016), extends the previous set-up to include a second immigration shock associated with fluctuations in unemployment in Australia—New Zealand's main neighbouring country. The results indicate that higher net immigration in New Zealand due to a higher unemployment rate in Australia leads to a higher unemployment rate in New Zealand, whereas higher net immigration for other reasons reduces unemployment in New Zealand.

Emigration from OECD countries to the rest of the world is routinely missing from this literature. More generally, there is a prevailing research focus on immigration rather than emigration, which can be partly explained by the absence of comprehensive data in emigration countries and by the fact that policies can influence immigration rates more easily than emigration rates. A notable exception is the study by Docquier et al. (2013), which constructs a database that provides bilateral migrant stocks by education level for 195 origin/destination countries for 1990 and 2000. The authors find that emigration had a negative effect on the wages of the less educated natives, ranging between 0% and −7%, and increased inequality within countries.[4] This study also documents that positive selection on skills and education characterises emigration from both poor and OECD countries.

Finally, regarding the macroeconomic determinants of migration, for which existing literature is still very limited, Lewis and Swannell (2018) have recently estimated a gravity model of the determinants of migration flows using pairwise data from around 160 origin countries to 35 advanced economy destinations over the period 1990–2013. When they interact the various explanatory variables with freedom of movement, they find that the elasticities of migration with respect to macroeconomic variables are not constant across country pairs. Under freedom of movement, the response to macroeconomic variables is stronger, and the response to distance and historical migrant stocks is weaker. However, the elasticity with regard to linguistic and historical variables remains constant. Migration flows are also higher to (from) destinations (origins) with stronger (weaker) expected GDP growth. In addition, greater labour market flexibility in destination countries is associated with higher inward migration.

In the macroeconomic theory with a focus on migration, reviewed more extensively in Chap. 7, earlier contributions include that by Canova and Ravn (2000), who studied the macroeconomic impact of unskilled migration in the neo-classical growth model, and that by Bentolila et al. (2008), who showed how immigration flattens the slope of the New Keynesian Phillips curve in Spain. In a two-country setting, Mandelman and Zlate (2012) have proposed a Dynamic Stochastic General Equilibrium (DSGE) model with immigration studying the role of remittances for business cycles in Mexico. More recent contributions, building on stylised DSGE models with net migration, include Bandeira et al. (2019), Smith and Thoenissen (2019), and Lozej (2019) with a focus on Greece, New Zealand, and Ireland, respectively, while Hauser and Seneca (2019) study the US case.

1.3 An Overview of the Chapters in This Volume

The contributions of this volume analyse, using empirical and theoretical methodologies, the effects of international migration in sending and receiving countries. The topics included touch upon several important issues in the current debates related to the labour market effects of migration for natives, the bi-directional relation between taxation and emigration, migration and the informal economy, business cycle amplification from migration, and brain waste.

The chapters are grouped in two main sections. The first section presents empirical evidence on topics such as the impact of immigration on productivity, the macroeconomic and fiscal consequences of migration in OECD countries, and brain waste. The authors of the chapters in the second section use as a workhorse (and also extend) the search and matching model, both in continuous and discrete time, to study topics related to the labour market effects of migration and its interaction with taxation. The chapters in the second section perform both steady-state and DSGE analysis, considering both Real Business Cycle and New Keynesian channels.

Starting with the section of the book on empirical evidence, the chapter by Llull ties the volume to the recent burgeoning literature on the microeconomic effects of immigration, coming mostly from labour economics. Llull presents a cross-country analysis of the impact of immigration on productivity and employment. The chapter begins by discussing how the large existing literature on the microeconomic effects of immigration informs the content presented here and how its findings can help solve existing disagreements within that literature. In terms of methodology, push-distance interactions provide relevant and exogenous variation for identification. The results obtained suggest that one percentage point increase in the immigrants' share in the population reduces GDP per capita by 2%, the employment rate by 0.89 percentage points, and average hours worked by 1.28%, while the unemployment rate rises by 0.55 percentage points. Back-of-the-envelope calculations based on a simple production framework provide a structural interpretation of these results. Estimates imply a semi-elasticity of native wages to immigration of −0.7 if the extensive margin of labour supply is ignored and +0.12 on the wages of those who remain working. The effect on immigrant wages is unambiguously negative.

In the next chapter, d'Albis and Boubtane provide empirical evidence on the macroeconomic and fiscal consequences of international migration for OECD countries. The authors use a panel of 19 countries over the period 1980–2015 to study the effects of increases in the net migration rate on per capita GDP and on both the employment rate and the share of working age in total population. Their main econometric tool of analysis is the SVAR model. Moreover, they study the effect of exogenous changes in fiscal balance by decomposing the effects of net taxes and public spending. The empirical evidence is discussed using recent findings of the theoretical literature.

In the last chapter of the first section, Barker discusses the economics of migrants experiencing brain waste. Brain waste, including underemployment, occurs when the country hosting a skilled migrant fails to fully recognise the skills of the worker. The workers experience a skill-job mismatch, relatively higher unemployment, or weaker powers in the labour market including lower wage levels. The problem of brain waste is of a varying severity across migrant host nations, influenced by migration policy and profile of the economy. The chapter presents a rich set of stylised facts with a focus on Canada as a destination economy for migrants.

The second section of the book offers a collection of essays using as a workhorse the search and matching model to study topics related to the labour market effects of migration and its interaction with taxation. In the first chapter of this section, Chassamboulli discusses recent research on the effect of immigration policies on job creation on the basis of a search and matching model in continuous time. New findings show that various types of immigrants can have a positive impact on employers' incentives to post vacancies and create new jobs, which benefits also competing natives. Policies that restrict the presence of foreign workers in the labour market are less beneficial to natives than policies that do not decrease immigration, but instead shift its composition towards the types of immigrants that benefit the natives the most. This chapter explores one such policy combination that eliminates illegal immigration but allows for foreigners to enter on temporary work permits. Chassamboulli shows that this policy can help attenuate the negative job creation effect of fewer illegal immigrants in the market.

In the following chapter, Kyrkopoulou and Palivos examine the interaction between the informal sector of the economy and undocumented immigration. For this purpose, they use a search and matching model in continuous time, with a formal and an informal sector. Native workers can work in both sectors, whereas undocumented immigrants can work only in the latter. Both native workers and firms choose optimally the sector in which they operate, balancing costs and benefits, for example, taxation versus unemployment benefits and severance payments in the case of workers and taxation and auditing versus subsidies in the case of firms. The chapter analyses and compares the effects of three types of policies, namely deterrence, incentive, and immigration policies, while also considering combinations of these policies.

The next chapter by Bandeira, Caballé, and Vella is motivated by the fiscal austerity measures implemented in peripheral countries of Europe during the recent debt crisis and the surge in emigration that these economies experienced. They make use of a small open economy model in discrete time, with search and matching frictions and sticky prices, in a DSGE framework. The authors first show that a negative productivity shock increases the job search abroad of the unemployed, with a positive short-run impact on the unemployment of stayers, while it also reinforces the negative consumption effects of the shock and therefore can lead to higher unemployment costs over time. They then study a particular type of fiscal consolidation: the one carried out through an increase in consumption tax rates. The goal is to shed light on the macroeconomic links between VAT hikes and emigration. The results indicate that VAT hikes induce a fall in private consumption demand, which reduces labour demand and increases emigration. The departure of emigrants reinforces the fall in internal demand and employment relative to an economy without labour mobility. This implies that, over time, the unemployment costs of tax-based consolidation are reinforced by emigration. However, these effects are significantly smaller than in the case of labour income tax hikes.

Continuing in a DSGE framework, Lozej studies in the following chapter the business cycle amplification resulting from migration using a search and matching model in discrete time. The chapter presents results to a positive productivity shock and a positive shock to matching efficiency, with both increasing the attractiveness of the economy as host for immigrants. Migration interacts with the domestic labour market through the increase in labour supply from immigration when labour market conditions improve and, consequently, labour market tightness increases. The chapter argues that this leads to an amplification mechanism when there are search frictions, because it becomes more profitable for firms to post vacancies when labour supply is abundant. Unlike in the standard Beveridge curve relationship, the number of searching workers in the labour market and the number of vacancies can move in the same direction, which leads to a sharp increase in employment and aggregate output. Compared to an economy where there is no migration, such mechanism can lead to a substantial amplification of business cycle fluctuations, which can also become more persistent.

Finally, in the last part of this book, a historian and a political scientist, Comte and Kyriazi respectively, evaluate the new insights that the contributions in this volume offer through the research methods of macroeconomists for other disciplines, namely history and political science. They show that macroeconomic research could help to develop the economic history of migration, the history of the European Union, and the history of the conflicts surrounding immigration. Conversely, they propose integrating in macroeconomic analysis the historical and political construction of labour markets. They detail how increasing politicisation of migration in the context of gradually eroding political borders calls for innovative thinking that transcends disciplinary boundaries. Last, they point to a number of ways in which macroeconomic findings could be more firmly anchored in their political and historical context and offer suggestions on how interdisciplinary collaboration can be enhanced through common projects on current debates in the field of migration studies.

Acknowledgements Financial support through the EU Horizon 2020 Marie Sklodowska-Curie Grant 798015 (EuroCrisisMove) is greatfully acknowledged. Harvey Stafford provided excellent research assistance for Section 1.1 of this chapter.

Notes

1. Eurostat's population statistics contain data on the stock and flows of migrants. Net migration statistics are also provided by taking the difference between the change in total population and the estimated change in the natural population, that is the change due to mortality and natality. The major advantage of this statistic is that it is available for the majority of EU countries and there is an extended time series. At the same time, certain limitations arise due to the fact that estimation of population changes depended on each country's administrative records, which are not always up to date. Therefore, statistical adjustments are often required (e.g. census-related revisions). Eurostat population statistics also contain comprehensive statistics (often since 2008) of the population by either citizenship or country of birth. This statistic directly captures migration and not on a residual basis. However, this statistic is again not without

limitations. Administrative records are often inaccurate, and furthermore, said records suffer from impact comparability.
2. Luxembourg is omitted due to its population of less than 1 million, which leads to a large immigrant share.
3. The European Economic Area unites EU member states with Iceland, Liechtenstein, and Norway (the EFTA) to form the 'single market', enabling the free movement of goods, services, capital, and people. Note that this statistic excludes the reporting country.
4. For additional studies focusing on emigration, rather than immigration, see the review of the literature in Chap. 7.

References

Armstrong, Jed, and Chris McDonald. *Why the drivers of migration matter for the labour market.* No. AN2016/02. Reserve Bank of New Zealand, 2016.

Bansak, Cynthia, Nicole B. Simpson, and Madeline Zavodny. *The Economics of Immigration*. Routledge, 2015.

Bandeira, Guilherme, Jordi Caballé, and Eugenia Vella, Fiscal austerity and Greek emigration: A missing link, Barcelona GSE Working Papers Series no 1075, 2019.

Bentolila, Samuel, Juan J. Dolado, and Juan F. Jimeno. "Does immigration affect the Phillips curve? Some evidence for Spain." *European Economic Review* 52, no. 8 (2008): 1398–1423.

Beyer, Robert CM, and Frank Smets. "Labour market adjustments and migration in Europe and the United States: How different?." *Economic Policy* 30, no. 84 (2015): 643–682.

Borjas, George J., and Barry R. Chiswick. *Foundations of Migration Economics*. Oxford University Press, 2019.

Borjas, George J., Barry R. Chiswick, and Benjamin Elsner. *Foundations of Migration Economics*. Oxford University Press, 2019: 659.

Borjas, George J. *Immigration Economics*. Harvard University Press, 2014.

Borjas, George J. "The labor demand curve is downward sloping: Reexamining the impact of immigration on the labor market." *The Quarterly Journal of Economics* 118, no. 4 (2003): 1335–1374.

Borjas, George J. "Immigration and welfare magnets." *Journal of Labor Economics* 17, no. 4 (1999): 607–637.

Canova, Fabio, and Morten O. Ravn. "The macroeconomic effects of German unification: Real adjustments and the welfare state." *Review of Economic Dynamics* 3, no. 3 (2000): 423–460.

Chiswick, Barry, and Paul W. Miller, eds. *Handbook of the Economics of International Migration: The Impact.* Elsevier, 2014.

Cortes, Patricia. "The effect of low-skilled immigration on US prices: evidence from CPI data." *Journal of Political Economy* 116, no. 3 (2008): 381–422.

d'Albis, Hippolyte, Ekrame Boubtane, and Dramane Coulibaly. "Immigration policy and macroeconomic performance in France." *Annals of Economics and Statistics/Annales d'Économie et de Statistique* 121/122 (2016): 279–308.

Docquier, Frédéric, Çağlar Ozden, and Giovanni Peri. "The labour market effects of immigration and emigration in OECD countries." *The Economic Journal* 124, no. 579 (2013): 1106–1145.

Dustmann, Christian, and Tommaso Frattini. "The fiscal effects of immigration to the UK." *The Economic Journal* 124, no. 580 (2014): F593-F643.

Dustmann, Christian, Tommaso Frattini, and Ian P. Preston. "The effect of immigration along the distribution of wages." *Review of Economic Studies* 80, no. 1 (2013): 145–173.

Dustmann, Christian, Albrecht Glitz, and Thorsten Vogel. "Employment, wages, and the economic cycle: Differences between immigrants and natives." *European Economic Review* 54, no. 1 (2010): 1–17.

Furlanetto, Francesco, and Ørjan Robstad. "Immigration and the macroeconomy: Some new empirical evidence." *Review of Economic Dynamics* 34 (2019): 1–19.

Hauser, Daniela, and Martin Seneca. *Labor Mobility in a Monetary Union.* No. 19–15. Bank of Canada, 2019.

Kiguchi, Takehiro, and Andrew Mountford. "Immigration and unemployment: A macroeconomic approach." *Macroeconomic Dynamics* 23, no. 4 (2019): 1313–1339.

Lach, Saul. "Immigration and prices." *Journal of Political Economy* 115, no. 4 (2007): 548–587.

Lewis, John, and Matt Swannell. *The Macroeconomic Determinants of Migration.* No. 729. Bank of England Staff Working Paper, 2018.

Lozej, Matija. "Economic migration and business cycles in a small open economy with matching frictions." *Economic Modelling* 81 (2019): 604–620.

Mandelman, Federico S., and Andrei Zlate. "Immigration, remittances and business cycles." *Journal of Monetary Economics* 59, no. 2 (2012): 196–213.

McDonald, Chris. *Migration and the housing market*. Reserve Bank of New Zealand, 2013.

Mueller, Charles F., and Edwin S. Millls. *The Economics of Labor Migration: A Behavioral Analysis*, Academic Press, 2013.

OECD. (2017). "Over-qualification rates of recent and settled migrants, 2015", in *International Migration Outlook 2017*, OECD Publishing, Paris, doi:https://doi.org/10.1787/migr_outlook-2017-graph33-en.

Ottaviano, Gianmarco IP, and Giovanni Peri. "Rethinking the effect of immigration on wages." *Journal of the European Economic Association* 10, no. 1 (2012): 152–197.

Peri, Giovanni. "The effect of immigration on productivity: Evidence from US states." *Review of Economics and Statistics* 94, no. 1 (2012): 348–358.

Sá, Filipa. "Immigration and House Prices in the UK." *The Economic Journal* 125, no. 587 (2014): 1393–1424.

Saiz, Albert. "Room in the kitchen for the melting pot: Immigration and rental prices." *Review of Economics and Statistics* 85, no. 3 (2003): 502–521.

Smith, Christie, and Christoph Thoenissen. "Skilled migration and business cycle dynamics." *Journal of Economic Dynamics and Control* 109 (2019): 103781.

Storesletten, Kjetil. "Sustaining fiscal policy through immigration." *Journal of Political Economy* 108, no. 2 (2000): 300–323.

Zimmermann, Klaus, and Thomas Bauer. *The Economics of Migration*. Edward Elgar Publishing, 2002.

Part I

Migration and the Macroeconomy: Empirical Evidence

2

The Impact of Immigration on Productivity

Joan Llull

2.1 Introduction

Immigration to the countries of the Organisation for Economic Co-operation and Development (OECD) has increased dramatically in recent years. This increase has motivated a large debate both in the political arena and among researchers regarding the consequences of immigrant inflows for the receiving economies. On the political arena, many political campaigns have drawn intensively on anti-immigration sentiment to gain votes (e.g. Trump, Brexit, Salvini, and many other presidential campaigns in Europe). Among researchers, a vast labour economics literature has analysed the effects of immigration on wages without reaching any consensus.[1] From a more aggregate perspective, fewer studies

J. Llull (✉)
MOVE, Barcelona, Spain

Universitat Autònoma de Barcelona, Barcelona, Spain

Barcelona GSE, Barcelona, Spain
e-mail: joan.llull@movebarcelona.eu

E. Vella et al. (eds.), *Understanding Migration with Macroeconomics*,
https://doi.org/10.1007/978-3-030-40981-4_2

have examined the economic effects of immigration on receiving countries, focusing on outcomes such as employment, income per capita, total factor productivity (TFP), and inflation (de la Rica et al. 2015).

This chapter provides a cross-country analysis of the impact of immigration on productivity. In particular, it analyses the effect of immigration on GDP per capita, employment rate, hours worked, and unemployment rate using aggregate variation across OECD destination countries. The analysis exploits exogenous variation from country of origin *push* factors (wars, political environment, demographic, and economic factors) leveraged across destination countries by the distance between origin and destination, which determines the choice of the destination country for immigrants that decide to move. Therefore, the variation is not given by the push factors or the distance themselves (which are collinear with fixed effects included in the regression), but by their interaction. For example, the Syrian war pushes more immigrants to Europe than to Australia.

In order to structurally interpret the results, this chapter provides an analytical framework based on a simple production function. This framework allows for some back-of-the-envelope calculations that also shed light on the predicted effects on wages or the marginal productivity of labour. This analysis allows to disentangle the separate effects on the productivity of natives and immigrants, and provides results that are more readily comparable with the large labour economics literature on wage effects of immigration.

First-stage regressions are estimated using bilateral immigrant stocks data collected by Llull (2016). The push-distance interactions provide relevant and arguably exogenous variation that allow for the identification of the results. Second-stage regression results suggest that a one percentage point increase in the share of immigrants in the population reduces the country's GDP per capita by 2%. Furthermore, employment effects are also important: a one point increase in the share of immigrants reduces the employment rate by 0.888 percentage points, reduces average hours worked by those individuals who stay employed by 1.28%, and increases the unemployment rate by 0.55 percentage points.

Back-of-the-envelope calculations based on the production framework introduced in this chapter suggest that the capital supply elasticity is not zero, but also not infinite. This result implies that immigration increases labour market competition because the increase in labour supply is not compensated by a large enough increase in the supply of capital. The downward wage pressure associated with the larger competition may or may not be shared between immigrants and natives. If immigrants and natives are perfect substitutes, the effect is distributed equally across the two groups. However, assuming that natives and immigrants are imperfect substitutes in production (as in Ottaviano and Peri 2012), the effect on native wages is ambiguous because the increase in the number of immigrants increases the demand for the (imperfectly substitutable) native labour. Given the estimated coefficients, the semi-elasticity of native wages to the immigrant share is estimated to be −0.7 if the extensive margin of labour supply is ignored (i.e. if we average in the zeros of natives who stop working) and 0.12 if we compute it only for the individuals who remain at work. Thus, the effect of immigration is large and negative for some natives (those who lose their jobs) and slightly positive for others (those who manage to keep them). Consistent with the literature and with theoretical predictions, the effect of immigration on the wages of immigrants is unambiguously negative.

An earlier version of the research reproduced in this chapter (Llull 2008) was among the first papers to explore the effect of immigration on GDP per worker in a cross-country setting.[2] Angrist and Kugler (2003) use data from European countries to identify the effect of immigration on employment, analysing the role of labour market (lack of) flexibility in channelling these effects. Building on the trade literature, Andersen and Dalgaard (2011) and Ortega and Peri (2014a, b) use cross-country variation to jointly estimate the long-run effects of trade and immigration on income. Using somewhat more structural approaches, di Giovanni et al. (2015) and Docquier et al. (2014) analyse similar questions. Like the previous two studies, di Giovanni et al. (2015) draw from the trade literature and conduct an evaluation of the global effects of international migration using a model of trade with varieties. Docquier et al. (2014) calibrate an aggregate model of the global labour market to fit bilateral stocks data across many countries of origin and destination.

An important concern for the identification of the effect of interest, which has also been raised in the labour economics literature, is the extent to which the inflow of migrants into the different markets is endogenous. In observational studies that do not exploit natural experiments, this has been a prominent complication that has been discussed in many papers. In the labour economics literature, most papers, pioneered by Altonji and Card (1991) and Card (2001), use past settlements of immigrants as instruments for subsequent inflows.[3] This approach has been widely criticized (e.g. see Borjas et al. 1997; Borjas 1999, 2003, 2014). In particular, if the unobservable factors that determine wages and attract immigrants are persistent over time, past settlements are likely to be correlated with current inflows. As noted above, this chapter uses variation in the interaction of push factors and distance to identify the effect. Methodologically, this approach is close to Angrist and Kugler (2003), who leverage the different stages of the Balkans War with distance to Yugoslavia to obtain cross-country over-time variation. It is also related to Llull (2018b), who uses the interaction of similar push factors as those used in this chapter with geographic and cultural distance further interacted with skill-cell dummies to obtain variation across skill-cells for a given country. Ortega and Peri (2014a, b) also use gravity-based instruments in migration regressions, but they do not exploit over-time variation in their predictions. More broadly, this chapter is also related to labour economics papers that exploit natural experiments as push factors (Card 1990; Hunt 1992; Glitz 2012; Dustmann et al. 2017; Monràs 2019).

The labour economics literature on immigration analyses the effect of immigration on wages and other outcomes by comparing different labour markets that face different levels of immigrant penetration. The studies in the literature differ in the way they define labour markets. Traditional studies use cross-city variation to identify the effects (e.g. Grossman 1982; Altonji and Card 1991; Card 2001). The papers following this so-called spatial approach tend to find negligible impacts of immigration on wages and employment. Other papers, pioneered by Borjas et al. (1997) and Borjas (2003), identify the effects at the national level defining labour markets in terms of skills (see also Aydemir and Borjas 2007, 2011; and Llull 2018b). The papers in the skill-cell approach tend to find sizeable effects. The variety of results obtained with the two approaches motivated a long-standing debate.

There are many potential reasons behind the different results in the literature. Dustmann et al. (2016) provide a unified theoretical framework that shows that the skill-cell and the spatial approaches identify different elasticities. Aydemir and Borjas (2011) state that an important part of the differences in the results are attributable to attenuation bias caused by measurement error in the immigrant shares at the local level. Borjas (2006) argues that spatial arbitrage can generate negligible effects in the spatial approach. Lewis (2011) shows that firms adjust their capital adoption decisions depending on immigration, which is another form of spatial arbitrage.

Following the framework in Dustmann et al. (2016), this chapter identifies the same coefficient as in the spatial correlations approach and yet provides results that are more in line with the findings in the skill-cell approach. This result can be the consequence of the absence of spatial arbitrage and measurement error at the cross-country level, and also of the less elastic capital supply at the national level (small versus large economies).

The remainder of this chapter is organized as follows. Section 2.2 explains the econometric model. Section 2.3 discusses the econometric framework and the differences between the cross-country and cross-metropolitan area spatial approaches. Section 2.4 introduces the data. Section 2.5 presents the estimation results, and Sect. 2.6 presents the results from the back-of-the-envelope simulations before concluding in Sect. 2.7.

2.2 Theoretical Framework

Consider the following production function:

$$Y_{it} = A_{it} K_{it}^{\alpha} \left(\theta N_{it}^{\rho} + (1-\theta) I_{it}^{\rho} \right)^{\frac{1-\alpha}{\rho}}, \tag{2.1}$$

where Y_{it} denotes GDP in country i and year t, A_{it} is TFP, N_{it} denotes the number of natives, and I_{it} denotes the number of immigrants. Capital is supplied according to $r_t = K^{\lambda}$, where r_t is the interest rate, and $1/\lambda$ is the capital supply elasticity (Dustmann et al. 2016).[4] Let the economy be characterized by a representative firm that produces output using the technology described in Eq. (2.1) and pays competitive wages and interest rates. In such context, equilibrium capital equals:

$$K_{it} = \left(\alpha A_{it}\right)^{\frac{1}{1-\alpha+\lambda}} L_{it}^{\frac{1-\alpha}{1-\alpha+\lambda}}, \tag{2.2}$$

where $L_{it} \equiv \left(\theta N_{it}^{\rho} + (1-\theta) I_{it}^{\rho}\right)^{\frac{1}{\rho}}$. Substituting Eq. (2.2) into (2.1), dividing by total population ($N_{it} + I_{it}$), and rearranging yields:

$$y_{it} \equiv \frac{Y_{it}}{N_{it} + I_{it}} = A_{it}\left(\alpha A_{it}\right)^{\frac{\alpha}{1-\alpha+\lambda}} \left(\theta\left(1-m_{it}\right)^{\rho} + (1-\theta) m_{it}^{\rho}\right)^{\frac{1-\frac{\alpha\lambda}{1-\alpha+\lambda}}{\rho}}. \tag{2.3}$$

where $m_{it} \equiv I_{it}/(I_{it} + N_{it})$ is the share of immigrants. Log-differentiating this expression gives, upon rearrangement:

$$\frac{d\ln y_{it}}{dm_{it}} = \left(1 - \frac{\alpha\lambda}{1-\alpha+\lambda}\right) \frac{(1-\theta) m_{it}^{\rho-1} - \theta\left(1-m_{it}\right)^{\rho-1}}{\left(\theta\left(1-m_{it}\right)^{\rho} + (1-\theta) m_{it}^{\rho}\right)}. \tag{2.4}$$

Noting that the denominator is positive, and the term in the first parenthesis ranges between $1 - \alpha$ (when $\lambda \to \infty$) and 1 (when $\lambda = 0$), the sign of the estimated semi-elasticity of interest depends on the sign of the numerator. In particular, a positive effect occurs if and only if:

$$(1-\theta) m_{it}^{\rho-1} > \theta\left(1-m_{it}\right)^{\rho-1} \quad \Leftrightarrow \quad \theta < \frac{m_{it}^{\rho-1}}{m_{it}^{\rho-1} + \left(1-m_{it}\right)^{\rho-1}}. \tag{2.5}$$

Simple comparative statics with Eq. (2.5) are informative. Ottaviano and Peri (2012) estimate the elasticity of substitution between natives and immigrants (within the same education-experience group) to average around 20. At the average immigration rate in the data used below, which is around 7%, the estimated effect on productivity should be positive iff

$\theta < 0.533$ and negative otherwise. The intuition is as follows. If natives and immigrants were perfect substitutes ($\rho = 1$), then the threshold would be 0.5: if we are adding less productive individuals, then the effect is negative, and if we are adding more productive individuals, then the effect is positive. The extra margin comes from the imperfect substitutability between natives and immigrants: even if immigrants are slightly less productive than natives, the partial complementarity with natives compensates this negative composition effect. If immigrants are much less productive than natives, the composition effect dominates. All in all, these composition and substitution effects determine whether the amount efficiency units per capita increases or decreases with the increase in the number of immigrants.

The other two parameters, α and λ, play a role in amplifying the positive or negative effects. A large elasticity of capital supply (small λ) implies that capital reacts more to changes in effective labour supply, and, hence, GDP per capita also reacts more. A large value of α makes labour relatively less important in determining GDP than capital, and, therefore, reduces the size of the reaction of GDP per capita to changes in the effective supply of labour.

As discussed in the introduction, a large literature in labour economics has estimated the effect of immigration on native wages (equivalent to native labour productivity in a competitive setting). Equation (2.4) describes the effect of immigration on overall productivity (GDP per capita). Additionally, this framework allows for the derivation of expressions for wages, which are more directly comparable with the estimates in the labour literature. In a competitive economy, workers are paid their marginal product. Therefore, native wages are given by:

$$w_{it}^{(N)} = \theta\left(1 - \frac{\alpha\lambda}{1-\alpha+\lambda}\right) A_{it} \left(\alpha A_{it}\right)^{\frac{\alpha}{1-\alpha+\lambda}} \left(\begin{array}{c}\theta\left(1-m_{it}\right)^{\rho} + \\ \left(1-\theta\right) m_{it}^{\rho}\end{array}\right)^{\frac{1-\rho}{\rho} - \frac{\alpha\lambda}{\rho(1-\alpha+\lambda)}}$$
$$\left(1-m_{it}\right)^{\rho-1}\left(N_{it}+I_{it}\right)^{\frac{-\alpha\lambda}{1-\alpha+\lambda}}. \qquad (2.6)$$

Noting that $d(N_{it} + I_{it})/dm_{it} = (N_{it} + I_{it})/(1 - m_{it})$ and log-differentiating the above expression gives:

$$\frac{dlnw_{it}^{(N)}}{dm_{it}}=\left(1-\rho-\frac{\alpha\lambda}{1-\alpha-\lambda}\right)\left[\frac{(1-\theta)m_{it}^{\rho-1}-\theta(1-m_{it})^{\rho-1}}{\left(\theta(1-m_{it})^{\rho}+(1-\theta)m_{it}^{\rho}\right)}+\frac{1}{1-m_{it}}\right]. \quad (2.7)$$

The corresponding expression for immigrant wages is given by an analogous expression to Eq. (2.6) in which the first term, θ, is replaced by $1-\theta$, and the penultimate term, $(1-m_{it})^{\rho-1}$, is replaced by $m_{it}^{\rho-1}$. Therefore:

$$\frac{dlnw_{it}^{(I)}}{dm_{it}}=\left(1-\rho-\frac{\alpha\lambda}{1-\alpha-\lambda}\right)\frac{(1-\theta)m_{it}^{\rho-1}-\theta(1-m_{it})^{\rho-1}}{\left(\theta(1-m_{it})^{\rho}+(1-\theta)m_{it}^{\rho}\right)} -\frac{(1-\rho)}{m_{it}}-\frac{\alpha\lambda}{1-\alpha-\lambda}\frac{1}{1-m_{it}}. \quad (2.8)$$

Equations (2.7) and (2.8) provide a metric that allows for the comparison of the results with those in the labour economics literature, by means of a simple back-of-the-envelope calculation. Theoretically, if $\lambda = 0$ (perfectly elastic capital supply) and $\rho = 1$ (natives and immigrants are perfect substitutes), the effect of immigration on wages of both natives and immigrants will be zero. This is so because all changes in labour supply are compensated by adjustments in physical capital. Imperfect substitutability between immigrants and natives makes natives to gain relative to immigrants. In particular, if $\lambda = 0$ and $\rho < 1$, natives wages increase and immigrant wages decrease by a similar amount, so that the average effect is zero. If, additionally, $\lambda > 0$, then immigrant wages unambiguously decrease, whereas the effect on native workers becomes ambiguous: the overall negative wage effects generated by the partial adjustment of capital may or may not be offset by the imperfect substitutability effects.

This implication highlights an important part of the empirical contribution below. Dustmann et al. (2016) provide a unified framework to understand the differences in estimates obtained in spatial and skill-cell approaches. Results from the spatial approach, the type of variation exploited in this chapter, crucially depend on the capital supply elasticity. The debate between Borjas (2003) and Ottaviano and Peri (2012) highlights that the importance of the capital supply elasticity and imperfect substitutability between immigrants and natives is also fundamental to understand the effects. Borjas (2013) shows that the overall effects on aggregate wages in the Borjas/Ottaviano-Peri structural frameworks is completely determined by the assumed capital supply elasticity (which Borjas assumes to be zero, and Ottaviano and Peri assume to be infinite). Lewis (2011) provides evidence of capital adjustments to immigration, suggesting that there is some, potentially imperfect, adjustment of capital. The analysis on GDP per capita from this chapter, based on Eq. (2.4) allows for indirect (back-of-the-envelope) inference on the capital supply elasticity.

Results presented below also provide evidence of the impacts of immigration on labour supply, both at the intensive and extensive margins. Such labour supply effects generate an effective overall increase in labour supply that is smaller than the increase in the number of individuals in the population. Assuming that the effects on labour supply are homogeneous across workers, this variation enters the wage equations through the change in the last term in Eq. (2.6). Let Δ_E denote the increase in effective labour (e.g. employment rate). In this case, the effective labour supply increase is $d(N_{it} + I_{it})/dm_{it} = (1 + \Delta_E)(N_{it} + I_{it})/(1 - m_{it})$. Therefore, Eqs. (2.7) and (2.8) rewrite as:

$$\frac{dlnw_{it}^{(N)}}{dm_{it}} = \left(1-\rho-\frac{\alpha\lambda}{1-\alpha-\lambda}\right)\frac{(1-\theta)m_{it}^{\rho-1}-\theta(1-m_{it})^{\rho-1}}{\left(\theta(1-m_{it})^{\rho}+(1-\theta)m_{it}^{\rho}\right)} + \frac{(1-\rho)}{1-m_{it}} - \frac{\alpha\lambda}{1-\alpha-\lambda}\frac{1+\Delta_E}{1-m_{it}} \tag{2.9}$$

and:

$$\frac{dlnw_{it}^{(I)}}{dm_{it}} = \left(1-\rho-\frac{\alpha\lambda}{1-\alpha-\lambda}\right)\frac{(1-\theta)m_{it}^{\rho-1}-\theta(1-m_{it})^{\rho-1}}{\left(\theta(1-m_{it})^{\rho}+(1-\theta)m_{it}^{\rho}\right)} - \frac{(1-\rho)}{m_{it}} - \frac{\alpha\lambda}{1-\alpha-\lambda}\frac{1+\Delta_E}{1-m_{it}}. \quad (2.10)$$

In words, a positive change in employment intensity implies a larger labour supply shock, which puts extra negative pressure on wages if $\lambda > 0$, and a negative change reduces downward wage pressures (for those individuals who work). If $\Delta_E = -1$, there is a perfect displacement effect, and the last term, which captures the labour supply effect, cancels.

2.3 Cross-Country Spatial Regressions

Analysing the economic effects of immigration requires a counterfactual comparison of a given labour market in the presence and in the absence of immigration. Because we are unable to observe the reality in such parallel worlds, comparing outcomes across different but similar markets is the only chance to identify these effects. A typical paper in the labour economics literature uses the following regression (Aydemir and Borjas 2011):

$$\omega_k = \phi m_k + \sum_h \varphi_h z_{kh} + \upsilon_k, \quad (2.11)$$

where ω_k is the outcome of interest in market k, and z_{kh} are control variables that may include period fixed effects, region fixed effects, skill-cell fixed effects, and/or any other variable that generates differences in wage levels across labour markets. Identification requires defining labour markets that are penetrated differently by immigrants and make before-after and across-groups comparisons to identify the effect.

This chapter estimates a similar regression for GDP per capita (and also some employment variables) defining labour markets as OECD countries. Dustmann et al. (2016) show in a unified framework that Eq.

(2.11) estimates a different native wage elasticity depending on the definition of labour market. In their expression, the spatial approach identifies how the overall inflow of immigrants affects native wages and employment of a given group. The focus on GDP per capita identifies yet a different parameter, described in Eq. (2.4).

The labour economics literature has estimated many versions of Eq. (2.11) using spatial variation. It is useful to discuss here the main empirical challenges and results they have encountered in order to define the empirical strategy to follow in this chapter. Seminal papers by Grossman (1982) and Borjas (1987) estimate elasticities from different production functions using Census data variation across Standard Metropolitan Statistical Areas (SMSAs) for 1970 and 1980, respectively. The common conclusion of their studies is that the elasticity of native wages with respect to immigration is very small (around −0.02). A similar conclusion is achieved by the majority of studies defining labour markets as metropolitan areas. One of the most influential papers in the literature, Card (1990), found very negligible effects of the large labour supply increase generated by the Cuban refugees that arrived during the Mariel Boatlift (in 1980) on the relative wages of Miami compared to other four control cities.[5] Other studies reached similar conclusions with different setups (LaLonde and Topel 1991; Altonji and Card 1991; Card 2001).

For years, economists have been trying to reconcile these results with the most simple demand and supply theoretical models that would imply that an increase in (homogeneous) labour supply should be associated with a decrease in equilibrium wages. Three types of empirical issues have been discussed as potential drivers of this result: endogeneity, spatial arbitrage, and measurement error.

The endogeneity concern arises because immigrants are more likely to settle in areas where labour market opportunities are more promising, and this can build a positive correlation between wage shocks and immigration that can bias the results. The estimation using panel data and controlling for permanent unobserved heterogeneity, as initiated by Altonji and Card (1991), is partially a solution, but is not enough, and an instrumental variables analysis is needed. Altonji and Card (1991) and Card (2001) propose a shift-share instrument that allocates aggregate inflows of immigrants in the United States into metropolitan areas based on the historical settlements of previous immigrants from the same country of origin. This approach has been as widely used in the literature as it has been criticized (e.g. see Borjas 1999, 2014). In particular, if economic shocks in a given region are persistent, the endogenous factors that attract immigrants today could be correlated with the factors that attracted immigrants in the past, which would break the exogeneity assumption.[6]

This chapter follows a different approach. In particular, it exploits the variation in costs of immigration across destination countries, summarized by distance, and the origin country-specific factors that drive individuals to move across countries, namely *push* factors such as wars, or political and economic conditions. These instruments are based on the so-called gravity equations, which are very often used in the international trade literature (e.g. Frankel and Romer (1999) use them to analyse the effect of trade on economic growth). In the economics literature, fewer papers have such gravity-based exogenous variation in a cross-country setting (Angrist and Kugler 2003; Llull 2008, 2011, 2018b; Ortega and Peri 2014a, b).[7]

Compared to the more standard gravity instrument (Frankel and Romer 1999; Ortega and Peri 2014a, b), there is an important difficulty that has to be circumvented. The estimation of a panel data model with fixed effects requires time variability of the instrument. In particular, fixed determinants (such as the distance between two countries) are collinear with country dummies and hence do not identify the desired effect. Likewise, push factors do not generate cross-destination variation and are collinear with time dummies. However, we can exploit the joint variation of these two different sources to find instruments that vary across destinations and over time. For example, a war in Syria pushes more people to Europe than to Australia. Put differently, a change in an origin country's living conditions does not equally affect all destination countries. Therefore, the variation from the interaction of a push factor and distance provides relevant exogenous variation that allows to identify the coefficients of interest.[8]

The estimation procedure is implemented in two stages. The first stage consists of a bilateral regression of push factors, distance, and their interaction (along with destination country and time fixed effects). In particular, the share of immigrants from country q in country i at time t, defined as $m_{iqt} \equiv I_{iqt}/N_{it} + I_{it}$, is given by:

$$
\begin{aligned}
m_{iqt} = {} & \beta_1 War_{qt} \times lnDistance_{iq} + \beta_2 PolityIV_{qt} \times lnDistance_{iq} + \beta_3 PolityIV_{qt}^2 \\
& \times lnDistance_{iq} + \beta_4 Pop_{qt} \times lnDistance_{iq} + \beta_5 PPP_{qt} \times lnDistance_{iq} \\
& + \beta_6 War_{qt} + \beta_7 PolityIV_{qt} + \beta_8 PolityIV_{qt}^2 + \beta_8 Pop_{qt} + \beta_9 PPP_{qt} \\
& + \beta_{10} \ln Distance_{iq} + \beta_{11} CommLang_{iq} + \beta_{12} Colony_{iq} \\
& + \beta_{13} Border_{iq} + \zeta_i + \upsilon_t + \epsilon_{iqt},
\end{aligned}
\qquad (2.12)
$$

where the different regressors are defined in Sect. 2.4. The second-stage estimation is a version of Eq. (2.11) in which the outcome is log GDP per capita, and where m_{it} is replaced by its predicted value from the first stage, namely $\hat{m}_{it} \equiv \sum \hat{m}_{iqt}$. In particular:

$$
lny_{it} = \gamma \hat{m}_{it} + \eta_i + \delta_t + \varepsilon_{it}. \qquad (2.13)
$$

An analogous version of this regression is estimated for different employment outcomes.

The second empirical issue that has been discussed in the literature is spatial arbitrage. In particular, if natives respond to the entry of immigrants into a local labour market by moving their labour to other areas, native wages are equalized across areas. Borjas (2006) finds that the measured impact of immigration on wages in local labour markets is attenuated by 40–60% for states and metropolitan areas respectively as a consequence of the native migration response. On the contrary, Card (2001) finds that intercity mobility rates of natives and early immigrants are insensitive to immigrant inflows. In the German context, Dustmann et al. (2017) find some evidence of geographical displacement, even though, in their context, "movement from and to non-employment is far more relevant than movement across areas" (p. 475). Borjas (2003, 2006), Cortés (2008), and Aydemir and Borjas (2011) estimate the skill-cell standard regressions for different geographical definitions of a labour market showing that the more locally is defined a labour market, the smaller are the effects that are estimated. Arbitrage is also a concern at the skill-cell level. In particular, results in Llull (2018a) indicate that native adjustments in skills are also important. Exploiting geographic variation, Lewis

(2011) shows that another important margin of adjustment is technology adoption, especially in the presence of capital-skill complementarities.

These concerns are mitigated in this chapter. One of the main advantages of the cross-country analysis is that countries are much more closed labour markets than cities: if there is a concern of native reaction to immigration by moving to other metropolitan areas as Borjas (2006) suggests, then such concern should vanish in a cross-country setting. Furthermore, the use of spatial variation alone reduces the concerns of arbitrage across skill groups. And finally, the analysis of effects on GDP per capita allows for indirect inference (through back-of-the-envelope calculations) on the intensity of adjustment of physical capital.

The third empirical issue is measurement error. Aydemir and Borjas (2011) show that the different spatial results at different levels of aggregation can be explained partially by attenuation bias due to measurement error in the computation of immigrant shares. Using restricted data from the Canadian census, these authors estimate larger negative effects of immigration relative to the elasticities obtained with public use samples. They also show that this conclusion can be extrapolated to the United States. However, as in Llull (2018b), this chapter's use of instrumental variables that are uncorrelated with this measurement error eliminates this concern. Furthermore, the accuracy of immigrant shares at the national level is much larger than at finer geographic definitions of the labour market.

The advantages of the cross-country analysis in tackling these three empirical issues come at some costs. First, it is difficult to conduct a direct analysis of wages due to the lack of cross-country wage data for a long period of time. Therefore, the analysis of the effects on productivity obtained from GDP per capita regressions cannot be complemented with a similar regression analysis on wages. Hence, conclusions for wages can only be extracted from back-of-the-envelope calculations based on Eqs. (2.7) through (2.10). Additionally, only the total stock of immigrants is observed, but not its disaggregation by educational levels or other categories, which prevents the estimation of the so-called mixed approaches, which combine spatial and skill-cell variation. It also prevents the use of production functions that are more comparable to those estimated by Borjas (2003) or Ottaviano and Peri (2012) for the United States or Manacorda et al. (2012) for the United Kingdom. Therefore, the conclusions below are somewhat harder to compare to those in the literature.

2.4 Data

Observing international migration is not easy. In general, origin countries do not collect statistics on the amount of people who leave the country, so the main source of data is at the destination. The fact that different countries count immigrants in different ways requires additional effort from the researcher to work on the comparability of the different statistics.

In recent years, several authors collected data from different sources to construct cross-country bilateral datasets (e.g. Docquier and Marfouk 2006; Özden et al. 2011; Llull 2016). Llull (2016) collected census-based data from National Statistical Offices of the 24 richest OECD countries.[9] The data contain stocks of immigrants by country of origin at 10-year frequency from 1960 to 2000. The purpose of that paper is to look at the determinants of bilateral migration. Therefore, the credibility of the estimates relies on the quality of migration data. Additionally, the paper estimates bilateral regressions with large amounts of observations. This chapter estimates cross-destination country regressions with few observations. Additionally, as the immigrant share is instrumented, measurement error is not as important as long as it is uncorrelated with the instrument, which is very plausible in this case. Under this premise, the database is extended to 5-year frequency. To this end, data from all destination countries that carry censuses every 5 years are included, and information from other sources like labour Force Surveys or, in recent years, small annual versions of censuses like the ACS in the United States are also added. For a small subset (21 country-time observations), the available census estimates are interpolated.[10]

Data are based on destination countries' censuses.[11] From each census, data on the stock of immigrants by country of birth or country of nationality are collected. The dataset contains information on stocks of immigrants from 188 countries of origin (sometimes in grouped categories) into each of the 24 listed OECD countries.[12]

This dataset has important advantages relative to other datasets in the literature. First, it covers 100% of stocks of immigrants in all of these destination countries, without imputations. Moreover, unlike some of the existing datasets (e.g. International Migration Database from the OECD), it contains data on stocks. For economic and statistical reasons, it is more attractive to work with stocks rather than flows: from an economics point of view, the marginal effects derived in Eqs. (2.4) and (2.7) through (2.10) are expressed in terms of immigrant shares. Econometrically, it has long been recognized that migration flow data are less reliable than stock data, because of the impossibility of evaluating emigration and return migration movements (Docquier and Marfouk 2006). Additionally, although censuses do not record all illegal immigrants, they do a much better job in counting them than issues of residence and work permits (especially when census data are physically collected directly at the dwelling). Finally, the dataset covers a wide time period (from 1960 to 2005).

There are a few comparability issues that are worth mentioning. They are unlikely to affect the analysis below because this source of measurement error is unlikely to be correlated with the instrument. First, the definition of immigrant is different across countries. Some countries define immigrants on the basis of the place of birth, while others base it on nationality. Although this may affect the comparison of stocks across destination countries, observations are likely to be comparable within countries, which provide the relevant variation since regressions include country fixed effects. Second, census dates vary across destination countries: roughly a half of them are carried in 0- and 5-ended years (1960, 1965, 1970, etc.) and the other half in 1- and 6-ended ones (1961, 1966, 1971, etc.). Dates are generally consistent, however, so the difference between two censuses is always of 5 or 10 years. The analysis below shows robustness to the date of measurement of the dependent variable.

Figure 2.1 shows the evolution of immigrant rates (i.e. stock of immigrants over population) across destination countries over the sample period. The same scale on the left axis is used in order to make the plots comparable. The level and slope of these curves is very different. The observed patterns are as follows: stable low-immigration countries (Korea and Japan), stable high-immigration countries (Australia, Canada and New Zealand), old immigration countries with a strong increasing trend (United States, Luxembourg, Switzerland, and the United Kingdom), old immigration countries with a slight decrease (Belgium and France), and new immigration countries (Spain, Italy, Austria, Greece, Portugal, and the Nordic countries).

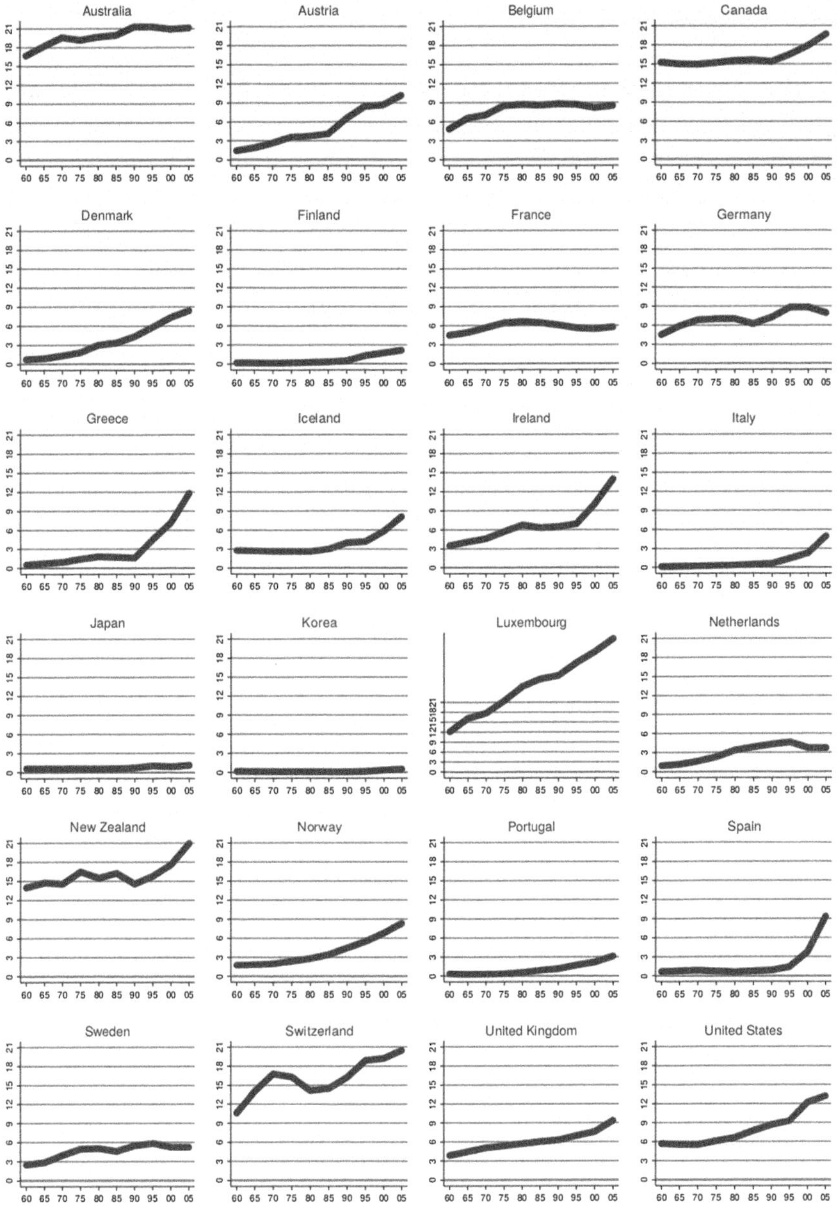

Fig. 2.1 Immigrant share (%) for a sample of OECD countries (1960–2005). Note: Black solid lines represent immigrant shares (in %), that is total stocks of immigrants in a given destination country over its total population. See main text for a data description. Immigrant share is plotted on the left axis, which is of common scale for all destination countries, ranging from 0% to 21% —it is compressed for Luxembourg due to its exceptionally large fraction of immigrants (40.3% in year 2005)

The different outcomes used in the second-stage regressions are obtained from different sources. GDP per capita comes from Penn World Tables 7.0 (PWT) and is measured at constant international dollars. Employment rates (total employment over population) and hours worked per worker come from the Total Economy Database (Conference Board). Unemployment rates come from OECD (Economic Outlook). For all dependent variables, different dates are used for different specifications (see Sect. 2.4).

Push factors are averaged over the period $t-5$ to $t-1$ and come from different sources. Four variables are considered: wars, Polity IV index, population, and purchasing power parity (PPP). The war variable is based on data from the Polity IV project (Center for International Development and Conflict Management 2006). This variable measures the fraction of months over the previous decade that the country was in any type of war. The autocracy-democracy index Polity IV comes from the same source. It ranges from −10 (autocracy) to 10 (democracy). Values of 0 indicate anocracy, some sort of instability and lack of control either by an autocratic or a democratic power. Population and PPP are obtained from PWT.

Distance variables include physical distance (great circle distance between the two capitals) and dummies for having a common language, a past colonial relationship, and a common border. Interactions with *push* factors are included only with distance. The distance variable is based on data from Rose (2004), extended to cover all the sample. The common language dummy was constructed using data by Alesina et al. (2003). A pair of countries is considered to share a particular language if that language is spoken by at least 10% of the population in each country of the pair. Those data are complemented with The World Factbook from the Central Intelligence Agency (2007). The colonial relationship dummy and the common border variable are also constructed using information from the CIA.

Finally, some of the regressions below control for trade (instrumented in the same way as migration). Bilateral trade data are obtained from Rose (2004) for 1960–1995 and from UN Comtrade for 2000 and 2005.

2.5 Estimation Results

This section presents the estimation results for the model and regressions presented in Sect. 2.3. Table 2.1 shows the estimation results from the first-stage regression (2.12). This regression is estimated with bilateral data on migrant stocks, described in Sect. 2.4. The data include 12,287 origin-destination-time observations, some of them representing grouped categories, which are weighted accordingly.

Overall, Table 2.1 shows a strong relevance of the instruments. The signs of the coefficients are also interpretable. The negative coefficient of the war interaction indicates that the effect of a war on migration (which is positive) is reduced when countries are far away. For example, the Syrian war pushes people to all countries, but more so to Europe than to Australia.

The Polity IV variable ranges from −10 (autocracy) to 10 (democracy), with intermediate values (around 0) representing societies where the central authority is weak or non-existent (anocracies). The findings in Llull (2016) suggest that anocracies favour migration, as risk-averse people have a dis-utility of living in such an unstable environment (individuals would also like to flee from autocracies, but migration is often more restricted in those contexts). To capture this non-linearity, Eq. (2.12) includes a quadratic on the index. Results confirm the findings in Llull (2016), and also show, through the interaction terms, that this quadratic relation is less strong for further away countries. Put differently, the fall of Gaddafi's autocratic regime in Libya and the subsequent situation of instability (anocracy) push more migrants to Italy than to the United States.

The last two variables used as push factors (population and PPP) are proxies for demographic and life quality measures. An increase in population increases the competition in the labour market, increasing, as a result, the likelihood of moving. This effect, however, is again mitigated by distance. PPP captures two different factors. From a long-run perspective, it is a measure of economic development of the origin country. Lower development levels are associated with larger gains from migration and, hence, larger migrant flows. Short-run (negative) shocks are a form of economic instability (e.g. hyperinflation, currency attacks, bad

Table 2.1 First-stage regression

Interactions:		
War x Log Distance	−0.806	(0.277)
Polity IV x Log Distance	−0.003	(0.007)
Polity IV^2 x Log Distance	0.005	(0.002)
Population x Log Distance	−0.111	(0.078)
PPP x Log Distance	0.309	(0.124)
Non-interacted terms:		
War	7.201	(2.387)
Polity IV	0.059	(0.059)
Polity IV^2	−0.036	(0.019)
Population	1.154	(0.652)
PPP	−2.718	(1.094)
Log distance	−0.978	(0.148)
Common language	2.970	(0.398)
Colony	0.351	(0.128)
Border	5.343	(0.704)
Observations	12.287	
Adjusted R^2	0.14	
F-statistic	18.46	
F-statistic (interactions only)	7.9	

Note: The regression includes destination country fixed effects and time dummies and it is estimated at the bilateral level (destination-origin-year). Demographic and political variables refer to origin countries at a point in time. Geographic variables refer to a country pair and are constant over time. F-statistic tests the joint significance of all coefficients. An F test for the joint significance of interactions is also reported. Robust standard errors in parentheses

economic policies, etc.) and are also positively associated with migration. Once again, however, this effect is larger for countries that are nearby, and it gradually decreases with distance.

Table 2.1 also shows results to tests of joint relevance of the instruments. The F-statistic for the joint significance of all excluded coefficients (all the coefficients except time and country dummies) is relatively large (18.6), clearly rejecting the null hypothesis of insignificance of all coefficients. The F-statistic for the joint significance of the interaction terms (the only subset of excluded instruments that remains non-collinear with the time and country dummies after aggregation) is slightly smaller (7.9), but still well above the Stock and Yogo's (2005) threshold for rejection of weak instruments if a maximum of 5% bias (towards Ordinary Least Squares, OLS) is allowed in the second stage (at the 5% significance level).

Table 2.2 Effect of immigration on GDP per capita

	Without trade		With trade	
1. Baseline (census date)	−2.061	(1.125)	−2.078	(1.125)
2. All in the same year	−1.958	(1.121)	−2.038	(1.263)
3. Four-year average	−1.947	(1.084)	−2.066	(1.228)
4. Least squares	−0.023	(0.720)	−0.012	(0.756)

Note: All regressions include country fixed effects and time dummies. All specifications estimated by 2SLS (see first-stage regression in Table 3.1). Right column includes trade as a control variable (instrumented with a bilateral first stage using the same instruments). Dependent variable: Log of GDP per capita at constant international dollars. All coefficients correspond to immigrant rate. Immigrant rate measured at Census dates (either at 1- and 6-ended years or at 0- and 5-ended ones). Specification 1 (baseline) measures the dependent variable at Census date as well. Specification 2 measures the dependent variable at 1- and 6-ended years. Specification 3 includes a 4-year average. And Specification 4 is the OLS estimate of the baseline specification. Number of observations: 240. Robust standard errors in parentheses

Table 2.2 presents the second-stage results for Eq. (2.13). All specifications are instrumented using the constructed instrument based on the aggregation of the first-stage regression in Table 2.1, except for the last row that presents OLS estimates. The baseline specification introduces the dependent variable at the corresponding census date, that is at the exact year immigrant share is observed. Results suggest an important effect of immigration on income per capita. In particular, 1 percentage point increase in the immigrant share reduces wages by 2%. Although precision is low, due to the small number of observations (24 × 10 = 240 obs.), this estimate is significantly different from zero. The structural interpretation of the results is discussed in the next section.

Two additional specifications are estimated to check the robustness of the results to the different measurement issues described in Sect. 2.4. The first of these two specifications, presented in the second row, adjusts the measurement of the dependent variable to the exact census date, as opposed to the 0- or 5-year-ended date that the census is assumed to represent. The second one, in the third row, replaces it by a 4-year average. In both specifications, results are virtually unchanged by these changes, which suggests that the timing of the data is unlikely to be a source of concern.

Another concern is that the instruments may be correlated with the error term because of their correlation with international trade. Indeed, Frankel and Romer (1999) or Ortega and Peri (2014a, b) use geographic instruments (in levels, not their interaction with distance) to instrument for trade. To account for this concern, the specifications in the second column of Table 2.2 reproduce the same regressions controlling for trade, which is also instrumented by the same variables. Point estimates are again virtually unchanged (even though precision falls in some cases). Therefore, results are robust to controlling for trade.

The last row of Table 2.2 presents the OLS regression coefficients. Point estimates are virtually zero, indicating an important positive bias. This bias is motivated for the non-random allocation of immigrants across destination countries. For example, Southern European countries were doing poorly compared to OECD countries from 1960s to 1980s and had virtually no immigrants, but their rapid convergence to the income levels of their European partners is associated with a drastic increase in the stock of immigrants in most of them (see Fig. 2.1).

Table 2.3 provides an analysis of the employment and labour supply effects. In particular, results are presented for three different outcomes using the same instrument and specifications. Each panel presents the results for a different outcome: employment rate, log hours worked, and unemployment rate.

Results in Table 2.3 suggest that 1 percentage point increase in the immigrant share reduces employment by about 0.8–0.9 percentage points, reduces average hours worked (conditional on working) by 1.2%, and increases unemployment by 0.5–0.6 percentage points. The latter is very consistent with the findings of Angrist and Kugler (2003) using similar sources of variation. The results on hours worked are in line with Borjas (2003), who finds a significant reduction in hours worked as a consequence of immigration. In all three cases, OLS estimates are considerably biased towards less severe effects of immigration. As in the case of wages, this bias indicates that immigrants migrate to the countries that offer better work conditions. The large magnitude of such biases motivates the use of instrumental variables in the estimation.

Table 2.3 Effects of immigration on employment, hours worked, and unemployment

	Without trade		With trade	
A. Employment rate (employed/population)				
1. Baseline (census date)	−0.888	(0.268)	−1.002	(0.256)
2. All in the same year	−0.849	(0.265)	−0.966	(0.255)
3. Four-year average	−0.754	(0.251)	−0.878	(0.240)
4. Least squares	0.601	(0.151)	0.579	(0.157)
B. Log hours worked				
1. Baseline (census date)	−1.281	(0.366)	−1.321	(0.403)
2. All in the same year	−1.267	(0.360)	−1.315	(0.397)
3. Four-year average	−0.450	(0.341)	−0.291	(0.347)
4. Least squares	−0.581	(0.166)	−0.593	(0.176)
C. Unemployment rate (unemployed/labour force)				
1. Baseline (census date)	0.550	(0.150)	0.566	(0.167)
2. All in the same year	0.512	(0.146)	0.541	(0.165)
3. Four-year average	0.513	(0.139)	0.578	(0.152)
4. Least squares	−0.117	(0.094)	−0.127	(0.097)

Note: All regressions include country fixed effects and time dummies. All specifications estimated by 2SLS (see first-stage regression in Table 3.1). Right column includes trade as a control variable (instrumented with a bilateral first stage using the same instruments). Dependent variables: employment rate, log hours worked, and unemployment rates. All coefficients correspond to immigrant rate. Immigrant rate measured at Census dates (either at 1- and 6-ended years or at 0- and 5-ended ones). Specification 1 (baseline) measures the dependent variable at Census date as well. Specification 2 measures the dependent variable at 1- and 6-ended years. Specification 3 includes a 4-year average. And Specification 4 is the OLS estimate of the baseline specification. Number of observations: 240. Robust standard errors in parentheses.

2.6 Structural Interpretation and Wage Effects: Some Back-of-the-Envelope Calculations

This section provides a set of back-of-the-envelope calculations that allow for a structural interpretation of the results and for inference on wage effects on natives and on immigrants. Table 2.4 summarizes the main results of this exercise. The top panel describes the main assumptions and data inputs used in the calculation. The central panel provides the parameters implied by these assumptions and the results in Tables 2.2 and 2.3. Finally, the bottom panel shows the implications for wage effects of immigration.

Table 2.4 Back-of-the-envelope calculations: Wage effects

Inputs	
Native-immigrant wage gap (Adserá and Chiswick 2007)	−0.401
Average immigration rate (data)	0.070
Elasticity of substitution (Ottaviano and Peri 2012)	20.000
Implied parameters	
Inverse elasticity of substitution (ρ)	0.950
Relative native efficiency (θ)	0.629
Capital share (α)	0.300
Inverse elasticity of capital supply (λ)	0.520
Wage effects	
Natives	−0.702
Immigrants	−1.466
Wage effects (netting out employment effects)	
Natives	0.126
Immigrants	−0.638

Note: Author's calculations using the expressions in the text and the inputs listed in the first panel

Borrowing from the findings of Ottaviano and Peri (2012), we fix the elasticity of substitution between natives and immigrants to 20, which implies that $\rho = 0.95$. Using this parameter, an estimate of θ can be obtained from the comparison of native and immigrant wages. Dividing Eq. (2.6) by the analogous expression for immigrant wages yields:

$$\frac{w_{it}^{(N)}}{w_{it}^{(I)}} = \frac{\theta}{1-\theta}\left(\frac{1-m_{it}}{m_{it}}\right)^{\rho-1} \tag{2.14}$$

Using data for EU-15 countries, Adserà and Chiswick (2007) estimate a native-immigrant (log) wage gap of 0.401 (Table 5.1). Substituting this estimate in the left-hand side of Eq. (2.14), and for an average immigrant rate of 7% (from the data), the implied value for θ is 0.629. Following many papers in the literature (e.g. Borjas 2003), we fix the capital share to $\alpha = 0.3$. Given all these parameters, we recover λ as the only unknown in an equation that equates the right-hand side of Eq. (2.4) to the baseline estimate in Table 2.2. The resulting value is 0.52. This value is different from the two extremes that have been considered in the literature, and suggests, as in Lewis (2011), that it is very important to account for capital adjustments in understanding labour market impacts of immigration.

Given these parameter values, the bottom panel provides simulated values for Eqs. (2.7) through (2.10). The first two values measure the wage semi-elasticity to immigration not taking into account labour supply adjustments. Therefore, this result implicitly averages in the "zeroes" for the individuals that stop working because of the extra immigration. The estimated semi-elasticities are obtained to be roughly −0.7 and −1.5. These values imply that a 1% increase in immigration reduces native wages by 0.7% and immigrant wages by 1.5%. These results are in line with the results obtained with the skill-cell approach (e.g. Borjas 2003; Aydemir and Borjas 2007; Llull 2018b) and, with the spatial approach, only with those computed for the groups of less skilled natives (e.g. Altonji and Card 1991; Dustmann et al. 2013).

The calculations obtained for Eqs. (2.9) and (2.10) account for the effect on employment, and, therefore, exclude the individuals that no longer work in the presence of immigration. The estimated effect on the employment rate in Table 2.3 is −0.888 (which is interpreted as Δ_E). Given this value, the implied wage correction is 0.828, which implies that the predicted effects for natives become slightly positive (0.126), and the ones for immigrants stay negative (−0.638). These results imply that the wages of the natives who remain employed after a 1% increase in the share of immigrants in the population increase by 0.1%, whereas those of the immigrants that stay at work decrease by 0.6%.

These results provide evidence of downward wage pressure (even on natives) after immigration. This is so because the capital supply elasticity is estimated to be less than infinity. This result is in contrast with most of the results in the literature using the spatial approach, which tends to find a negligible effect. This discrepancy can be the result of several factors. First, the spatial arbitrage (e.g. Borjas 2006) is unlikely to operate at the cross-country level. Second, metropolitan areas are likely to be small open economies, whereas countries are more likely to influence the capital markets. And third, the attenuation bias generated by measurement error (Aydemir and Borjas 2011) is unlikely to apply here both because of the higher accuracy at the national cross-country level and also because the instrumental variables used in this chapter are likely uncorrelated with the measurement error in the computation of immigrant shares.

2.7 Conclusions

This chapter provides a cross-country analysis of the impact of immigration on productivity. In particular, it analyses the effect of immigration on GDP per capita, the employment rate, hours worked, and the unemployment rate using aggregate variation across OECD destination countries. The analysis exploits exogenous variation from the interactions of push factors at origin and distance between origin and destination countries. The push-distance interactions provide relevant and arguably exogenous variation that allows for the identification of the results. Second-stage regression results suggest that 1 percentage point increase in the share of immigrants in the population reduces the country's GDP per capita by 2%. Furthermore, employment effects are also important: a one point increase in the share of immigrants reduces the employment rate by 0.888 percentage points and average hours worked by those individuals who stay employed by 1.28%, and increases the unemployment rate by 0.55 percentage points.

In order to structurally interpret the results, this chapter provides an analytical framework based on a simple production function. This framework allows for back-of-the-envelope calculations that also shed light on the predicted effects on wages or the marginal productivity of labour. These calculations suggest that the capital supply elasticity is not zero, but also not infinite. This result implies that immigration increases labour market competition because the increase in labour supply is not compensated by a large enough increase in the supply of capital. Given the estimated coefficients, the semi-elasticity of native wages to the immigrant share is estimated to be −0.7 if the extensive margin of labour supply is ignored (i.e. if we average in the zeros of natives who stop working) and 0.12 if we compute it only for the individuals who remain at work. Thus, the effect of immigration is large and negative for some natives (those who lose their jobs), and slightly positive for others (those who manage to keep them). Consistent with the literature and with theoretical predictions, the effect of immigration on the wages of immigrants is unambiguously negative.

These results are only a first step towards stronger policy implications. In particular, it would be interesting to understand whether the large effects on employment are driven by institutions, as suggested by Angrist and Kugler (2003). Furthermore, more freedom of capital mobility, and the recent access to the capital markets of large countries, such as China, may increase the capital supply elasticity, which could reduce the negative effects on GDP per capita. Finally, it would be useful to study the role of policies that redistribute the gains of those who benefit from immigration (e.g. the capitalists or the immigrants themselves) to those whose labour market prospects are negatively affected.

Acknowledgements This chapter is mostly based on earlier research included in two working papers: Llull (2008, 2011). Furthermore, Llull (2008) was based on the author's MPhil thesis and Llull (2011) was based on a chapter of the author's PhD dissertation. The author is indebted to Manuel Arellano and Stéphane Bonhomme for their encouragement and advice. He is also grateful to Marco Alfano, Samuel Bentolila, Guillermo Caruana, Nacho Conde-Ruiz, Jorge de la Roca, José L. Groizard, Claudio Michelacci, Pedro Mira, Josep Pijoan-Mas, Joan C. Rosselló, and seminar participants at CEMFI, Economic Bureau of the Spanish Prime Minister, and SAEe for helpful comments and discussions on the earlier working papers. Excellent research assistance by Marta Aguilera and Anqi Shan is gratefully appreciated. This work has been supported by the European Research Council (ERC), through Starting Grant n. 804989, the Generalitat de Catalunya, through the SGR grant 2017-SGR-1765, the Spanish Ministry of Science, Innovation, and Universities and FEDER, through grant PGC2018-094364-B-I00, and the Severo Ochoa Programme for Centers of Excellence in R&D, though grant SEV-2015-0563.

Notes

1. See Borjas (2003), Ottaviano and Peri (2012), Dustmann et al. (2013), and Llull (2018a, b) among many others.
2. See Llull (2011) for another version that has been cited in the literature.
3. A notable exception is provided by some specifications of Peri and Sparber (2009), which instead use distance to leverage inflows of Mexican workers across different US states.

4. Borjas (2013) also discusses, in a theoretical framework, the importance of the capital supply elasticity in predicting theoretically the effects of immigration on wages.
5. Borjas (2017) and Borjas and Monràs (2017) revisited this and other natural experiments and disputed some of the results.
6. Borjas (2003) introduced the skill-cell approach, which defines labour markets in terms of skills, rather than spatially. That paper argues that, even though endogeneity is still a potential concern, it is less so than in the spatial approach. Llull (2018b), using exogenous sources of variation that are in a similar spirit to those explained below, shows that endogeneity is also a concern in the skill-cell approach.
7. Beyond its use as instruments, gravity-based migration models have been popularized in the migration literature. Beine et al. (2015) provide a comprehensive review of this literature.
8. Llull (2016) estimates a model in which the importance of income gains in determining migration are heterogeneous between country pairs. Angrist and Kugler (2003) interact dummies for the different phases of Balkans War with distance as an instrument to analyse the consequences of immigration on employment in Europe. Ortega and Peri (2014a, b) interact push factors with immigration laws as an instrument in analysing the effect of immigration on different production factors.
9. These countries include Australia, Austria, Belgium, Canada, Denmark, Finland, France, Germany, Greece, Iceland, Ireland, Italy, Japan, Korea (Rep.), Luxembourg, Netherlands, New Zealand, Norway, Portugal, Spain, Sweden, Switzerland, United Kingdom, and United States.
10. In some cases, the data are grouped for several origin countries. The extreme case is when only the total stock of immigrants is observed. Llull (2016) presents a wide discussion on the importance of this issue. The implication for the present study is that some observations from the first-stage regression enter as a group and are accordingly weighted (using the number of countries in the group as the weight). The instruments are grouped consequently. The asymptotic properties of the second-stage estimator are unaffected by this issue.
11. Nordic countries replaced their censuses in 1970s and 1980s for continuous population registers.
12. These countries include all Member States of United Nations except Andorra, Liechtenstein, Monaco, Myanmar, Marshall Islands, Nauru, San Marino, Timor-Leste, and Tuvalu (none of them are available in

Penn World Tables). Additionally, they include the dependent territories of Taiwan, Macao, Hong Kong, Bermuda, and Puerto Rico. Netherlands Antilles and Serbia and Montenegro are considered as sole countries, even though Montenegro gained its independence from Serbia in 2006 and the Netherlands Antilles, dependent territory from the Netherlands, dissolved in 2010 into Curaçao, Sint Marteen, and three special municipalities.

References

Adserà, Alicia, and Barry R. Chiswick. 2007. "Are There Gender and Country of Origin Differences in Immigrant Labor Market Outcomes across European Destinations?" *Journal of Population Economics,* 20:496–526.

Alesina, Alberto F., Arnaud Devleeschauwer, William E. Easterly, Sergio Kurlat, and Romain Wacziarg. 2003. "Fractionalization." *Journal of Economic Growth,* 8:155–194.

Altonji, Joseph G. and David E. Card. 1991. "The Effects of Immigration on the Labor Market Outcomes of Less-skilled Natives." In *The Effects of Immigration on the Labor Market Outcomes of Less-skilled Natives,* edited by John M. Abowd and Richard B. Freeman, 201–234. Chicago: The University of Chicago Press.

Andersen, Thomas B. and Carl-Johan Dalgaard. 2011. "Flows of People, Flows of Ideas, and the Inequality of Nations." *Journal of Economic Growth* 16:1–32.

Angrist, Joshua D. and Adriana Kugler. 2003. "Protective or Counter-Productive? Labour Market Institutions and the Effect of Immigration on EU Natives." *Economic Journal,* 113:F302-F331.

Aydemir, Abdurrahman and George J. Borjas. 2007. "Cross-Country Variation on the Impact of International Migration: Canada, Mexico, and the United States." *Journal of the European Economic Association,* 5:663–708.

Aydemir, Abdurrahman and George J. Borjas. 2011. "Attenuation Bias in Measuring the Wage Impact of Immigration". *Journal of Labor Economics,* 29:69–112.

Beine, Michel, Simone Bertoli, and Jesús Fernández-Huertas Moraga. 2015. "A Practitioners' Guide to Gravity Models of International Migration." *The World Economy,* 1–15.

Borjas, George J. 1987. "Immigrants, Minorities, and Labor Market Competition." *Industrial and Labor Relations Review,* 40:382–392.

Borjas, George J. 1999. "The Economic Analysis of Immigration." In *Handbook of Labor Economics*, edited by Orley C. Ashenfelter and David E. Card, 1697–1760. Amsterdam: North-Holland Publishing Company.

Borjas, George J. 2003. "The Labor Demand Curve Is Downward Sloping: Reexamining the Impact of Immigration on the Labor Market." *Quarterly Journal of Economics*, 118:1335–1374.

Borjas, George J. 2006. "Native Internal Migration and the Labor Market Impact of Immigration." *Journal of Human Resources*, 41:221–258.

Borjas, George J. 2013. "The Analytics of the Wage Effect of Immigration." *IZA Journal of Migration*, 22:1–25.

Borjas, George J. 2014. *Immigration Economics*. Cambridge: Harvard University Press.

Borjas, George J. 2017. "The Wage Impact of the Marielitos: A Reappraisal." *International and Labor Relations Review*, 70:1077–1110.

Borjas, George J., Richard B. Freeman, and Lawrence F. Katz. 1997. "How Much Do Immigration and Trade Affect Labor Market Outcomes?" *Brookings Papers on Economic Activity*, 1997: 67.

Borjas, George J. and Joan Monràs. 2017. "The Labor Market Consequences of Refugee Supply Shocks." *Economic Policy*, 32:361–413.

Card, David E. 1990. "The Impact of the Mariel Boatlift on the Miami Labor Market." *Industrial and Labor Relations Review*, 43:245–257.

Card, David E. 2001. "Immigrant Inflows, Native Outflows, and the Local Labor Market Impacts of Higher Immigration." *Journal of Labor Economics*, 2001:22–64.

Center for International Development and Conflict Management. 2006. "Polity IV." Data in digital form available on Internet, CIDCM, University of Maryland, College Park.

Central Intelligence Agency. 2007. "The World Factbook." Central Intelligence Agency (CIA), Washington DC.

Cortés, Patricia. 2008. "The Effect of Low-Skilled Immigration on U.S. Prices: Evidence from CPI Data." *Journal of Political Economy*, 116:381–422.

Docquier, Frédéric, and Abdeslam Marfouk. 2006. "International Migration by Educational Attainment, 1990-2000". In *International Migration, Remittances and the Brain Drain*, edited by Çağlar Özden and Maurice W. Schif, 151–200. New York: Palgrave Macmillan.

Docquier, Frédéric, Çağlar Özden, and Giovanni Peri. 2014. "The Labour Market Effects of Immigration and Emigration in OECD Countries." *Economic Journal*, 124:1106–1145.

Dustmann, Christian, Tommaso Frattini, and Ian Preston. 2013. "The Effect of Immigration along the Distribution of Wages." *Review of Economic Studies,* 80:145–173.

Dustmann, Christian, Uta Schönberg, and Jan Stuhler. 2016. "The Impact of Immigration: Why Do Studies Reach Such Different Results?" *Journal of Economic Perspectives,* 30:31–56.

Dustmann, Christian, Uta Schönberg, and Jan Stuhler. 2017. "The Impact of Immigration on Local Labor Markets: Evidence from the Opening of the Czech-German Border." *Quarterly Journal of Economics,* 132:435–483.

Frankel, Jeffrey A. and David Romer. 1999. "Does Trade Cause Growth?" *American Economic Review,* 89:379–399.

di Giovanni, Julian, Andrei A. Levchenko, and Francesc Ortega. 2015. "A Global View of Cross-Border Migration." *Journal of the European Economic Association,* 13:168–202.

Glitz, Albrecht. 2012 "The Labor Market Impact of Immigration: A Quasi-Experiment Exploiting Immigrant Location Rules in Germany." *Journal of Labor Economics,* 30:175–213.

Grossman, Jean B. 1982. "The Substitutability of Natives and Immigrants in Production." *Review of Economics and Statistics,* 64:596–603.

Hunt, Jennifer. 1992. "The Impact of the 1962 Repatriates from Algeria on the French Labor Market." *Industrial and Labor Relations Review,* 45:556–572.

LaLonde, Robert J. and Robert H. Topel. 1991. "Labor Market Adjustments to Increased Immigration." In Labor *Market Adjustments to Increased Immigration,* edited by John M. Abowd and Richard B. Freeman, 167–200. Chicago: The University of Chicago Press.

Lewis, Ethan G. 2011. "Immigration, Skill Mix, and Capital-Skill Complementarity." *Quarterly Journal of Economics,* 126:1029–1069.

Llull, Joan. 2008. "The Impact of Immigration on Productivity", CEMFI Working Papers 0802.

Llull, Joan. 2011. "Reconciling Spatial Correlations and Factor Proportions: A Cross-Country Analysis of the Economic Consequences of Immigration", mimeo, CEMFI.

Llull, Joan. 2016. "Understanding International Migration: Evidence from a New Dataset of Bilateral Stocks (1960-2000)." *SERIEs – The Journal of the Spanish Economic Association,* 7:221–255.

Llull, Joan. 2018a. "Immigration, Wages, and Education: A Labour Market Equilibrium Structural Model." *Review of Economic Studies,* 85:1852–1896.

Llull, Joan. 2018b. "The Effect of Immigration on Wages: Exploiting Exogenous Variation at the National Level." *Journal of Human Resources,* 53:608–622.

Manacorda, Marco, Alan Manning, and Jonathan Wadsworth. 2012. "The Impact of Immigration on the Structure of Wages: Theory and Evidence from Britain." *Journal of the European Economic Association,* 10:120–151.

Monràs, Joan. 2019. "Immigration and Wage Dynamics: Evidence from the Mexican Peso Crisis." *Journal of Political Economy,* forthcoming.

Ortega, Francesc and Giovanni Peri. 2014a. "Openness and Income: The Roles of Trade and Migration." *Journal of International Economics* 92:231–251.

Ortega, Francesc and Giovanni Peri. 2014b. "The Aggregate Effects of Trade and Migration: Evidence from OECD Countries", In *The Socio-Economic Impact of Migration Flows: Effects on Trade, Remittances, Output, and the Labour Market,* edited by Andrés Artal-Tur, Giovanni Peri, and Francisco Requena-Silvente, 19–51. Switzerland: Springer International Publishing.

Ottaviano, Gianmarco I. P. and Giovanni Peri. 2012. "Rethinking the Effect of Immigration on Wages." *Journal of the European Economic Association,* 10:152–197.

Özden, Çağlar, Christoper R. Parsons, Maurice W. Schiff, and Terrie L. Walmsey. 2011. "Where on Earth is Everybody? The Evolution of Global Bilateral Migration 1960-2000." *World Bank Economic Review,* 25:12–56.

Peri, Giovanni and Chad Sparber. 2009. "Task Specialization, Immigration, and Wages." *American Economic Journal: Applied Economics,* 1:135–169.

de la Rica, Sara, Albrecht Glitz, and Francesc Ortega. 2015. "Immigration in Europe: Trends, Policies, and Empirical Evidence", In *Handbook of the Economics of International Migration,* edited by Barry R. Chiswick and Paul W. Miller, 1303–1362. Amsterdam: North-Holland Publishing Company.

Rose, Andrew K. 2004. "Do We Really Know That the WTO Increases Trade?." *American Economic Review,* 94:98–114.

Stock, James H. and Motohiro Yogo. 2005. "Testing for Weak Instruments in Linear IV Regression." In *Identification and Inference for Econometric Models: Essays in Honor of Thomas Rothenberg,* edited by Donald W. K. Andrews and James H. Stock. 80–108. Cambridge: Cambridge University Press.

3

Macroeconomic Consequences of International Migration for OECD Countries

Hippolyte d'Albis and Ekrame Boubtane

3.1 Introduction

According to United Nations (2019), OECD countries host more than 40% of all immigrants worldwide. Moreover, the share of immigrants in the population of those countries has increased from 7% in 1990 to 14% in 2019. Because global population trends show a predicted concentration of young people in Africa, immigration figures are likely to rise. This chapter analyses the effects of international migration on the macroeconomic and fiscal situation of host countries. This point is important because most OECD countries structurally run public deficits. Moreover, opinion polls show that whatever the position of natives toward

H. d'Albis (✉)
Paris School of Economics, Paris, France

CNRS, Paris, France
e-mail: hippolyte.dalbis@psemail.eu

E. Boubtane
University Clermont Auvergne, Clermont-Ferrand, France
e-mail: ekrame.boubtane@uca.fr

E. Vella et al. (eds.), *Understanding Migration with Macroeconomics*,
https://doi.org/10.1007/978-3-030-40981-4_3

immigrants, the cost for public finances appears as the main economic concern associated with international migration. For instance, according to the European Social Survey (2014), 52% of European natives agree with allowing many or some immigrants from poorer countries outside Europe to come and live in their home country. Among them, 30% believe that, on balance, immigrants take more (in terms of health and welfare services used) than they add (in terms of taxes payed), and 18% believe that immigrants generally take jobs away from native workers. Among those who say they want few or no immigrants, these proportions are 61% and 45%, respectively.

The empirical assessment of the links between migration and the economy faces several challenges. First of all, the reality of migration is complex: immigrants do not form a homogeneous group of people, whether in terms of length of residence, reason for migration, or socio-economic characteristics. They do not necessarily have the same characteristics as non-immigrants. The reality of the economy is also complex: there are multiple links between economic variables, which can be direct or indirect, through spillovers most notably.

There are also statistical challenges. Migration statistics are often criticized for not capturing all immigrants particularly because of the irregular entry of foreigners. However, this type of problem is not unique to migration data; it is echoed in the undeclared work not captured in employment figures, and even in the unrecorded transactions left out of GDP. Fundamentally, migration policy deals with persons who are nationals from one country—the country of origin—who wish to settle for a period in another country—the host country. When the host country grants permission to settle permanently in its territory, for whatever reason (professional, educational, family, humanitarian), the immigrant can access the formal labor market and public services (education, transport, social protection), which (s)he contributes to financing like the rest of the resident population of that country. Migration policy evaluation thus considers the economic effects of the flows of migrants who have been granted permission to stay in the host country. For many countries, however, there is a real problem of collecting long-term statistical data on all immigrants and their socio-economic characteristics according to their date of arrival in the host country. Finally, immigrants are part of the resident population and the economic variables related to them are not recorded in the National Accounts separately from those of the non-immigrant population.

The other issue, to be found in all the research literature on migration economics, is how to establish a direction of causality. The interactions between the economic or budgetary situation of the host country and its migration flows are potentially bidirectional: public expenditure, for example, is likely to rise with migration flows and also to increase those flows. This statistical bias is often addressed by using in the estimates an instrumental variable that is correlated with migration flows but not correlated with public expenditure and the other variables that may affect them. Clemens and Hunt (2017), however, have recently shown that different instrumental variables possessing the good properties may lead to different interpretations of the effect of migration on wages.

More specifically, the study of the effects of migration on public finances raises two main methodological issues. It is clearly a macroeconomic question, but is usually addressed from an accounting point of view. Following Blau (1984)'s pioneering article, many studies have computed the costs and benefits of immigrants and compared them with the native-born population. These researches use microeconomic surveys and administrative sources to determine individual mean figures that are aggregated to evaluate the respective net contribution to public finances of the two groups. Such evaluations are heavily dependent on the quality of the sources used and unfortunately often rely on surveys whose prime purpose is not to assess the situation of immigrants. External validation is also complex because it is not possible to compare their results with data obtained from national accounts since these are not broken down by origin of resident population. More problematically, these cost-benefit analyses ignore the interactions among economic variables and thus disregard the consequences that immigrants may have on the economic situation of the rest of the population.

This chapter discusses two categories of migrants. The analysis focuses primarily on the flow of migrants who have been granted permission to settle permanently in the host country (either for an indefinite period or at least one year). Due to data restrictions, this flow is approximated by net migration, which represents the difference between the entry and exit of people in a given year. The analysis will also touch upon the flow of asylum seekers, whose residence permit is provisional while their application for international protection is being examined. If the asylum application is refused, the person is denied the right of asylum, which means that the host country does not grant permission to settle, and asks the asylum seeker to leave its territory. If the application is accepted, the host country allows the asylum seeker to settle permanently on humanitarian grounds, thus becoming a permanent immigrant.

After having established the conceptual framework for analyzing the effects of migration flows in host countries, we will present the results of our previous empirical studies which consider the effects on living standard, employment, unemployment and public finances. We will then generally discuss the findings by placing them in the context of relevant literature.

3.2 Macroeconomic Consequences of Immigration: Some Theoretical Insights

Theoretical reasoning allows us to define the problem and perceive the challenges. First, consider the standard of living in the host country, measured by the ratio of domestic production to the resident population, which is the main indicator of a country's economic activity. It is a function of the amount of capital mobilized for productive activities, that is productive capital, and the amount of labor used, that is total employment. It is clear that flows of permanent migrants are a component of population growth in host countries. In addition, most migrants are of working age and have, upon arrival to the host country, a certain level of training and knowledge acquired in their country of origin. Immigration therefore increases the working-age population in the host country, therefore labor supply, and it is likely to influence productive capital: thus, having effects on domestic production and possibly on per capita production levels. These effects are closely linked to the substitutability of production factors, particularly between resident workers and new immigrants, and also to the host country's economic environment.

One theoretical argument could assume that, upon arrival, immigrants are very similar in terms of qualifications to resident workers and they are likely to replace them; immigrants and resident workers are then assumed to be substitutable. Assuming constant returns to scale, this implies that as a result of immigration, wages per worker decline while capital returns increase. And if there is no wage adjustment, the unemployment rate increases, all else equal. More precisely, total employment, and consequently production, increases as a result of the arrival of migrants. If productive capital is constant, the increase in total employment would be greater than the increase in production (due to capital dilution), and ultimately labor productivity decreases. The effect of immigration on per capita output is therefore ambiguous: it depends on the respective magnitude of its effect on productivity and per capita employment. If the latter is unchanged, the immigration's effect on living standard corresponds to its effect on productivity, and is therefore negative. On the other hand, if per capita employment increases following the arrival of migrants, the potential decline in labor productivity can be offset by the increase in per capita employment, provided that migrants' participation in the host country's labor market is sufficiently high. If the productive capital increases, labor productivity also increases, which reinforces immigration's positive effect on living standard.

A second theoretical argument assumes that, upon arrival in the host country, immigrants have skills that enable them to occupy jobs that are complementary to those held by national workers. For example, jobs for which there are unmet labor needs in the host economy. Immigrants thus constitute a flexible source of labor which makes it possible to respond quickly to labor market needs and to compensate, in part, for the low geographical and occupational mobility of national workers. Migration does influence labor supply, but it is also likely to influence the labor demand of companies. The latter can take advantage of the low bargaining power of immigrants to offer them lower wages. In this context, potential profits increase following the arrival of immigrants, companies increase their demand for labor, and the employment prospects of the native population improve (Moreno-Galbis and Tritah 2016).

Nevertheless, empirically assessing the degree of substitutability or complementarity between production factors is complex; it depends on assumptions made about an economy's functioning, and on the reference period considered. Evaluation of substitutability's effects on labor and capital perfectly illustrates these challenges, which have been a subject of discussion in literature dating back to the 1960s (Cette et al. 2019). The implications of the value of the elasticity of substitution between capital and labor are important. High elasticity means that it is easy for the economy as a whole to replace capital with labor and vice versa, depending on the relative cost of labor relative to capital. Some studies have found an elasticity greater than 1, suggesting strong substitutability between capital and labor, but most have concluded that elasticity is less than 1. This debate reveals the difficulties of assessing elasticities even when data are available from National Accounts. It is therefore understandable that it is extremely difficult to assess the elasticity of substitution between different categories of workers, let alone between immigrants and the rest of the population. And there are other difficulties: the availability of representative data on immigrant workers by qualification level, and the sensitivity of the results to the qualification categories as defined. One shortcoming of general equilibrium models applied to the assessment of migration effects is precisely that their results depend crucially on the elasticity between immigrants and the rest of the population; an elasticity that we do not know.

For public finances, the relevant indicator is the fiscal balance, which is the difference between general government revenue and expenditure. One part of annual public revenue, social contributions, gives rise to rights to future public expenditure, social benefits. Similarly, part of the public expenditure in a year, for example education expenditure, is likely to generate future public revenue by improving future employment prospects. Public finance analysis thus requires to consider the effects over time, for successive generations of immigrants. In a given year, flows of permanent migrants increase the number of taxpayers and all taxes (direct or indirect taxes, social contributions), but their effect on per capita income is ambiguous as indicated above. Immigrants allowed to settle in the host country benefit from public services and public expenditure, which are also likely to increase. The effect of migration flows on the fiscal balance is on principle ambiguous and yet is crucially linked to the effects of immigration on domestic production.

At this stage, a theoretical analysis of the results does not provide a clear conclusion. However, a conceptual framework highlights the importance of the economic environment and immigrants' participation in economic activities as soon as they arrive in the host country. Theoretical effects rely upon assumptions, hence the importance of supplementing them with an empirical analysis of migration flows based on available data.

3.3 An Empirical Analysis Using a Panel of OECD Countries

To assess immigration's economic and fiscal impacts, empirical studies use available data and standard tools used in economics. They consider direct and indirect links between public expenditure and revenue, output per capita, employment and unemployment on the one hand; and, migration flows on the other hand. Many studies, which use alternative data sources and different methodologies, show that migration flows have a positive overall effect on gross domestic product per capita, thus improving the average standard of living in the host country. This positive effect can be explained by the effects that immigration can have on innovation, productive capital and employment. More recently, we have shown that the effect on public finances is also positive. Below is the methodological framework we have used in several recent articles and we present our econometric results.

3.3.1 Data

The data used in our papers come mainly from the OECD and Eurostat databases which are publicly available; this approach ensures the accessibility and comparability of each study's data. For most countries, the accurate economic and demographic data are available annually over a limited time period and are insufficient to analyze the macroeconomic effects of international migration in a given country. Thus, we consider a panel framework that allows us to conduct an accurate analysis on annual data for a sample of OECD countries which are selected in order to have a set of long-span data. More precisely, we consider all the OECD member countries which signed the Convention on the OECD before the beginning of the period examined and for which the demographic and economic data used in the corresponding study are available over the whole sample period.

For instance, our study of the fiscal consequences of international migration was conducted on a sample of 19 OECD countries: Australia, Austria, Canada, Belgium, Denmark, Finland, France, Germany, Ireland, Iceland, Italy, Japan, the Netherlands, Norway, Spain, Sweden, Portugal, the United Kingdom and the United States. For these countries, the fiscal data used the literature on fiscal multipliers (e.g. Beetsma et al. 2006) are available from 1980. Thus, our sample includes yearly observations from 1980 to 2015 for 19 countries and can be used to replicate the findings of the fiscal policy literature (Blanchard and Perotti 2002; Perotti 2005; Beetsma et al. 2006, 2008; Beetsma and Giuliodori 2011). The idea is to establish in the first stage the suitability of our empirical model with regard to the recent findings in the literature concerning the economic effects of fiscal policies. We then analyze the economic and fiscal effects of international migration.

In line with the literature on fiscal multipliers (e.g. Beetsma and Giuliodori 2011), we compute the first variable, government purchases, as the sum of general government final consumption expenditure and general government fixed capital formation. The second variable, transfers paid by the general government, is computed as the sum of social security benefits and other current payments. The third variable, tax revenues collected by the general government, includes direct and indirect taxes on production and imports, social security contributions and other current transfer receipts. Out of those three variables, we define (i) net taxes as the difference between tax revenues received and transfers paid by the general government; (ii) public spending as the sum of the government purchases and transfers, and (iii) the fiscal balance as the difference between general government revenues and spending. We also consider GDP, total employment and the unemployment rate. All these variables are expressed in real terms.

The originality of our approach is to consider the effects of international migration in the model used in the fiscal policy literature. To this end, we consider the net flow of migrants using net migration data. To the best of our knowledge, this data is the only annual data available over the period 1980–2015 for the 19 OECD countries we consider. Net migration is calculated as the difference between the total change and the natural change of the "usual resident" population. Net migration then accounts for the difference between the number of immigrants and the number of emigrants. It does not make a distinction between nationals and foreigners.

Note that most available data on international migration are related to the population of immigrants, for which data is usually obtained from population censuses. This data is usually available for limited periods, mostly at ten-year intervals. The available data at five-year intervals is built by interpolating ten-year intervals (see, for instance, Brücker et al. 2013). Furthermore, net migration data generally suffer from fewer comparability issues than data on inflows and outflows of foreigners published by the OECD and Eurostat. Comparability is indeed difficult as national systems of registering permanent entries and exits are heterogeneous. Each OECD country uses its available sources (population registers, international passenger survey, residence permits etc.) to compute entries (since 1990 only) but a minority of countries collects information on exits. The limitation of available national statistics on foreigners in OECD countries is a well-known problem (see Lemaître et al. 2006, for a discussion on the sources and methods of harmonized statistics on inflows) and the OECD has undertaken initiatives to harmonize the statistics on inflows of foreign nationals. However, this harmonized data is only available since 2007 for 18 OECD countries of our sample. Conversely, net migration data is based on population and vital statistics, which is much more comparable. We also consider two additional demographic variables; total population and working-age population.

3.3.2 Methodology

We set up a structural VAR model to draw inference on the macroeconomic effects of international migration, following a methodology developed in the empirical fiscal policy literature that started with the seminal paper of Blanchard and Perotti (2002). Given the available time-series data, we consider a panel VAR as in Alesina et al. (2002). Our empirical model is specified as follows:

$$Z_{it} = A(L)Z_{it} + v_i + \lambda_i t + f_t + \varepsilon_{it} \text{ for } i = 1, \ldots, N \text{ and } t = 1, \ldots, T$$

where Z_{it} is the vector of endogenous variables, $A(L)$ is a matrix polynomial in the lag operator L, v_i is the vector of country fixed-effects, $\lambda_i t$ represents country-specific time trends, f_t is the common time-specific effect and ε_{it} is the vector of residuals satisfying $E(\varepsilon_{it}) = 0$, $E(\varepsilon_{it}\varepsilon'_{it}) = 0$ and $E(\varepsilon_{it}\varepsilon'_{j\tau}) = \Omega$ for $i \neq j$ or $t \neq \tau$.

This empirical model is estimated using the bias-corrected fixed-effects technique developed by Hahn and Kuersteiner (2002) in order to deal with the short T dynamic panel data bias (also known as the Nickell (1981) bias). This technique is appropriate when the sizes of the time dimension T and the cross-sectional dimension N are of the same order of magnitude, i.e., when $0 < N = T < \infty$ (as is always the case in our papers). As argued by Hahn and Kuersteiner (2002), since their approach does not require a preliminary consistent estimator, it may therefore be perceived as an implementable version of Kiviet's (1995) bias-corrected fixed-effects estimator of the single equation. More importantly, it is suitable for $VAR(p)$ models with orders higher than 1. Moreover, the Monte Carlo experiment conducted by Hahn and Kuersteiner (2002) showed that the efficiency of the bias-corrected estimator measured by the root mean squared error often dominates that of the generalized method of moments estimator. To set the lag length of the system, we use the Akaike information criterion and the Bayesian information criterion.

To choose the appropriate VAR model (in level or in first difference), we consider the stationarity properties of the variables. To this end, we use the second-generation panel unit root test developed by Pesaran

(2007) that accounts for cross-sectional dependence. This methodology, with the null hypothesis of the presence of a unit root in all series, is based on augmenting the usual augmented Dickey-Fuller (ADF) regression with the lagged cross-sectional mean and its first difference to capture the cross-sectional dependence. Panel unit root tests fail to accept the null hypothesis of the unit root on detrending the variables (with country-specific linear trend). So, we consider a VAR model on variables in levels while controlling for country heterogeneity (by including country-specific effects and country-specific time trends) and cross-country interdependence (by including year-specific effects).

After estimating the VAR coefficients, we establish causal relationship between variables by identifying structural shocks based on Cholesky decomposition. This identifying scheme relies on the assumption that variables ordered first in the VAR can impact the other variables contemporaneously, while variables ordered later can affect those ordered first only with lags.

In other words, we make assumptions about the contemporary impacts of the shocks specifying which variables may be influenced in period t by a change in another variable in the same period t, while no restriction is placed on the variables for dates after t. Precisely, a structural shock, or innovation, to one variable can impact at time t this variable and the other variables ordered afterwards, and from $t + 1$, all the variables of the system. In our papers, we consider that migration can contemporaneously affect the economic performance of the host country, and it is assumed to respond to it only with a lag. This assumption is supported by an international migration process where the decision to migrate is generally taken on the basis of the host country's economic conditions over the previous years. As pointed out by Smith and Thoenissen (2019), this identifying assumption seems reasonable given that moving from a country can be a lengthy process. Concerning the economic and fiscal variables, the ordering we choose is the same as the one chosen in the literature.

In this recursive identification scheme, results depend on the order of the variables. Thus, the assumption of ordering migration variable first is key and is justified by the fact that the decision to migrate is generally made before the year during which migrants settle in the host country.

Although this justification is highly plausible, we conduct two robustness checks. First, we consider the role of anticipation. Even if the decision to migrate is generally taken before immigration, one cannot exclude the idea that the migration decision may be based on migrants' expectations. On the other hand, we may imagine that private agents in the host country also form expectations on future immigration inflows and react to them. This is taken into account in the VAR analysis (due to its intrinsic dynamic structure), insofar the most relevant variable (GDP) considered in these expectations is included in the VAR (Stock and Watson 2001). Furthermore, we include "forward-looking" variables in the VAR, which are supposed to contain information about the future effects of shocks. Second, we propose an alternative identification strategy that is not recursive and employs *sign restrictions* (see Fry and Pagan 2011, for a review of the estimation of SVAR with sign restrictions). This approach was recently was used by Furlanetto and Robstad (2019) to analyze the macroeconomic effects of immigration in Norway. In the absence of a strong theoretical basis, it is not easy to choose the appropriate sign restrictions on macroeconomic variables in order to identify migration shocks. With that in mind, we consider an identification scheme based on sign restrictions with a penalty function criterion proposed by Faust (1998) and Uhlig (2005) to identify monetary policy shocks.

To analyze the macroeconomic effects of international migration, we consider a number of specifications depending on the economic and fiscal variables of interest. For instance, the baseline specification in line with the literature on fiscal multipliers including our migration variable is given by the following system:

$$Z_{it} = \left[log\left(1+m_{it}\right), log\left(g_{it}\right), log\left(nt_{it}\right), log\left(y_{it}\right) \right]'$$

where g_{it} is government purchases per capita, nt_{it} is net taxes per capita and y_{it} is GDP per capita. Because the ratio of net migration to population (m_{it}) can be negative, we add one to express the variable in logarithm.

Following standard practice in the literature, we assume that government purchases can impact contemporaneously net taxes and GDP, while changes in net taxes and GDP can, at best, impact government purchases with a lag. Net taxes are allowed to have a contemporaneous impact on GDP, and may be influenced by GDP only with a lag. This identifying assumption is justified by institutional knowledge on fiscal policy that is as follows: (i) decisions on changing government purchases are generally taken in the Budget Act that is presented before the new fiscal year, while adjustments during the current year may be considered as negligible (Beetsma et al. 2006, 2008; Beetsma and Giuliodori 2011) and (ii) net taxes include both cyclically sensitive components (some spending items such as social benefits and other current receipts) and discretionary components under the government's control that are also determined in the Budget Act before the new fiscal year.

In the literature, the fiscal balance is expressed as share of GDP: $\frac{nt-g}{y}$ and its response is computed as:

$$\frac{nt}{y}\left[\widehat{\log(nt)}-\widehat{\log(y)}\right]-\frac{g}{y}\left[\widehat{\log(g)}-\widehat{\log(y)}\right]$$

where $\widehat{\log(nt)}$, $\widehat{\log(g)}$ and $\widehat{\log(y)}$ are the impulse responses of the logarithm of net taxes per capita, of the logarithm of government purchases per capita and of the logarithm of GDP per capita, respectively. The ratios $\frac{nt}{y}$ and $\frac{g}{y}$ are approximated by the overall sample mean.

We are aware that transfers include some items that are cyclically sensitive. The estimation of the baseline model using cyclically adjusted net taxes, instead of unadjusted net taxes, gives roughly the same impulse responses (see Beetsma and Giuliodori 2011; d'Albis et al. 2018, for more discussion of this issue).

Note that our model was able to replicate the results from recent studies on the macroeconomic effects of fiscal stimulus. More specifically, we compare the stimulating effect of a government purchases increase in our model that includes the net flow of migrants with the findings of previous studies (Beetsma et al. 2006, 2008; Beetsma and Giuliodori 2011) and we find that our estimates are quite similar (see d'Albis et al. 2019a, Appendix A-2 for more details). Our model can therefore be used to analyze the macroeconomic effects of migration shocks.

3.3.3 Results

Let's begin with the effects of the net flow of migrants on the average standard of living of OECD countries. To take into account the labor market, we extend our baseline model to include the logarithm of the unemployment rate. The impulse response functions following a migration shock are presented in Fig. 3.1.

Figure 3.1 shows that, following the migration shock, GDP per capita increases significantly in the year of that shock and the improvement

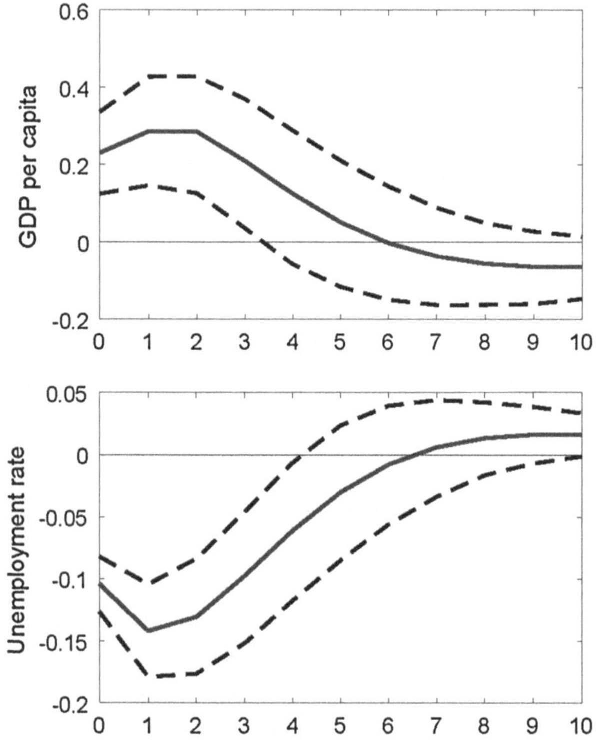

Fig. 3.1 Impulse responses of output and unemployment following a migration shock. Notes: The solid line gives the estimated impulse responses. Dashed lines give the 90% confidence intervals generated by Monte Carlo with 5000 repetitions. The size of the migration shock is set to 1 person per 1000 inhabitants. The response of GDP per capita is in percentage change. For the unemployment rate (u), the response is in percentage points change. This figure refers to the following specification: $Z_{it} = [log(1 + m_{it}), log(g_{it}), log(nt_{it}), log(y_{it}), log(u_{it})]'$

remains significant after three years. The unemployment rate decreases significantly in the year of the shock and for three years after the shock. These findings are consistent with previous empirical studies, such as Boubtane et al. (2013a) and Ortega and Peri (2014).

The net flow of permanent migrants improves the average standard of living and enhances job opportunities in the OECD countries. In order to disentangle the effects of international migration on GDP per capita, we consider in the baseline specification the decomposition of GDP per capita into three components: the share of working-age, the ratio of total employment to the working-age population (namely, the employment rate) and the GDP per person employed (labor productivity according to national accounts).[1] The impulse response functions following a migration shock are presented in Fig. 3.2.

The ratio of working-age to total population significantly increases after a migration shock from the year of that shock and for at least four years. This result is expected given that migrants are mainly of working-age. The employment rate significantly increases after a migration shock from the year of that shock and remains significant for at least seven years. The response of labor productivity is not significant during the four years after the migration shock and becomes negative from the fifth year after the shock. The positive response of GDP per capita to a migration shock obtained in our baseline specification is thus driven by the demographic effect that materializes through an increase in the share of working-age population and a positive response of the employment rate.

With regard to public finance, we analyze the fiscal effects of the net flow of migrants using our baseline specification. The impulse response functions to a migration shock are presented in Fig. 3.3.

Following the migration shock, government purchases per capita rise significantly in the year of the shock and for five years after. Net taxes per capita also increase from the year of the shock and for three years after the shock. Consequently, the fiscal balance improves significantly in response to an exogenous shock that increases the net flow of migrants. The improvement remains significant after two years.

Note that our results are robust to the issues related to anticipations and to the use of an alternative identification strategy based on sign restrictions, discussed above.

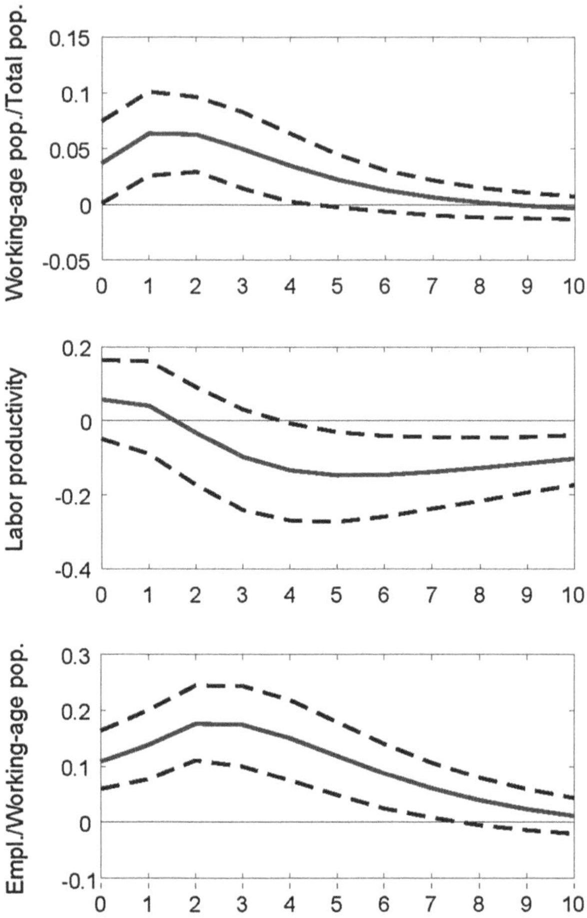

Fig. 3.2 Impulse responses of additional variables following a migration shock. Notes: The solid line gives the estimated impulse responses. Dashed lines give the 90% confidence intervals generated by Monte Carlo with 5000 repetitions. The size of the migration shock is set to 1 person per 1000 inhabitants. The response of labor productivity (*pdty*) is in percentage change. For the employment rate (*er*) and the working-age to total population ratio (*wa*), the responses are in percentage points change. This figure refers to the following specification: $Z_{it} = [log(1 + m_{it}), log(wa_{it}), log(g_{it}), log(nt_{it}), log(pdty_{it}), log(er_{it})]'$

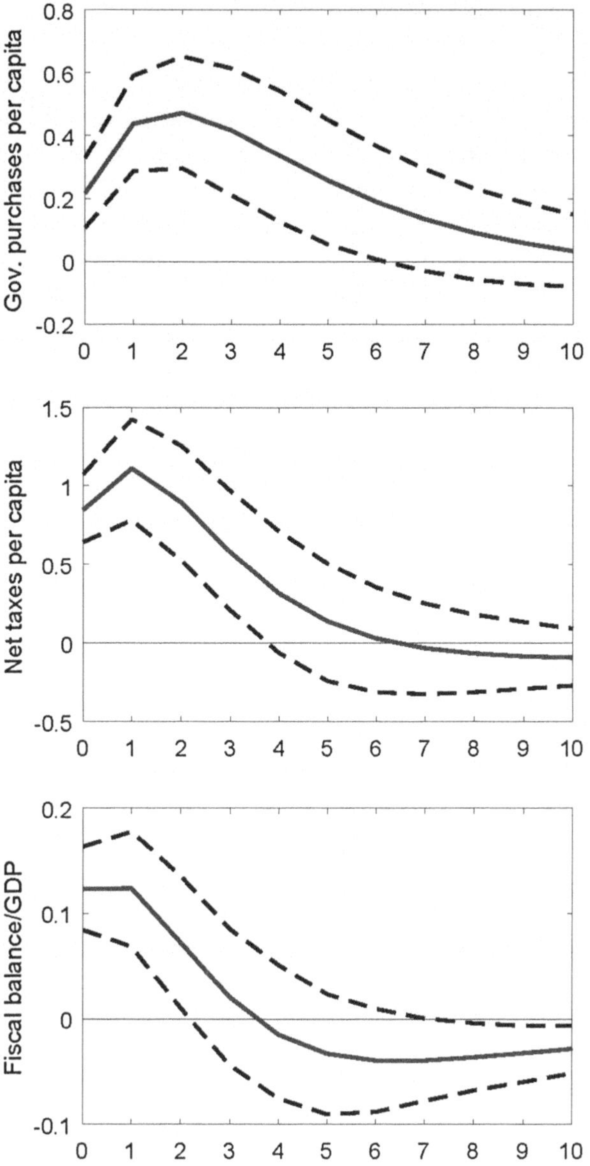

Fig. 3.3 Impulse responses of fiscal variables to a migration shock. Notes: The solid line gives the estimated impulse responses. Dashed lines give the 90% confidence intervals generated by Monte Carlo with 5000 repetitions. The size of the migration shock is set to 1 person per 1000 inhabitants. The responses of net taxes per capita and government purchases per capita are in percentage change. For the fiscal balance to GDP ratio, the response is in percentage points change. This figure refers to the baseline specification

An important issue in OECD countries is the effect of international migration on labor market conditions. We thus go beyond our baseline model and consider now the effect of the net flow of migrants on public spending on labor market policies. These expenditures can be found in both the government purchases and in the transfers paid by the government. Thus, we group those two components of government expenditures into one variable named public spending. In the baseline specification, our fiscal variables are here public spending (including transfers) per capita (*ps*) and tax revenues per capita (*re*) in two additional specifications. Using the OECD Social Expenditure Database (SOCX) decomposition of public expenditure, we study the effect of a migration shock considering the SOCX data social policy areas related to labor market: *active labor markets programs* and *unemployment* (see Adema et al. 2011, for the methodological aspects of the OECD SOCX data). We consider two additional variables: active labor market programs spending per capita (*als*) and unemployment spending per capita (*us*).[2] Figure 3.4 shows the impulse response functions of those two variables following a migration shock.

Public spending on active labor market increases, while spending associated to unemployment benefits decreases. These results interestingly clarify the effects of the net flow of migrants on the labor market. As newcomers, migrants are necessarily more likely to benefit from a public accompaniment during their job search, which represents a cost for public finances. However, because of their contribution to the reduction of unemployment rate, migrants do reduce the expenditure associated with unemployment benefits. Thus, the resident population benefit from a migration shock even if public spending dedicated to active labor market policies increases.

The arrival in Europe of more than one million people who applied for asylum in 2015 has raised concerns about the economic and fiscal impact of asylum seekers. We consider a sample of 15 Western European countries which are the main host countries of asylum seekers (89% in 2015) from 1985 to 2015. The flow of asylum seekers is measured as the number of first applications, pending at the end of the year, made by people who state that they are unable to return to their country of origin due to a well-founded fear of being persecuted. Data is from Eurostat. The

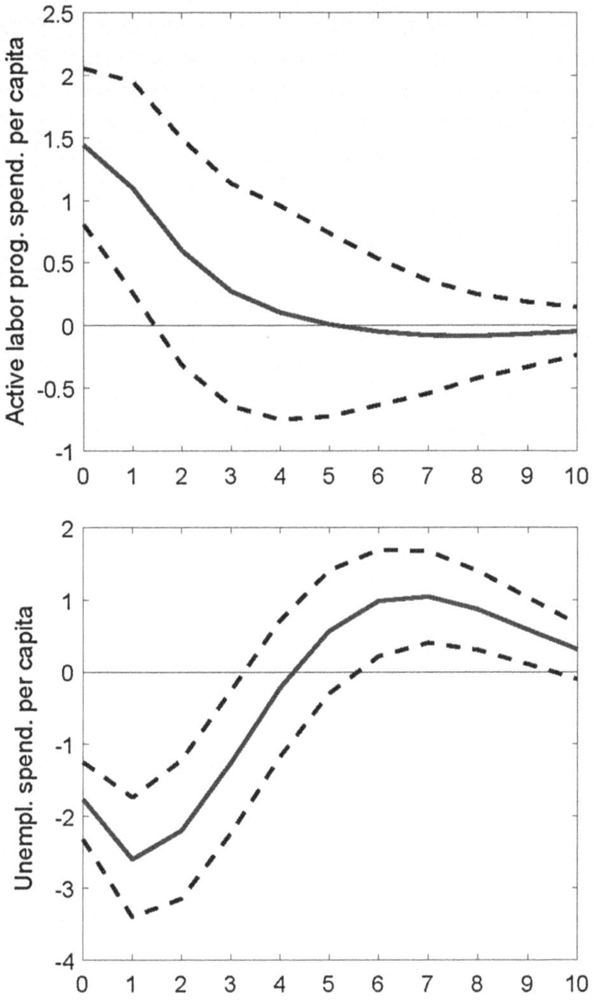

Fig. 3.4 Impulse responses of public spending on labor market policies following a migration shock. Notes: The solid line gives the estimated impulse responses. Dashed lines give the 90% confidence intervals generated by Monte Carlo with 5000 repetitions. The size of the migration shock is set to 1 person per 1000 inhabitants. The responses of per capita spending on labor market policies are in percentage change. This figure refers to the following specifications: $Z_{it} = [log(1 + m_{it}), log(ps_{it}), log(als_{it}), log(re_{it}), log(y_{it})]'$, $Z_{it} = [log(1 + m_{it}), log(ps_{it}), log(us_{it}), log(re_{it}), log(y_{it})]'$

lodging of an asylum application with a country entitles the applicant to reside legally in that country while the application is being processed but generally does not entitle the applicant to work and does not necessarily lead to being granted refugee status. We extend our baseline model including unemployment and the flow of asylum seekers in the system. The impulse response functions following a shock to the flow of asylum seekers are presented in Fig. 3.5.

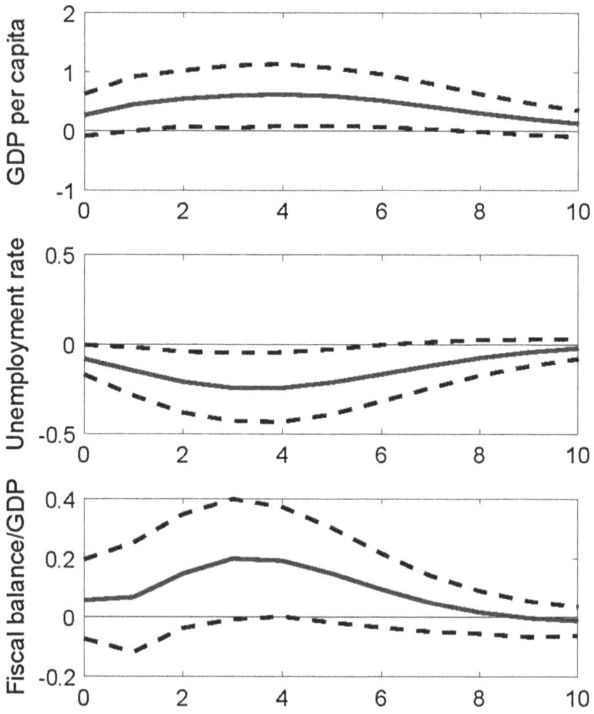

Fig. 3.5 Impulse responses following a shock to the flow of asylum seekers. Notes: The solid line gives the estimated impulse responses. Dashed lines give the 90% confidence intervals generated by Monte Carlo with 5000 repetitions. The size of the migration shock is set to 1 asylum seeker per 1000 inhabitants. The responses of net taxes per capita and government purchases per capita are in percentage change. For the fiscal balance to GDP ratio, the response is in percentage points change. This figure refers to the following specification, where *as* is the ratio of the flow of asylum seekers to population: $Z_{it} = [log(1 + as_{it}), log(1 + m_{it}), log(g_{it}), log(nt_{it}), log(y_{it}), log(u_{it})]'$

We are occasionally told that granting asylum seekers entry brings significant costs for host countries, but over the period in our study, i.e. 1985–2015, we found no statistical evidence suggesting a worsening of economic conditions in Western European countries, whether in terms of standard of living, unemployment or public finances. After several years, there may be a slight positive effect as asylum seekers granted permanent residence take up employment and contribute actively to the economy of their host country.

3.4 Discussion

The results presented above are part of a literature that has been developing in recent years on the macroeconomic assessment of the effects of immigration in host countries. An important contribution is made by Ortega and Peri (2014) who show that the immigrant population contributes to the improvement of total factor productivity. These authors analyze the effects of bilateral migration flows by taking into account geographical factors. They use variations in the immigrant population between 188 countries using census data from around the 2000s. They show a positive effect on the standard of living that is linked to an increase in overall productivity, explained by the immigrant population's diversity and positive contributions to innovation. The diversity of immigrants' countries of origin reflects the diversity of their qualifications, complementary to those of the native population, whose effects are beneficial for the host economy. In addition, immigrants contribute to innovation and research and development activities: they are researchers or founders of innovative companies. Their total contribution can nevertheless be underestimated because the mixing of different and complementary ideas can result in an increase in the contribution of native people to innovation. Ortega and Peri (2014) show that an increased share of immigrants in the population increases the number of patents filed per capita in host countries. Finally, the study shows that immigrants do not have significant effects on income disparity in the host population (measured by the Gini coefficient) or on income distribution between those with the highest and lowest incomes.

In addition, the average standard of living increases when immigrants arrive with knowledge acquired in the country of origin and contribute to the productive capital of the host country. This result was highlighted by Boubtane et al. (2016) in a study that uses both variation across countries and variation over time. The article analyses the effects of migration flows from data of 22 OECD countries covering the years 1987–2006 and shows that this positive effect is linked to the human capital contribution of recent migration flows. Indeed, recent immigrants are relatively more skilled than the resident population, nearly 30% of recent immigrants have a higher level of education than that of resident population, and they contribute to the productive capital of OECD host countries. In another study using a different approach, migration's positive effect on living standard in the 22 OECD countries is confirmed by taking into consideration the potential impact of migration flows on the labor market. This study uses the time series approach which, unlike the approaches used in the two studies mentioned above, does not require the use of theoretical restrictions to estimate the causal effects of migration flows (Boubtane et al. 2013a, b). This approach, introduced by Christopher Sims, is widely used to assess the aggregate effects of macroeconomic policies. Its main advantage is that it allows statistical data to speak for itself by imposing very few theoretical assumptions. We adapt this approach to the analysis of immigration's economic effects, a subject for which there is no consensus among economists. The results indicate that migration flows increase per capita output on average in OECD countries and improve employment prospects for native and immigrant populations. Indeed, the arrival of new immigrants contributes to reducing the unemployment rate of native-born people and also that of immigrants in OECD countries. These results are consistent with those generally obtained in the literature and suggest that immigrants upon arrival occupy jobs that are generally complementary to the jobs held by all workers.

D'Albis et al. (2019a) also show that the increase in per capita output is linked to the positive effect of immigration on the employment rate—the ratio of total employment to the working-age population. On the one hand, flows of permanent migrants are mainly composed of people of working age; 80% of the immigrant population in OECD countries is aged between 15 and 64 in 2017. The share of working-age population increases with immigration. On the other hand, permanent migrants authorized to settle for professional purposes have a job or a promise of employment upon arrival. The others also enter the labor market mainly with jobs that are complements to those held by resident workers. Our results therefore suggest that the increase in total employment is greater than the increase in the working-age population, hence the positive effect of immigration on the employment rate and standard of living.

One of the shortcomings of the previous studies is that they use a panel of countries, which can always be suspected of being heterogeneous, and which above all only gives an average response (i.e. for an average country in the panel) and does not allow a specific country analysis. Country analyses, which require quality databases, are then useful. For example, an assessment of the macroeconomic effects of immigration in France also shows an improvement in the average standard of living. In a first study using monthly data for metropolitan France from 1994 to 2008, we highlight a positive effect on per capita production of flows of immigrants coming from countries of the European Economic Area (d'Albis et al. 2016). Overall, immigrants arriving in France, particularly those who have arrived in the family context and who come from developing countries, enter into stressful occupations (e.g. personal services or the construction sector) and are likely to occupy jobs that rather complement those of resident workers. Our second study, based on annual regional data (of France's 22 former regions) from 1990 to 2013, confirms these results and shows that immigration has a positive effect on the average standard of living in the French regions and has no significant effects on the housing market (d'Albis et al. 2019b).

On the public finance side, several studies have analyzed the fiscal impact of immigration. Accounting studies provide an approximation of the distribution of public revenue and expenditure between the immigrant population and the non-immigrant population for a given year. Depending on the year, the estimated relative budget balance of the immigrant population may be positive or negative, but it remains relatively low. These accounting studies do not take into account interdependencies between different economic variables. The links between these variables are not simple accounting relationships, they involve a multitude of links that can be direct or indirect, which are the subject of economic analysis. To take into account all of immigration's effects on public finances, several studies apply standard tools. One approach uses a macroeconomic model that represents the economy as a whole. This type of model can be used to simulate the impact of economic policies or external shocks (such as an increase in the price of oil). The results obtained are linked to theoretical assumptions and elasticity values used to simulate the effects, but this type of model allows for a rich analysis and details a multitude of direct and indirect links between economic variables. In a recent study, Aubry et al. (2016) propose a multi-country model that they calibrate using data from 34 OECD countries for two years (2000 and 2010). The results of their simulations of immigration's economic and fiscal effects indicate a positive average impact. A second approach uses the time-series method and considers the effects of migration flows on government's various expenditures and revenues. The data is aggregated directly from the National Accounts and covers the entire resident population. This model is typically used to assess the impact of fiscal policies on public finances, but we adapt it for the analysis of immigration effects (d'Albis et al. 2018, 2019a). Our results indicate that the flow of permanent migrants increases per capita production as well as public expenditure and revenue as a proportion of population. The increase in public revenues following the arrival of immigrants is greater than the increase in public spending, and so the budgetary balance in relation to national production increases. The fiscal impact of permanent migrant flows is positive and can be explained by the "demographic dividend" generated by migration. Indeed, migration flows increase the proportion of people of working age in the population, which has many favorable economic and fiscal consequences. Migration changes the population's age structure, resulting in a decline in per capita public transfers while per capita public revenues increase. Some types of public spending increase, particularly on family and children, while others decrease, particularly on pensions and spending on older people. All in all, the effect is positive and the public finance balance improves with migration.

The aforementioned studies focus on migrants authorized to settle permanently in OECD host countries. The arrival in Europe of more than one million asylum applicants in 2015 has raised concerns about the economic and fiscal impact of these flows. To answer this question, we consider the economic and fiscal effects of asylum seeker flows in 15

European countries between 1985 and 2015 (d'Albis et al. 2018). We use the time-series approach based on annual data and our results indicate that no negative effects are observed on either macroeconomic variables or public finances. The fiscal impact of asylum seekers is not significant and the effect on living standards is positive even three to five years after arrival, when some are granted permanent asylum and can fully participate in the economic activities of their European host countries.

3.5 Conclusion

An increase in the flow of permanent migrants has a positive effect on OECD economies: GDP per capita increases significantly for four years, the unemployment rate falls and the budget balance sharply improves.

With respect to the flow of asylum seekers, we find no deterioration in the economic conditions of western European countries, namely living standards, unemployment or the budget balance. After a number of years, there may be a rather slight positive effect, due to the fact that some asylum seekers granted long-term residency contribute to the host country's economy by working. However, we note that immigrants, especially asylum seekers, are not here to "boost" European economies. International migration raises a number of social, cultural and political issues in host countries, and also tough diplomatic problems within Europe. This is why it is crucial to present empirical evidence rejecting the notion which associates migrants and asylum seekers with an economic burden.

This research could be pursued in many directions. In particular, the inequality issue is crucial. This is relevant as any increase in inequality may reinforce the opposition to globalization in general and international migration in particular. In a recent paper (d'Albis et al. 2019c) we analyze the impact of migration flows on the inequality between capital and labor. Variation in this inequality probably correlates with disparity between the income of the richest and poorest, because capital is more concentrated in corporate profits, which are less equally distributed than wages (IMF 2017). Our results suggest that immigration reduces this inequality.

Notes

1. Note that log GDPPop = log GDPEmpl + log EmpWork. age pop. + log Work. age popPop. Using the notation of the estimated model (Fig. 3.2): log (yit) = log (pdtyit) + log (erit) + log (wait).
2. The estimation sample covers 19 OECD countries over the period 1990–2013 for the model including spending on active labor market programs. For the model including unemployment spending, the estimation sample covers 18 OECD countries over the period 1990–2013.

References

Adema, W., Fron, P., Ladaique, M. 2011. "Is the European welfare state really more expensive? : Indicators on social spending, 1980–2012; and a manual to the OECD Social Expenditure Database (SOCX)". *OECD Social, Employment and Migration Working Papers* 124.

d'Albis H., Boubtane E. and Coulibaly D. 2016. "Immigration Policy and Macroeconomic Performances in France". *Annals of Economics and Statistics* 121–122: 279–308.

d'Albis H., Boubtane E. and Coulibaly D. 2018. "Macroeconomic evidence suggests that asylum seekers are not a "burden" for Western European countries". *Science Advances*: 4.

d'Albis H., Boubtane E. and Coulibaly D. 2019a. "Immigration and Public Finances in OECD Countries". *Journal of Economic Dynamics and Control* 99: 116–151.

d'Albis H., Boubtane E. and Coulibaly D. 2019b. "International Migration and Regional Housing Markets: Evidence from France". *International Regional Science Review* 42(2): 147–180.

d'Albis H., Boubtane E. and Coulibaly D. 2019c "Demographic Changes and the Labor Income Share" *PSE working Paper.*

Alesina, A., Ardagna, S., Perotti, R., Schiantarelli, F. 2002. "Fiscal policy, profits, and investment". *American Economic Review* 92: 571–589.

Aubry A., Burzynski M. and Docquier F. 2016. "The welfare impact of global migration in OECD countries". *Journal of International Economics* 101: 1–21.

Beetsma, R., Giuliodori, M. 2011. "The effects of government purchases shocks: Review and estimates for the EU". *The Economic Journal* 121: F4–F32.

Beetsma, R., Giuliodori, M., Klaassen, F. 2006. "Trade spill-overs of fiscal policy in the European Union: A panel analysis". *Economic Policy* 21: 639–687.
Beetsma, R., Giuliodori, M., Klaassen, F. 2008. "The effects of public spending shocks on trade balances and budget deficits in the European Union". *Journal of the European Economic Association* 6(2/3): 414–423.
Blanchard, O.J., Perotti, R. 2002. "An empirical characterization of the dynamic effects change in government spending and taxes on output". *Quarterly Journal of Economics* 117: 1329–1368.
Brücker H., Capuano, S., Marfouk, A. 2013. "Education, gender and international migration: Insights from a panel-dataset 1980–2010". *mimeo.*
Boubtane E., Coulibaly D. and Rault C. 2013a. "Immigration, Growth and Unemployment: Panel VAR Evidence from OECD Countries". *Labour: Review of Labour Economics and Industrial Relations* 27(4): 399–420.
Boubtane E., Coulibaly D. and Rault C. 2013b. "Immigration, Unemployment and Growth in the Host Country: Bootstrap Panel Granger Causality Analysis on OECD Countries". *Economic Modelling* 33: 261–269.
Boubtane E., Dumont J.-C., and Rault C. 2016. "Immigration and economic growth in the OECD countries 1986–2006". *Oxford Economic Papers* 62: 340–360.
Blau, F. D. 1984. "The use of transfer payments by immigrants". *Industrial and Labor Relations Review* 37(2): 222–239.
Cette, G., Koehl, L. and Philippon, T. 2019. "Labor shares in some advanced economies". *NBER Working Paper* 26136.
Clemens, M A and Hunt, J. 2017. "The Labor Market Effects of Refugee Waves: Reconciling Conflicting Results". *CEP Discussion Paper* 1491.
European Social Survey Round 7 Data. 2014. Data file edition 2.1. NSD—Norwegian Centre for Research Data. Norway Data Archive and distributor of ESS data for ESS ERIC.
Faust, J. 1998. "The robustness of identified VAR conclusions about money". *Carnegie-Rochester Conference Series on Public Policy* 49: 207–244.
Fry, R., Pagan, A. 2011. "Sign restrictions in structural vector autoregressions: A critical review". *Journal of Economic Literature* 49 (4): 938–60.
Furlanetto, F., Robstad, Ø, 2019. "Immigration and the macroeconomy: Some new empirical evidence". *Review of Economic Dynamics* 34: 1–19.
Hahn, J., Kuersteiner, G., 2002. "Asymptotically unbiased inference for a dynamic panel model with fixed effects when both n and T are large". *Econometrica* 70: 1639–1657.

IMF, 2017. "Understanding the downward trend in labor income shares". In World Economic Outlook: Gaining Monentum. *International Monetary Fund*, Publication Services. Washington.

Kiviet, J. F., 1995. "On bias, inconsistency, and efficiency of various estimators in dynamic panel data models". *Journal of Econometrics* 68: 53–78.

Lemaître, G., Liebig, T, Thoreau, C. 2006. "Harmonised statistics on immigrant inflows-preliminary results, sources and methods". Report OECD, Paris.

Moreno-Galbis, E. and Tritah, A. 2016. "The effects of immigration in frictional labor markets: Theory and empirical evidence from EU countries". *European Economic Review* 84: 76–98.

Nickell, S. J. 1981. "Biases in dynamic models with fixed effects". *Econometrica* 49: 1417–1426.

Ortega, F. and Peri, G. 2014. "Openness and income: The roles of trade and migration". *Journal of International Economics* 92(2): 231–251.

Pesaran, M. H., 2007. "A simple panel unit root test in the presence of cross-section dependence". *Journal of Applied Econometrics* 27: 265–312.

Perotti, R., 2005. "Estimating the effects of fiscal policy in OECD countries". *CEPR Discussion.*

Smith, C., Thoenissen, C. 2019. "Skilled migration and business cycle dynamics". *Journal of Economic Dynamics and Control*, 108, forthcoming.

Stock, J. H., Watson, M. W. 2001. "Vector Autoregressions". *Journal of Economic Perspectives* 15, 101–115.

Uhlig, H., 2005. "What are the effects of monetary policy on output? Results from an agnostic identification procedure". *Journal of Monetary Economics* 52: 381–419.

United Nations, Department of Economic and Social Affairs. Population Division, 2019. "Trends in International Migrant Stock: The 2019 revision". United Nations database, POP/DB/MIG/Stock/Rev.2019.

4

The Economics of Brain Waste

Emily R. Barker

4.1 Introduction

In the last 30 years, the levels of migration worldwide have increased significantly. There are now 258 million people living outside their country of birth. According to research by the United Nations, the international stock of migrants increased by 17% between 2000 and 2017 (United Nations 2017). The four main reasons for migration are economic, political, social, and environmental. Economic migration is based on seeking improved employment opportunities. Political migration is escaping conflict or authoritarian regimes. Social migration relates to family reunification. And environmental migration is leaving areas which are becoming or will be uninhabitable in the future.

Countries that are net hosts of migrants are predominantly advanced economies.[1] These advanced economies have dominating industries that are shifting towards high-skilled, which often leads to gaps in the labour

E. R. Barker (✉)
Department of Economics, The University of Sheffield, Sheffield, UK
e-mail: erbarker1@sheffield.ac.uk

E. Vella et al. (eds.), *Understanding Migration with Macroeconomics*,
https://doi.org/10.1007/978-3-030-40981-4_4

market. The need for skilled workers, and migration when these gaps form, is ever increasing, particularly in the areas of technology. In this chapter, we analyse the economic impacts of brain waste for countries that are net hosts of migrants.[2] We focus on Canada, a country that experiences notably high levels of brain waste and has been recognised at a federal level. Once called "A nation of immigrants", Canada is one of the most ethnically diverse countries in the world. Even though the majority of migrants are happy in Canada—since of the migrants eligible for Canadian citizenship, 86% had acquired citizenship—still there are a large number that are unable to use their full potential in comparison to migrants. This is the highest rate amongst similar countries (Fung et al. 2019).[3]

The story of brain waste follows that brain drain is the loss of human capital to the sending nation. The country that hosts the migrant and their human capital has brain gain. However, brain waste occurs when the gain of human capital is not maximised in the host country. Brain waste consists of underemployment and increased involuntary employment in comparison to natives. Underemployment is when a worker is employed in a job for which they are overqualified, a skill-job mismatch, paid less than their native equivalent, employed only part-time when full-time is desired, and experiences higher labour market frictions.

4.2 Migration Compact

The topic of migration is frequently debated in both political and economic contexts and has increased in its importance dramatically in recent decades. Before 2018, there was no common approach to migration which was dealt with on a sovereign basis. However, in 2018, the United Nations put forward a migration compact that targeted a common approach to migration internationally. The not legally binding pact aims to manage migration at multiple geographical levels and optimise the benefits of migration for the sending and host nations. The "UN Global Compact for Safe, Orderly and Regular Migration" contained 23 objectives that cover all types of migration: economic, political, social, and environmental. Three of the objectives are particularly relevant to the integration of economic migrants:

Objective (16) Empower migrants and societies to realize full inclusion and social cohesion
Objective (17) Eliminate all forms of discrimination and promote evidence-based public discourse to shape perceptions of migration
Objective (18) Invest in skills development and facilitate mutual recognition of skills, qualifications and competences
UN Global Compact for Safe, Orderly and Regular Migration – Paragraph 16 (United Nations 2018)

Of the three objectives, Objective (16) and Objective (18) relate most strongly to brain waste. Part of the problem of brain waste occurs when migrants are not fully integrated into society, not just in the labour market. By integrating migrants fully, society gains as a whole through their human capital, economic activities, and community contributions. Objective (17) is important because of its recognition of discrimination of migrants that extends beyond racism. This pact was adopted by the United Nations, even though a small group of nations either voted against it or abstained. A notable vote against the pact came from the United States of America, which in part attests to the current administration's negative stance on immigration. The others that voted against it are Hungary, the Czech Republic, Poland, and Israel, while the 12 countries that abstained were Algeria, Australia, Austria, Bulgaria, Chile, Italy, Latvia, Libya, Liechtenstein, Romania, Singapore, and Switzerland. The reasons for voting against were largely conclusive, since these countries have openly opposed migration. Hungary and Poland were notable in their response to the European migration crisis of 2015 when there was an influx of refugees from the Middle East and northern Africa that arrived in southern Europe and went on to claim refugee status in countries across Europe. The reasons for abstaining mostly surrounded political pressures including that the pact had not been approved by domestic parliaments. As it has been adopted, it at least lays the foundations for governments worldwide to optimise migration, whether they are net senders or hosts of migrants.

4.3 The Importance of Migration

For many developed western countries, the role migration plays in population growth is very notable. There are some countries, such as Germany, where migration is the only source of population growth because the natural population change is negative.[4] In Canada, immigration counts for 80% of population growth in 2017–2018, and is predicted to be the only source of population growth by 2030 as the declining birth rate does not meet the replacement ratio amongst native born Canadians.

Another reason supporting migration in developed countries is the increasing dependency ratio due to an ageing population.[5] As the number of retirees increases, the ratio of workers to retirees decreases, and the number of elderly citizens requiring care increases, the role of economic migrants is ever more significant. Figure 4.1 shows how data supports this.[6] The first indicator, shown by the blue bar, is the percentage of the labour force that is aged 50 or older. The labour force is ageing slowly, the average is 32.3%, which shows that a third of the workforce is coming up for retirement in the next 15–16 years.[7] Skilled workers often take early retirement, compared to the average citizen. In addition to skill gaps that

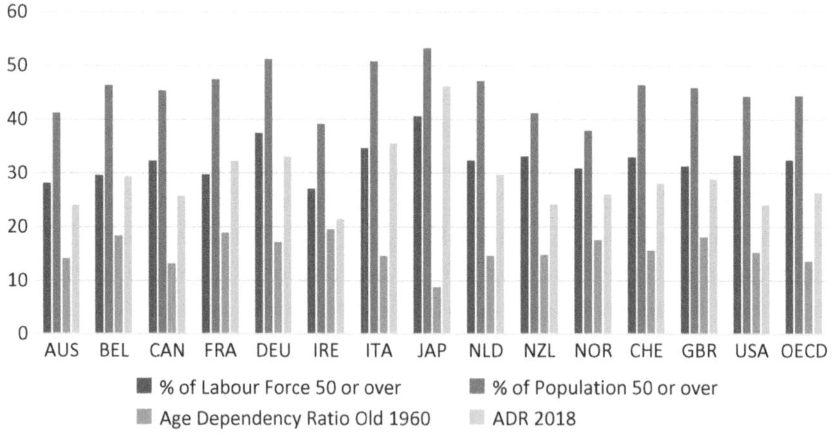

Fig. 4.1 Demographics of the ageing population. (Source: OECD statistics for labour force and population by age (2018) and World Bank Data Portal for old age dependency ratio for 1960 and 2018)

form in many countries, early retirement is an incentive to focus on high-skilled migration. Since more young people are postponing joining the labour force to continue education, there is not a sufficient replacement rate without migration. This will result in the increase of the pensioners-to-workers ratio. The second indicator is the percentage of the population who are 50 years or older. The average for which is 44.3% with three countries, Germany, Italy, and Japan, having more than half of their population aged over 50.

The third and fourth bars on the graph show the old age dependency ratio in 1960 and again in 2018. In 1960, the average across OECD countries was 13.6% which by 2018 had nearly doubled to 26.3%. The average of the 14 countries presented in 1960 was 15.7% which has risen to 29.2%. In the same time period, the young dependency ratio for the average of the countries presented (OECD) has fallen from 44.7% (48.1%) in 1960 to 26.1% (27.4%).[8] These figures show how the dependencies have shifted from young people to an almost equal balance between the two groups. If the trends continue, there will be more old dependents than young, which is concerning for the future.

In this chapter, we focus on economic migration, the policies of migration, and brain waste. Countries that are able to target migration through points-based visa programmes often focus on migrants that are young and high-skilled. However, as (Reitz 2013) comments, the focus by the Canadian government on high-skilled migration, particularly tertiary educated migrants, has left critical gaps between the migration focus and the profile of the Canadian labour market. He categorises them into three gaps. The first is the migrants who experience brain waste, more specifically underemployment as they do not work in a job that directly matches their skill profile. Secondly, there is actually an increase demand for low-skilled labour. These are typically trades and similar low-level occupations which do not require tertiary education. Finally, there is a rise of illegal immigration for these low or unskilled workers that fill the gaps in the labour market left by Canadians. He also believes that there is a third aim for increasing migration, called "nation building", which refers to the concept of increasing the size of the population.

4.4 Migration Patterns and the History of Migration in Canada

Immigration to Canada has been a significant part of their profile since the nineteenth century. Historically, immigrants arrived from the United Kingdom, Ireland, and France. Statistics Canada provides data on emigration from 1951 quarter 3, however, immigration data is available at a quarterly frequency from 1946.[9] The path of net migration is largely determined by immigration, since emigration has remained relatively constant in comparison, as shown in Fig. 4.2. Since the turn of the century, Canada has admitted on average 200,000–250,000 migrants per year, or 0.8% of the population. In more recent years, since the latest drive to increase economic migration, annually over 300,000 immigrants are being admitted, equivalent to 1% of the population. This is projected to rise by 20,000 each year. Only in two years, 1961 and 1962 was net migration negative.

One of the reasons for the increasing levels of migration, particularly economic migration, is the rise in immigrants from Asia. Figure 4.3 shows the change in immigration patterns to Canada. At the beginning

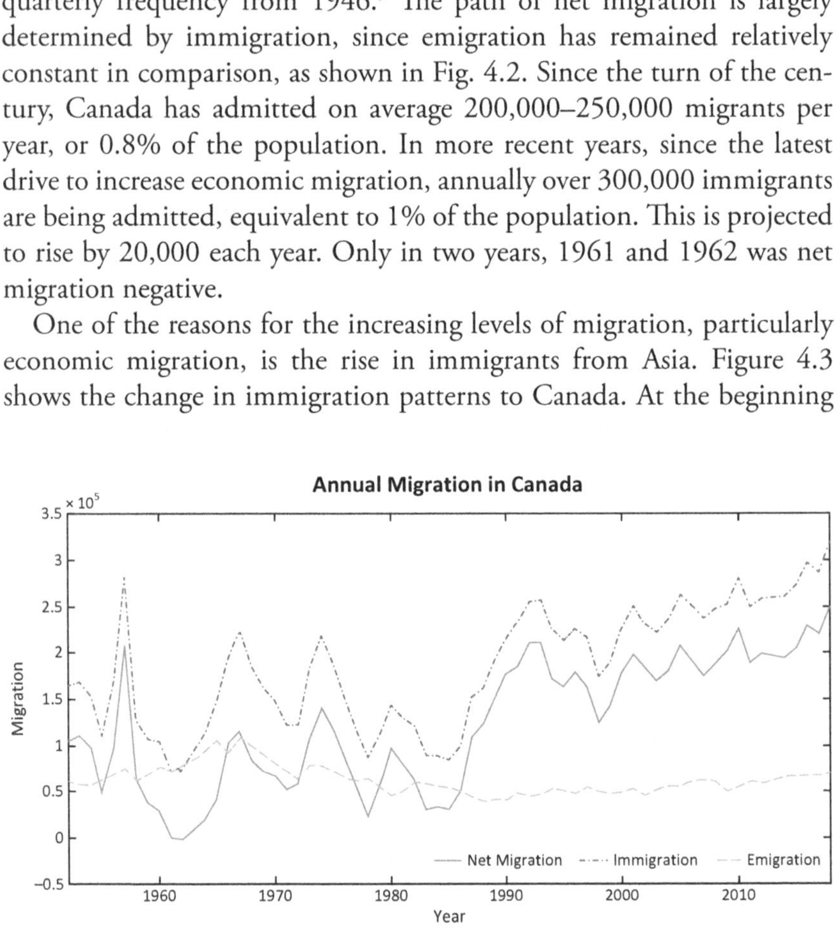

Fig. 4.2 Annual figures for immigration, emigration and net migration in Canada 1952–2018. (Source: Statistics Canada)

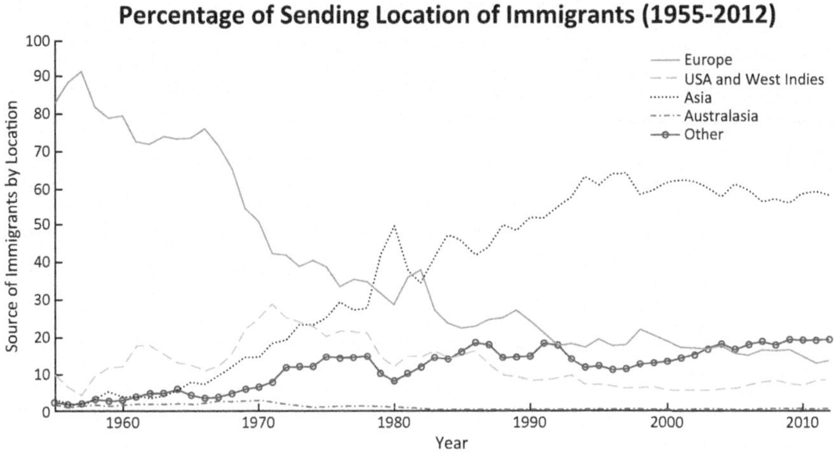

Fig. 4.3 The percentage of immigrants in Canada from Europe (solid line); USA and West Indies (dashed); Asia (dotted); Australasia (dash dot); and other (solid circle). (Source: Statistics Canada)

of the sample, 1955, in excess of 80% of immigrants originated in Europe. That figure has fallen to approximately 13.7% in 2012.[10] The fall in the percentage has two key factors: firstly, the fall in migration from Europe in absolute figures. Secondly, migration from Asia has increased dramatically from 3.3% in 1955 to 58% in 2012.

The breakdown of the figures shows that India, Hong Kong, Vietnam, and the Philippines were the biggest senders of migrants from Asia at the beginning of the sample available.[11] However, these have been overtaken by Chinese migrants that accelerated from the late 1980s to account for over half of all Asian immigrants. This number is expected to grow as there is a push for an increase in international students, and the increased mobility of Chinese citizens and other emerging economies.

The rise in other countries predominantly comes from an increase in African and South American countries as their citizens, too, become increasingly mobile. At the start of the sample, "Other countries" contributed 2.3% of the immigrants to Canada, by 2012, it made up to 19.4%. The important factor here is that both Asian, South American, and African countries have first languages other than English or French, and that the skill recognition is likely to be poor since these are countries that are not regarded as a skill qualification or education equivalent to Canada.

Ferrer and Riddell (2008) identify the problems associated with education attained outside Canada for the immigrants. They use data from the 1981, 1991 and 2001 census to analyse the rewards to human capital of immigrants. Results show that education and work experience in the country of origin is of a significantly lower value than the Canadian experience gained by natives who are directly comparable. One promising aspect, or potential for migrants, is that the increase in earnings for the workers with this education and experience compared to workers without, is greater for migrants than for natives.

In the province of Quebec, part of French speaking Canada, there is an informal rule *"domaines de formation privilèges"* that employers give points towards the ranking of education at bachelor level or above. The countries that are included in this select group of countries providing education to an equivalent standard to Canada is the United States of America, northern and western European countries, Australia, New Zealand, Japan, and Israel. These countries do not provide half of the economic migrants to Canada anymore, meaning that, even with some exceptions such as immigrants from these origin countries attained a degree in one of these countries or anomalous countries, there is a large number of immigrants already at a disadvantage and experiencing brain waste.

The three biggest cities in Canada: Toronto (Ontario), Montreal (Quebec), and Vancouver (British Columbia) are the main destinations for immigrants. Of the 286,479 permanent residents admitted in 2017, 111,925 of them were located in the province of Ontario. Ontario's largest trading partner is the state of Michigan in the United States to which it shares a border.[12] Quebec hosted 52,338 of the applicants, Alberta hosted 42,094, and British Columbia hosted 38,433.[13] Toronto is the country's financial district, Montreal is the biggest French speaking city in Canada that is home to the largest inland port in the world, and Vancouver is becoming one of the technological hubs of the world as it seeks to become the Silicon Valley of Canada. This is one of the schemes targeted by the most recent immigration programme which takes on the fact that the immigration to the United States, or technology giants based in Silicon Valley, is much tighter. Many of the big technology companies have set up offices in Vancouver as a result of incentives and ability to attract some of the world's best talent. Montreal is one of the global hubs for artificial intelligence, and the home of aerospace headquarters plus the Canadian space agency. All three of which require very high-skilled workers who are not in huge supply domestically. Some firms are made up of more than a third migrants. For these sectors that add billions to the economy, evidence of brain waste can be a concern for would be migrants. In 2017, four of the top five visa applications were related to the technology sector: "information systems analysts and consultants; software engineers; [and] computer programmers and interactive media developers" (Hussen 2018). The fifth was financial auditors and accountants. These all represent high-skilled professions. The country's capital city, Ottawa, is one of the top ten destinations, however due to its relatively smaller size compared to the other major cities in Canada, the attraction of immigrants is related to industry and population size.

The destinations within Canada have changed steadily over the past 20 years. In 1997, only 10% of economic migrants landed in provinces other than Ontario, British Columbia, and Quebec. By 2017, this figure had risen to 34% (Hussen 2018). For further context of the scale of city migration, just 39% of economic immigrants settled outside of Toronto, Montreal, or Vancouver. Cities tend to attract high-skilled migrants, while low-skilled migrants are focused outside of the city. The facts presented above highlight the shift towards high skill migration.

4.5 Migration Schemes

The countries that use schemes to target economic migrants, such as Canada, have two types of migration patterns, one to ease labour market shortages, particularly of low-skilled, and the other is high-skilled migration that increases the skillset of the country. The points-based system was first introduced in 1967, and there are programmes set out by the government every few years that aim to increase economic migration.

There have been several programmes that aim to ease labour market shortages, particularly in lower skilled industries. Low-skill migration is typically associated with short-term migration. The most notable programmes, at federal and provincial level, where immigrants are welcomed include "Federal Skilled Worker", the "provincial Nominee", and "Temporary Foreign Worker".

The "Federal Skilled Worker" programme was a nationwide scheme, rather than provincial, that aimed at bringing skilled workers to the country. This was focused on long term migration and filling skills gaps. Points were awarded based upon education, language proficiencies in either of the official languages English or French, work experience, age, whether a job secured in Canada, and adaptability. If there is a job secured before arrival, it overruled some of the attached conditions. This was entirely replaced with the "Express Entry" programme in 2015.

The Canadian government launched a "Temporary Foreign Worker Scheme" in 1973 that aimed to ease labour market shortages in low-skilled industries. This is an employer focused scheme rather than a federal one. Visas are dependent on having a job and passing further criteria associated with the visa including a "Labour Market Impact Assessment" (LMIA) that the Employment and Social Development Canada (ESDC) will evaluate before granting a visa. There are different subcategories based on the type of employment, business worker, caregiver, or agricultural worker.

Gaps left by the high-skilled migration programmes, and not fulfilled by the "Temporary Foreign Worker", were the target of the "Federal Skilled Trades" programme. To qualify under this scheme, the workers had to have two or more years of full-time work in one of the skilled trades, a minimum language proficiency in either English or French, and an offer of full-time employment for one or more years.

The "Provincial Nominee Programme" allows each province to have their own migration programme, the two non-participants were Quebec and Nunavut.[14] saw an increasing number of migrants arriving in the west, to Vancouver and Calgary rather than Toronto.

These programmes now run alongside or under the "Express Entry" programme. In this most recent programme, the relative shortage of labour caused Canada to relax its immigration policy for the "Express Entry" programme, which notably meant that having a job was not necessarily a pre-requisite to having a working visa, or had less weighting than previous programmes. The introduction of the "Express Entry

Programme" committed the government to spending CA$440 million (£250 million) from 2017 to 2019 to increasing immigration over three years from 310,000 in 2018 to 340,000 in 2020; equivalent to 0.84%. This target had already been achieved and has since been extended for 2020 and 2021. Part of the change in this programme to the others was the shifting of points awarded between the different categories. As a result of this programme, there was a 130% increase in the number of applications for citizenship between October 2017 and June 2018 (Hussen 2018).

A characteristic of Canada that differs from other major migrant host countries is that there are two official languages operating simultaneously that rank equally on federal visa applications.[15] In a comparison between Australia and Canada, Clarke and Skuterud (2013) find that a possible reason for the relatively higher brain waste status is that a knowledge of English is not essential, that is, English and French are weighted equally, and there is not as high emphasis on language skills as there is in Australia. New Zealand is one of the immigration systems that has the highest weighting on official language skills. The language barrier, one of the biggest barriers for migrants to overcome when moving to a country with an official language different from their mother tongue, is comprehension of the language.

The problem of language proficiency for migrants is illustrated in Ferrer et al. (2006). There is a difference in literacy skills between natives and migrants, quite a significant one in the favour of natives. However, for a directly comparable native, a migrant does not have a lower return to that level of proficiency. There is a high importance on literacy skills. Notably, there is a lower return to a university education gained abroad than in Canada. However, this is not controlled for specific countries. As a conclusion to their results, if immigrants had equivalent literacy scores as natives, the wage differential would decrease by 20%. For university, or highly educated workers, it would eliminate more than 50% of the wage gap. This result is surprising since the high-skill workers are most likely to have the highest language skills.

Of these migration programmes that have been implemented, most have focused on temporary migration. The most recently landed migrants are the ones who experience the highest levels of brain waste. If migration programmes were more balanced between the long and the short-term migration, then the problem of brain waste might not be as significant. One way of reducing brain waste is if the focus of migration programmes was towards long-term migration. This is more apparent with the "Express Entry" programme; however, previous long-term migration programmes have been followed by short-term ones showing that lessons have not been learned.

4.6 A Diminishing Hope of Convergence for Recently Landed Migrants

To what extent does the period of arrival influence the degree of brain waste the average migrant is subject to? Put simply, quite a lot. As already established, the amount of Canadian work experience can help influence the wage differential between migrants and natives. Migrants who have been landed a long time, prior to the new millennium especially, experience lower levels of brain waste. And those who arrived prior to 1980 experience almost insignificant levels of brain waste as they have had the time to fully integrate into Canadian society and build up in excess of 30 years Canadian work experience. This may also include Canadian education, as some could be children brought here with their parents and received some or all of their education in Canada. However, as the gap between earnings of natives and newly landed migrants have increased, there is research to suggest that earnings will never converge, unlike previous generations of migrants.

Research by Barker (2020) based on the 2016 Canadian census shows the difference in participation rates, unemployment rates, and wages between the immigrants who have arrived at different years, and naturalised citizens, or natives. One explanation for the reason that more recent immigrants experience higher levels of brain waste, is that their qualifications are less likely to be gained in Canada. Most skilled professions take years of training. Therefore, the migrants who suffer from brain waste the most, migrants that have landed in the last five years, are most likely to have received their highest level of education outside of Canada or are in a lower skilled profession that does not take as long to qualify for.

Using data from the 2016 census, we analyse the wage differentials between natives, migrants who have attained education in Canada and migrants who were educated outside of Canada.[16] For simplicity, we use the median employment income of workers (male and female) who are employed by firms (hence excluding self-employed workers). The comparison being between natives and migrants with degrees at bachelor level or above obtained in Canada, migrants earn on average between 3% and 7% less. When we compare with migrants who gained their degree outside of Canada, their earnings are on average between 20% and 25% less.[17] The distinction of migrants receiving their university degree inside or outside Canada has a significant effect on wages. The effect on low-skilled workers is not as clear. Depending upon the area of employment, the wage gap can be significant or small. Most estimates range between 15% and 25%. One of the explanations why the higher skilled workers experience on average less brain waste is that they have higher bargaining power over wages with firms. The low-skilled migrants are some of the most vulnerable in the labour market.

Green and Worswick (2017) using earnings show that, while the immigrant selection system seems to produce higher skilled inflow of workers, the data suggests otherwise. Additionally, there are problems for all new labour market entrants, not just migrants as previous not covered. They argue that discussions are required as to whether the migration schemes should be employer focused, such as "Temporary Foreign Worker", or whether new immigrants should be dependent upon that employment to remain in Canada.

4.7 Underemployment

Underemployment is one of the largest factors of brain waste. There are a number of studies that recognise that the non-recognition of qualifications is one of the major barriers for migrants to overcome. Approximately one in eight migrants worldwide believe that the non-recognition of qualifications it the biggest barrier to full integration to the economy (UNESCO 2018). Analysis of the German labour market for migrants by Brücker et al. (2018) finds that immigrants with recognised qualifications are 45% more likely to be employed. In terms of labour income per hour, this can be 40% higher than migrants who have not had their qualifications recognised. The problem is present in the United Kingdom too, where the average migrant is more highly qualified than the native equivalent. Lisenkova and Sanchez-Martinez (2016) use data for the United Kingdom to show how migrants are relatively more skilled than natives and often take jobs below their skill level. Their analysis looks at the effects on the United Kingdom with different migration policies following its exiting of the European Union (EU).[18]

In illustrating how different types of migration affect a country, we compare the participation rates calculated by Lisenkova and Sanchez-Martinez (2016) and those by Barker (2020).[19] In the United Kingdom, the employment rates on average are highest for the migrants from the new EU countries.[20] It is the immigrants from non-EU countries that have the lowest. When the populations are broken down into skill qualification, in the categories of high, medium, and low, UK citizens have the lowest proportion of high qualifications, and the highest proportion of low qualifications. In terms of qualifications, the story is similar for Canada. The share of migrants who have a degree at the bachelor level or above is 32.5% compared to natives at 19.65% (see Table 4.1). The differences in both countries can partially be explained by the different age composition since migrants are younger in profile and more educated. In terms of brain waste, for the United Kingdom, at all levels, natives receive higher earnings than both the new EU and non-EU. For EU15 countries, at high and medium-skill occupations they earn more but at low-skill occupations the natives earn more.

The non-recognition of qualifications has a highly detrimental effect on the migrants who are skilled in a certain field, such as medical, teaching, and legal professionals. One notable example is the "taxi driver syndrome", that is, the case where qualified medical doctors are employed as taxi drivers since their medical training qualifications are not recognised in the host nation. Cases such as this mean that highly skilled migrants are employed in positions that underutilise their skills, and due to the specificness of the profession it can be that they in effect have no skills, or very low skills, that are useful in the labour market. There has been extensive research into the role particularly in the medical profession. For

Table 4.1 Upper panel: The relative and cumulative size of skill level by highest certificate, diploma or degree for total, native, and immigrant citizens; Lower panel: Participation and unemployment rates by skill. (Barker (2020))

Highest level of qualification	Total population		Native		Immigrant	
	Relative	*Cumulative*	*Relative*	*Cumulative*	*Relative*	*Cumulative*
No certificate, diploma or degree	18.29	18.29	18.78	18.78	17.38	17.38
Secondary (high) school diploma or equivalency certificate	26.45	44.74	27.53	46.3	23.25	40.63
Apprenticeship or trades certificate or diploma	9.78	54.52	10.89	57.2	6.91	47.54
College, CEGEP or other non-university certificate or diploma	19.39	73.91	20.66	77.86	16.17	63.71
University certificate or diploma below bachelor level	2.84	76.75	2.49	80.35	3.75	67.47
University certificate, diploma or degree at bachelor level or above	23.25	100	19.65	100	32.53	100
	Participation	*Unemployment*	*Participation*	*Unemployment*	*Participation*	*Unemployment*
Total qualifications	65.19	7.72	66.39	7.67	62.10	7.68
No certificate, diploma or degree	38.32	13.5	39.78	14.45	34.08	10.04
Secondary (high) school diploma or equivalency certificate	63.59	9.46	65.86	9.54	57.41	8.8
Apprenticeship or trades certificate or diploma	70.38	7.84	72.47	7.94	60.65	7.24
College, CEGEP or other non-university certificate or diploma	74.28	6.01	75.69	5.79	69.24	6.65
University certificate or diploma below bachelor level	67.89	6.07	67.24	5.4	69.33	7.08
University certificate, diploma or degree at bachelor level or above	78.05	5.38	79.29	4.21	76.34	7.12

instance, Bourgeault and Neiterman (2013) explain how the increased difficulty of international medical graduates to secure employment at the appropriate level has decreased partly due to the change in migration patterns as discussed in Sect. 4.4 (Migration Patterns). In the 1970s, the majority of immigrants that held medical qualifications spoke English and originated in English speaking countries such as the United Kingdom, Ireland, or the United States. This usually meant that their qualifications were easily recognised as these countries were of the level of education that employers see as equivalent to Canada. They could often be fast-tracked to achieve Canadian accreditation. The new immigrants with non or only partially recognised skills face years of re-examination that have high monetary costs associated with it.

Using the 2006 census, Aydede and Dar (2016) create an index that links fields of education with occupations for natives and then compare it with migrants to analyse the matching quality. The focus of the analysis is on internationally educated migrant workers. In comparing the efficiency of the matches, they approximate the cost of the skill-job mismatch using the change in earnings had they had the same matching efficiencies as natives. The results showed a persistent poor matching quality for migrants who were educated outside of Canada and a small cost to the economy in terms of lost wages.

4.8 Unemployment

Migrants are likely to be higher skilled, younger, and experience higher unemployment rates at a given skill level while having a lower participation rate. Using data from the 2016 census, Barker (2020) calculates the different unemployment and participation rates for natives and migrants at different education levels.[21] The upper panel of Table 4.1 shows the relative size of the population by their highest certificate, diploma, or degree for the total economy, native residents and immigrants. The most distinct difference is for the number of people who have a university certificate at bachelor level or above. The population average is 23.25%. However, broken down into natives and immigrants it is 19.65% for natives and 32.53% for immigrants meaning that on average the immigrant worker is more highly qualified.

When we examine the participation and unemployment rates of natives and migrants in the lower panel of Table 4.1, there is a distinct difference. It is generally assumed that low-skill workers have the lowest participation rates and highest unemployment rates. In comparison to natives at each skill level, it is assumed that migrants have lower participation and higher unemployment. For the majority of skill levels this is true. For participation rates, the skill level is only violated with the "university certificate or diploma *below* bachelor level". However, as it is such a small classification of highest level of qualification, this is not as anomalous as one would assume. Some analysis argues that the participation of the most highly skilled migrant workers is actually higher. The data for 2016 suggests that migrants are still marginally ahead. For the unemployment rates, migrants have a lower unemployment rate for the three lowest classifications of highest qualification. This is perhaps because they receive the lowest levels of unemployment insurance, if any, and are known to take up short-term work. This is raw data presented, no fixed effects or subcategory for different industries which goes part way to explain the different results. A reason for the difference in participation rates is described in Hilgenstock and Koczan (2018).

4.9 The Wage Question

How much individuals earn is an uneasy topic between workers, however, an interesting topic economically as evidence shows that on average migrants earn a lower wage per hour of work. The spread is even further between the most recent immigrant and non-immigrant workers. Aydemir and Skuterud (2008) show that there is a sorting of migrant workers into different sectors than natives and that wage differentials occur.

Green and Worswick (2012) examine economic development in terms of how human capital investment effects differ between natives and immigrants by comparing the earnings data when they enter the labour market at the same time. In using an earnings measure and matching immigrant arrivals with taxation data, the authors find that there is a gap between the earnings of natives and immigrants. The first data used was from the 1980s, where the entry earnings decreased. In the 1990s, these fell even further signalling that foreign experience is less meaningful. This relates to the earlier discussion on the origin of migrants. There are only a few countries that employers recognise as an equivalent standard of education and experience to Canada. The results suggest that there is concern over the issues all new migrants face, not just earnings, and policies should also aim at the targeting of labour market entrants not just migrants. This indicates that there is a problem of brain waste for migrants, and underemployment of natives.

Hou and Picot (2016) provide an assessment of the earnings of immigrants with and without Canadian work experience. One of their results find that the pre-landing Canadian work experience increases the wages levels of immigrant men. The effect for women was very significant too, such that it was the highest contribution on the positive effect of their earnings. A note of this is that the pre-landing Canadian work experience tended to be of a high-skill type.

Kaushal et al. (2016) compare longitudinal data for employment and earnings of men in Canada and the United States between migrants and natives. Using fixed effects, the authors find that immigrants do not have any growth in terms of employment, real wages, and hours worked, whereas men born and educated in Canada do. This is slightly contrasting to the United States; however, the key difference is that the immigrants in the United States are the proportion of low-education immigrants. In relation to the participation rate, for Canadian immigrants there is evidence of early retirement for immigrants who landed 20 years or more previously.

4.10 The Gender Bias

The difference in all aspects of the labour market is more significant between males and females compared to their non-immigrant counterparts. There have been different explanations for the reasoning behind this, primarily that females arrive on a family visa and more likely to be outside of the labour force to look after family. The increased difficulty in finding a job is a small deterrent.

Research by Uppal and LaRochelle-Cote (2014) shows that among internationally educated immigrants who are university graduates, 48% of women and 3% of men worked in occupations that usually required a high school education or less in 2006. By 2011, these numbers were 43% and 35%, respectively.

In terms of the principal applicant for an economic visa, there is a heavy weighting towards men. Of the economic applicants in the years 2015, 2016, and 2017, the percentages of men who were the principal applicant were 57%, 58%, and 56%, respectively. The significance is greater in terms of wages. For 2014, the average employment earnings of the principal applicant in the year of first landing was CAN$ 56,000 for men compared to CAN$32,000 for women, the growth of which provides an even greater difference. Immigrant men earnings grew on average CAN$12,000, while women's earnings grew CAN$3000 Hussen (2018). In percentage terms, the corresponding figures were 21.4% for men and 9.4% for women. When we relate participation rates and the type of visa, it is unsurprising that 94% of the principal applicants for the caregiver visa category were female.

4.11 The Macroeconomic Consequences

The degree of the costs from brain waste varies by country. On a macroeconomic scale, for example, estimates for losses in the United States put US$39 billion in lost wages and US$10.2 billion in lost tax revenue (Batalova et al. 2016). In context, the United States government collected US$3.18 trillion, of which US$1.07 trillion was from payroll taxes by firms and employees. This means that of the payroll tax, US$10.2 billion is approximately 1%. These estimates are difficult to calculate; however, the size of the problem can at least be recognised. For Canada, an estimate in 2012 put the total loss from brain waste at CAN$2 billion to CAN$15 billion per annum.

The link between fiscal policy and migration was studied in Storesletten (2000) who investigated how migration policy might deal with the ageing baby boom generation. The author shows that an increase in migration creates a net government gain due to the younger profile of migrants.

In Canada, over 50% of migrants are aged 25–39 at the time of arrival. Analysis by Barker (2020) examines the effects of migration on government consumption, investment, and the debt holdings in per capita terms in a VAR model with Canadian data from 1980. The migration shock is found to be expansionary for output and also reduces government's net liabilities.

Rowthorn (2008) shows how highly skilled immigrants can make a large fiscal contribution, while unskilled migrants either make a lower level of fiscal contribution or even pose a net fiscal cost. Amongst the advanced economies, his estimates of the net fiscal contributions by immigrants are in the region of plus or minus 1% of GDP. When high-skilled migrants are employed at a level equivalent to their qualifications, there is a greater level of capital-skill complementarity, which enables a higher domestic rate of productivity growth. The demonstration of the underemployment of migrants is shown in Saleheen and Shadforth (2006). The increase in migration and employment of workers increases the return on capital due to the capital-labour ratio. If firms underemploy their workers, they are losing out on some of the productivity and returns on investment.

Ruist (2015) shows the fiscal cost of refugees in Sweden, the country that has had the highest refugee per capita rate in the EU. Theoretical analysis by Stähler (2017) examines the effect of the refugee crisis of 2015 in Germany. The relation to brain waste is examined as the author examines, when the refugees are eventually employed, by what level of productivity they contribute. If they remain at lower levels of productivity, the outcome is a reduction in per capita GDP.

The impact of the political economy on deficit bias and immigration are explored in an OLG model in Ben-Gad (2018). In the context of the United States, the model demonstrates how a government with a short-term focus and knowledge of future immigration flows are more prepared to use debt and low taxation for long periods of time. This is regardless of whether higher taxes will be required in the future. Even if the decision is not deliberate in evaluating whether to increase taxation today or postpone it until future generations, the fact is that the United States federal deficit is increasing. The 2019–2029 forecast puts the current debt to GDP ratio at 78% for 2018 and is predicted to rise to 93% at the end of 2029, which is the highest level since the end of World War Two

(Congressional Budget Office 2019). Higher levels of brain waste reduce government revenues; hence reducing brain waste is a way to decrease tax burdens of future generations.

This chapter has discussed how much of the effects of brain waste are felt through wages. Whether this be a lower wage level compared to natives, or underemployment, any loss of income to the household has a negative effect on their expenditures. With lower levels of job stability and wages, this issue can extend beyond consumption. Migrants are more likely to find it hard to access financial capital, whether to set up their own business, a loan, or a mortgage to buy housing, which reduces the possibility of innovation. In some countries, the influx of migrants can cause house prices to rise. For example, McDonald (2013) and Smith and Thoenissen (2019) examine the role of migration and house prices in New Zealand, where an increase in migration has been blamed for the increase in house prices. Whilst their results suggest otherwise, there has been a shift so that only residents and citizens can buy houses to live in. This is when housing is in short supply; however, in countries such as Canada and the United States there is greater space and supply. Certain large cities can prove an anomaly. The point is that with less access to financial capital, there are fewer gains to be made and this puts increased pressure on the rental market. The migrants having lower incomes compared to natives, and reduced access to capital, are less likely to invest in firms and hence provide investment, thus preventing the economy from expanding.

Using the national income identity, we have outlined why there are lower levels of GDP due to lower wages for migrants: lower levels of consumption and investment plus reduced fiscal revenue through taxation reduces the fiscal budget and hence expenditure. The reduction in labour income also prevents higher levels of remittances that are sent by some migrants to family that remain in the country of origin.

As described by Dungan et al. (2013), the exchange rate receives opposing pressures. Remittances would cause a depreciation of the dollar but the funds brought in by migrants would cause an appreciation. Following an increase in immigration, more imports are required to meet the demands of citizens. Their simulation indicates a negative impact of immigration on the current account balance.

4.12 Conclusion

In this chapter, we have discussed how the economics of brain waste has negative effects for an economy. For the migrants, they lose out in terms of lower wages, higher unemployment rates, lower job security rates, skill-job mismatches, financial wealth, and lower levels of innovation. Firms lose out because they are not fully utilising the human capital available to them, experience relatively higher rates of inefficiency and lower levels of investment, and have unhappy employees if they are unable to use all of their skills. The economy suffers as a whole as there is less consumption and investment. General targeting of increasing economic migration, rather than skill-specific, can fill labour market gaps. However, it can lead to overfilling of some and shortages remaining in others. The granting of economic visas without a confirmation of employment to commence on arrival makes migration more attractive to potential immigrants, but opens up the opportunity for additional circumstances of brain waste. Eliminating brain waste is unlikely to occur completely due to the complexities and imperfections in the economy and labour market. However, laying the foundations for improved migration schemes to match migrants to areas of the labour market with precise shortages fills the gap and can create an economic stimulus. As the baby boom generation reaches retirement age, the birth rates decline, and natural population change decreases, immigration will play an even more vital role in the economy. Learning to target the right sectors for immigration and geographical locations will help reduce brain waste and make immigration more efficient.

Acknowledgements This chapter is based on part of my doctoral research (Barker, Essays in the Macroeconomics of Migration, 2020) which is circulated under the title "The Migrants" Plight: A Skill-Job Mismatch. Brain waste in Canada". Financial support for the PhD thesis is greatly appreciated from the Economic and Social Research Council (ESRC) under grant number ES/J500215/1.

Notes

1. A notable exception is Saudi Arabia that hosts a large number of migrants, but is not classified as an advanced economy.
2. We define net migration as immigration minus emigration due to its inward nature.
3. This is in part due to the simplicity of which it is possible for immigrants to acquire Canadian citizenship. For a number of migrant host countries, it is a lengthy, difficult and expensive process.
4. Author's own calculations using data from the Federal Statistics Office in Germany (DESTATIS). Natural population change is equal to births minus deaths.
5. The dependency ratio is defined as the ratio of the number of dependants, aged 0–14 and 65+, to the total population aged 15–64. The old dependency ratio is those 65+, and young 0–14.
6. Figure 4.1 shows four data sets for selected OECD countries, labelled with their World Bank country code. Australia, Belgium, Canada, France, Germany, Ireland, Italy, Japan, Netherlands, New Zealand, Norway, Switzerland, the United Kingdom, and the United States of America. We also include the average for OECD countries.
7. Dependent upon the retirement age in each country. The state retirement age is increasing amongst OECD countries as the law react to the ageing populations.
8. The OECD averages differ from the average of the countries presented as countries that have joined in the last 30 years including former USSR countries, Chile, Mexico, and South Korea that have slightly younger populations on average in comparison.
9. We present the annualised data, rather than quarterly, as it is more easily comparable to other major migrant host nations. Time series data on migration is often short and at an annual frequency.
10. The data is from Statistics Canada, Table 051-0006 with time periods 1955 quarter 1 to 2013 quarter 2. The percentages are the author's own calculations. The category 'Other Countries' includes countries from the continents of Africa and South America, and Other North America countries. Specific data for these three is only available from 1982.
11. The (partial) breakdown of the figures from Asia is available from 1982.
12. The three largest cities in the province of Ontario are Toronto (province capital city), Ottawa (capital city of Canada), and Hamilton.

13. Calgary, Alberta is the fourth biggest city in Canada by population, but the province of Alberta received the third most permanent residents in 2017. It is marginally greater than British Columbia.
14. The exclusion of Nunavut is insignificant as the territory only received 40 of the 286,479 permanent residents admitted in 2017.
15. For provincial level programmes, the weighting on English or French is subject to change. Particularly in Quebec that operates different systems to the rest of Canada.
16. The data is sourced from table 98-400-X2016280 by Statistics Canada.
17. There is insufficient data to make a reliable comparison of migrants who attained their highest qualification outside of Canada to migrants who achieved their highest qualification outside of Canada.
18. The research was published on the 24th May 2016, *before*, the United Kingdom's referendum on exiting the European Union. At time of writing, the United Kingdom is still a member of the European Union.
19. Lisenkova and Sanchez-Martinez (2016) use the "employment rate", whereas Barker (2020) uses the "participation rate".
20. New EU countries include the A8 countries, Cyprus, Malta, Bulgaria, and Croatia.
21. Data is taken from table 98-400-X2016198_English of the 2016 Census (source: Statistics Canada). The highest certificate, diploma, or degree uses IDs 2, 3, 5, 8, 9, 10, and identifier 1 is for total. Migrants includes immigrants and non-permanent residents from all different year of arrival. The author's own calculations.

References

Alexander, C., Burletun, D., & Fong, F. (2012). *Knocking Down Barriers Faced By New Immigrants To Canada. Fitting the Pieces Together.* Special Report, TD Economics. Retrieved June 05, 2019, from https://www.td.com/document/PDF/economics/special/ff0212_immigration.pdf

Aydede, Y., & Dar, A. (2016). The cost of immigrants' occupational mismatch and the effectiveness of postarrival policies in Canada. *IZA Journal of Migration, 5*(9). doi:https://doi.org/10.1186/s40176-016-0057-z

Aydemir, A., & Skuterud, M. (2008). The Immigrant Wage Differential within and across Establishments. *International Labour Relations (ILR) Review, 61*(3), 334–352.

Barker, E. R. (2020). *Essays on the Macroeconomics of Migration*. Unpublished doctoral dissertation, University of Sheffield, Department of Economics, Sheffield, United Kingdom.

Batalova, J., Fix, M., & Bachmeier, J. D. (2016). *Untapped Talent: The Costs of Brain Waste amongst Highly Skilled Immigrants in the United States*. Migration Policy Institute, New American Economy, and World Education Services, Washington DC.

Ben-Gad, M. (2018). On the Political Economy of Deficit Bias and Immigration. *Economic Journal, 128*(September), 2191–2221.

Bourgeault, I. L., & Neiterman, E. (2013). Integrating International Medical Graduates: The Canadian Approach to the Brain Waste Problem. In T. Triadafilopoulos (Ed.), *Wanted and Welcome?. Immigrants and Minorities, Politics and Policy*. New York, NY, USA: Springer. doi:https://doi.org/10.1007/978-1-4614-0082-0_8

Brücker, H., Romiti, A., Glitz, A., & Lerche, A. (2018). Occupational Recognition and Immigrant Labor Market Outcomes. *IZA Discussion Papers 12030*.

Clarke, A., & Skuterud, M. (2013). Why do immigrant worker in Australia perform better than those in Canada? Is it the immigrants or their labour markets? *Canadian Journal of Economics, 46*(4), 1431–1462.

Congressional Budget Office. (2019). *Deficits and Debt*. The Budget and Economic Outlook: 2019 to 2029.

Dungan, P., Fang, T., & Gunderson, M. (2013). Macroeconomic Impacts of Canadian Immigration. Results from a Macro Model. *British Journal of Industrial Relations, 51*(1), 174–195.

Ferrer, A., & Riddell, W. C. (2008, February). Education, Credentials, and Immigrant Earnings. *The Canadian Journal of Economics, 41*(1), 186–216.

Ferrer, A., Green, D. A., & Riddel, W. C. (2006). The effect of literacy on immigrant earnings. *Journal of Human Resources, 41*(2), 380–410.

Fung, L., Douwere, G., & Liu, H. (2019). *The Impact of Immigrant Business Ownership on International Trade*. Statistics Canada. Ottawa, Canada: Statistics Canada.

Green, D. A., & Worswick, C. (2012). Immigrant earnings profiles in the presence of human capital investment: Measuring cohort and macroeconomic effects. *Labour Economics, 19*(2), 241–259.

Green, D., & Worswick, C. (2017). Canadian economics research on immigration through the lens of theories of justice. *Canadian Journal of Economics, 50*, 1262–1303.

Hilgenstock, B., & Koczan, Z. (2018). *Storm Clouds Ahead? Migration and Labour Force Paritícpation Rates in Europe.* IMF Working Paper 18/148, International Monetary Fund.
Hou, F., & Picot, G. (2016). *Changing Immigrant Characteristics and Entry Earnings.* 11F0019M No. 374, Statistics Canada, Research and Evaluation, Citizenship and Immigration Canada and Institute for Research in Public Policy.
Hussen, A. (2018). *Annual Report to Parliament on Immigration.* Immigration, Refugees, and Citizens Canada.
Kaushal, N., Lu, Y., Denier, N., Shu-Huah Wang, J., & Trejo, S. J. (2016). Immigrant employment and earnings growth in Canada and the USA: Evidence from longitudinal data. (K. F. Zimmermann, Ed.) *Journal of Population Economics, 29*(1), 1249–1277.
Lisenkova, K., & Sanchez-Martinez, M. (2016). The long-term macroeconomic effects of lower migration to the UK. *NIESR Discussion Papers, 460.*
McDonald, C. (2013). *Migration and the housing market.* Reserve Bank of New Zealand. Wellington, New Zealand: Reserve Bank of New Zealand Analytical Notes AN2013/10.
Reitz, J. G. (2013). Closing the Gaps Between Skilled Immigration and Canadian Labor Markets: Emerging Policy Issues and Priorities. In T. Triadafilopoulos (Ed.), *Wanted and Welcome?, Immigrants and Minorities Politics and Policy* (pp. 147–163). New York, NY, USA: Springer Science+Business Media. doi:https://doi.org/10.1007/978-1-4614-0082-0_8
Rowthorn, R. (2008). The fiscal impact of immigration on the advanced economies. *Oxford Review of Economic Policy, 24*(3), 560–580.
Ruist, J. (2015, December). The Fiscal Cost of Refugee Immigration: The Example of Sweden. *Population and Development Review, 41*(4), 567–581.
Saleheen, J., & Shadforth, C. (2006). The Economic Characteristics of Immigrants and Their Impact on Supply. *Bank of England Quarterly Bulletin, 2006*(Winter), 373–385.
Smith, C., & Thoenissen, C. (2019). Skilled migration and business cycle dynamics. *Journal of Economic Dynamics and Control, 109.*
Stähler, N. (2017). *A model-based analysis of the macroeconomic impact of refugee migration to Germany.* Deutsche Bundesbank Discussion Paper 05/2017.
Storesletten, K. (2000). Sustaining Fiscal Policy through Immigration. *Journal of Political Economy, 108*(2), 300–323.
UNESCO. (2018). *What a waste: Ensure migrants and refugees' qualifications and prior learning are recognized.* Paris: UNESCO.

United Nations – Department of Economic and Social Affairs – Population Division. (2017). *International Migrant Stock: The 2017 revision*. Retrieved May 30, 2019, from United Nations: https://www.un.org/en/development/desa/population/migration/data/estimates2017/estimates17.asp
United Nations (2018). *Global Compact for Safe, Orderly and Regular Migration*. New York City: United Nations.
Uppal, S., & LaRochelle-Cote, S. (2014). *Overqualification among recent university graaduates in Canada*. Statistics Canada – Insights on Canadian Society, Catalogue no. 75–006-X. Statistics Canada.

Part II

Migration and the Macroeconomy: A Search and Matching Approach

5

Immigration and Job Creation

Andri Chassamboulli

5.1 Introduction

Large inflows of immigrants to the United States and other Western countries have put immigration at the centre of the recent political debate. Proposals for increasing immigration restrictions are becoming more common in recent years, while opposition to immigration has been rising in many countries. This backlash to immigration may to a large extent be cultural, resting on issues that have little to do with economics, but anti-immigration politics are often based on the argument that immigration has a negative effect on natives' employment and wages. This argument, however, is often not consistent with findings in the literature. There is no consensus that immigrants indeed take jobs from natives. Some studies find, by contrast, that immigrants help create new jobs for natives. In order to understand the potential of these anti-immigration policies to benefit the native workers, we need to address first the basic

A. Chassamboulli (✉)
University of Cyprus, Nicosia, Cyprus
e-mail: andrichassamboulli@ucy.ac.cy

E. Vella et al. (eds.), *Understanding Migration with Macroeconomics*,
https://doi.org/10.1007/978-3-030-40981-4_5

question of whether or not immigrants indeed take jobs from native workers or help, instead, create new jobs, some of which are taken by natives. In light of rising anti-immigration politics, addressing this question has become even more important.

A large empirical literature on the effects of immigration on labour market outcomes has not reached a clear conclusion (see for an overview e.g. Lewis and Peri 2015; Peri 2016). The debate has centred mainly on the elasticity of substitution between immigrants and native workers. Findings consistent with the view that immigrants hurt natives' wages and employment are based on the idea that immigrants and natives 'compete' for the same jobs, because they have similar skills. Others find a negligible or even a positive effect on natives' labour market outcomes and argue that immigrants' labour services complement those of native workers. That is, immigrants increase demand for native workers in complementing sectors. But the link between immigration and job creation is not that simple. This idea, which is based on the canonical model of labour demand and supply, omits several important features of reality, crucial to our understanding of how immigration affects the labour markets.

Recent literature examining the effect of immigration on the labour market departs from the neoclassical approach and uses models that allow for search frictions in the labour market (e.g. Pissarides 2000). In these models, job creation responds to the incentives provided by the market. Firms will open more vacancies and create new jobs when labour costs are low, while potential gains from new jobs are large. Within such a framework, we can account explicitly for the effect of immigration on job creation incentives. New findings show that various types of immigrants can have, for different reasons, a positive impact on employers' incentives to post vacancies and a positive job creation effect on even competing natives, that is on natives who search for jobs similar to those that immigrants take. We discuss in this chapter recent studies of the labour market effect of immigration based on the search and matching model and explain how the search-equilibrium approach can improve our understanding of how immigration policies affect the labour market.

The neoclassical approach does not account for the effects of immigration on job creation incentives and the employment opportunities of native workers. In the canonical model, there is always full employment and workers are paid their marginal product, meaning that the same wage is paid to all workers with similar skills. In reality, however, wages are not set competitively. Employers cannot immediately fill their job vacancies and have to incur recruitment costs. Similarly, it takes time for workers to find jobs and unemployment exists. Given that search frictions exist, matches of employers with workers generate rents to be shared between them, and thus wages are bargained. Wages reflect not only the worker's marginal product, but also his outside option. Incentives for sectors to grow and firms to expand by opening new vacancies and create new jobs depend also on workers' outside option, wages, recruitment costs, and other labour costs, which influence the rents that matches (jobs) generate. Such effects, which are not present in the neoclassical model, may generate a positive relation between immigration and job opportunities for native workers, in not only complementing sectors, but also in sectors that employ mainly immigrant workers.

A common perception about immigrants, also used in policy debates, is that they take jobs that natives with similar skills and qualifications would otherwise take. That is, immigrants crowd out competing natives. But this is not necessarily the case if large benefits from hiring immigrant labour induce employers to open more vacancies per unemployed worker, so that some of these new jobs go to natives. Immigrants come to a foreign country mainly to find a job and they will choose to stay as long as they can find a job. Coming from disadvantaged countries, they benefit in terms of better labour market prospects, only because employers in the host country are willing to offer them jobs. Employers, on the other hand, are willing to employ immigrant workers only if they can benefit from it. The long-lasting existence of immigration documents that immigrants can indeed find jobs, which means that employers also benefit from their presence in the labour market. This advantage that employers gain from hiring immigrants may in turn translate into higher job creation that benefits also competing natives. There is clearly a link between the presence of immigrants in the labour market and the possibility of a positive job creation effect. Despite the common perception that immigration takes jobs away from natives, deeper thinking into the forces supporting the long-lasting existence of the immigration phenomenon may reveal that there is more to it than just simple competition for jobs.

While most of the empirical research on immigration focuses on its impact on natives' wages, there are a few studies showing evidence of a positive impact of immigration on job creation and employment of native workers. Zavodny (2011) finds that high-educated immigrants, especially those working in science, technology, engineering and mathematics (STEM) fields, and immigrants on temporary work permits, skilled or unskilled, boost employment for US natives. Further, she finds no evidence that other types of immigrants, either undocumented or on family unification visas, hurt the employment of US natives. Recently, Orrenius et al. (2020), using data from the National Establishment Time-Series (NETS) database, show that immigrants contribute to job creation, business survival and growth.

Another important dimension often overlooked in the literature is the heterogeneity that may exist among immigrants themselves. The neoclassical approach focuses mainly on the skill characteristics of immigrants; whether they complement or substitute for native labour, and views immigration as an exogenous shift in labour supply that changes the skill composition of the labour force. But there are also important differences among immigrants themselves, which cannot be captured by a simple shift in the relative supply of certain skills. Immigrants can be documented or undocumented, they can be former students who obtained education in the host country, or new entrants that lack the language skills and face limited skill transferability, they can be entering through different pathways either accompanying family or simply to work, documented or not, either with a job or without a job facing different labour market prospects, different conditions for staying in the country, different visa durations and different return probabilities. Besides immigrants' skills, other characteristics relating to immigrants' entry paths and conditions for stay are also important for our understanding of how immigration and policies used to control it affect natives' labour market outcomes. We need to understand what types of immigrants can generate more jobs for native workers and which characteristics or conditions, beside skills, are responsible for this.

The literature examining the consequences of immigration sometimes distinguishes between undocumented and documented immigration. For instance, Palivos (2009) and Liu (2010) focus on the welfare effects of illegal immigration while Chassamboulli and Peri (2015) examine the consequences of policies restricting illegal immigration. More recently, interest in studying the consequences of high-skilled immigration to the US has grown as the number of high-skilled immigrants in the US has been increasing. Bound et al. (2017) and Jaimovich and Siu (2017) emphasize the strong impact of highly skilled foreigners entering the US labour force through the H-1B programme on innovation and economic growth in the long run. However, there is room for further research on the potentially differential effects of different types of entry paths and immigrant characteristics on natives' labour markets. One such attempt, by Chassamboulli and Peri (2019), discussed further below, differentiates among the most relevant channels of immigration to the US: employment-based, family-based and undocumented.

Finally, research on the effects of immigration should not overlook the role of immigration policies and the design of the immigration system. Most studies on the effects of immigration consider changes in the number of immigrants as if immigrants are an exogenous policy variable. But the government cannot control directly the number of immigrants entering or staying in the country. It can only set the rules for admitting foreigners into the country, the possible channels of entry (e.g. employment-based or family-based), the conditions to remain in the country (e.g. stay conditional on having a job or the right to remain indefinitely in the country) and decides the degree of enforcement of these rules. When considering the potential effects of reducing immigration on native workers, we need to take into account, first, whether actual immigration policies can effectively reduce the number of immigrants and, second, whether the policies themselves, irrespective of how they affect the number of immigrants, will have any disrupting effects on the labour market. Moreover, the rules and conditions the government sets, together with immigrants' incentives, generate the observed number of immigrants, but more importantly, they shape their composition in terms of skills/productivity, bargaining power, duration of stay and other features, which are important for how immigrants affect the host economy. For instance, an immigration programme can be 'merit-based', admitting immigrants based on productivity or skill selective, directing immigrant inflows towards the sectors and the jobs that are mostly needed. Likewise, immigrants' access to welfare benefits, employment conditions or conditions for stay in the country, can influence their bargaining position in wage setting, and thus the employers' surplus from hiring them, with important consequences on incentives to open new vacancies and create new jobs. Research examining the impact of immigration or the design of immigration policies should not overlook such dimensions.

The rest of the chapter is divided into two main sections. In Sect. 5.2 we discuss the recent literature that analyses the labour market effects of immigration using the search and matching model of the labour market. We explain how analysing immigration within this framework offers new insights into the effects of immigration and of immigration policies on the labour market. Next, in Sect. 5.3 we develop a model of immigration between two countries, representing the US and the rest of the world, and we use it to analyse the effects of a specific policy combination that aims to reduce illegal immigrants in the US, while increasing opportunities for unskilled foreigners to enter the US on temporary work permits. The model that we develop is based on existing literature that applies the search and matching framework to the immigration context.

5.2 Immigration in a Simple Search and Matching Model

5.2.1 The Job Creation Effect of Immigration

A recent strand of literature uses models of the labour market that account for search frictions to understand the effects of immigration on natives' labour market outcomes (e.g. Liu 2010; Chassamboulli and Palivos 2013, 2014; Chassamboulli and Peri 2015, 2019; Moreno-Galbis and Tritah 2016; Battisti et al. 2018; Liu et al. 2017). In these models, unemployment exists due to search frictions, and wages are the outcome of bargaining and reflect not only the workers' productivity (marginal product) but also their outside option. Job creation responds to the incentives provided by the market and the unemployment rate changes accordingly. We explain here how analysing immigration within this framework offers new insights into the effects of immigration and of immigration policies on the labour market.

Within the standard search and matching model, the job creation condition—the condition that describes how job creation responds to the incentives provided by the market—equates the expected cost of posting a job vacancy (the expected recruitment cost) to the expected profit of a new job (an employer-employee match). The expected recruitment cost increases as the number of vacancies per unemployed worker increases, because then it will take longer for employers to find workers to fill their vacancies. That is, a higher ratio of vacancies to unemployed means a lower job filling rate for firms and therefore higher recruitment costs on average. The expected profit of a new job, on the other hand, depends on: (i) the worker's marginal product (productivity),[1] (ii) the worker's outside option (the value of searching for a job), and (iii) the expected duration of the job (match). Apparently, larger productivity and expected job duration imply larger profits to the employer, while the worker's outside option affects the employer's profits negatively. A better outside option allows the worker to bargain for a higher wage, which in turn lowers the employer's share of the match surplus. When expected profits increase relative to the expected recruitment costs, firms open more vacancies per unemployed worker and job creation increases. More vacancies per unemployed worker then mean higher job finding rates and lower unemployment rates for workers participating in that market. It also implies higher wages, since with higher job creation workers' outside option improves, which means they can bargain for higher wages.

The presence of immigrants in the labour market can alter incentives to create jobs through all these channels: recruitment costs, productivity, wages, job duration. Consider a labour market that consists of n sub-markets. Sub-market i of this labour market recruits workers of skill type i and produces a labour input y_i, which is then used together with other labour inputs to produce the final good. The production structure is such that the different labour inputs produced in each of these sub-markets are complements. Suppose that in this sub-market i there are natives and different types of immigrants (e.g. documented, undocumented, temporary, permanent), all of skill type i searching for jobs. Let t denote the type of worker. Assume that firms cannot direct their search towards the one or the other type of worker (due to legal restrictions or incomplete information). If this is the case, then firms may match with either type of worker at rate $\frac{u_{it}}{u_i}$ where u_{it} is the number of unemployed workers of type t searching for jobs in market i and u_i is the total number of unemployed workers searching for a job in that market. With the presence of immigrants, the job creation condition takes the following form:

$$\frac{c_i}{q(\theta_i)} = \sum_t \frac{u_{it}}{u_i} J_{it} \tag{5.1}$$

where c_i is the flow recruitment cost (i.e. the flow cost of keeping a vacancy open), θ_i is the tightness in market i (i.e. the ratio of vacancies to unemployed), $q(\theta_i)$ is the job filling rate and J_{it} is the value of a match with a type t worker to the firm. The left-hand side represents the average recruitment cost and the right-hand-side the expected profit from a new job. If expected profits increase relative to recruitment costs, then θ_i increases, meaning that workers searching in this market can more easily find jobs, and their unemployment rate decreases.

Notice that the expression for expected profits is the weighted average of the value of each possible match J_{it}. In its simplest form, the value of a match with a type t worker is given by:

$$J_{it} = \frac{p_{it} - w_{it}}{r + s_{it}} \tag{5.2}$$

where p_{it} is the worker's productivity, w_{it} the worker's wage, r is the interest rate and s_{it} the separation rate (i.e. the probability that the match will break up). The presence of immigrants in the market can alter the expected profits of new jobs through two main channels. First, immigration-induced changes in the skill composition of the labour force will alter workers' productivities p_{it}. An increase in the relative supply of skills i will lower p_{it} and vice versa, when the relative supply of skills i decreases. Second, through changes in the weights $\frac{u_{it}}{u_i}$ put on each type of match in the right-hand-side of Eq. (5.1). An increase in the share of a certain type of immigrant in the pool of unemployed workers of skill type i will shift weights in Eq. (5.1) away from all other values and towards the value of a match with that type of immigrant. Employers' expected profits will increase if the surplus they generate from employing that immigrant is larger than from employing any other type of worker and vice versa.

If all types of workers (immigrants or natives) participating in this market generate the same surplus (i.e. $J_{it} = J_i \; \forall \; t$), meaning that wages, separation probabilities and productivity are all the same across all worker types (that is, $w_{it} = w_i$, $p_{it} = p_i$, and $s_{it} = s_i$,) then the presence of immigrants affects job creation incentives only through its impact on p_i. An immigration-induced increase in the relative supply of skills i will lower the marginal product of skill type i, p_i, and vice-versa if the relative supply of skills i decreases. The latter occurs when the new immigrants have different skills than the natives participating in this market, which means that they are searching in a different market, or when immigrants just choose to direct their search in a different market that produces a different labour input. This is the standard channel present in the canonical model. The only difference here is that we know explicitly that a decrease in productivity will increase the unemployment rate of workers participating in the market, because it will lower employers' profits and induce them to open fewer vacancies per unemployed worker. If, however, the increase in immigration is skilled balanced, that is, it leaves the relative supply of skills intact, then it will have no effect on marginal product, nor on employer's profits, and job creation will remain the same. Notice that immigration-induced changes in the relative supply of skills involve distributional effects. They might hurt one type of labour whose supply becomes relatively more abundant, but benefit that whose supply becomes more scarce, as long as complementarities between different skill types exist. For instance, an immigration-induced increase in the relative supply of skill i will lower p_i but may increase productivity in sub-market j, p_j, given that skills j and skills i complement each other in the production process.

It is very unlikely, however, that immigrants are identical to natives in all other aspects, even if they have the same skills. In fact, employers may benefit from the presence of immigrant workers in the labour force in several different ways depending on immigrant type (employment-based, family-based, undocumented etc.). So even when an immigration influx is skill-balanced, meaning that it does not affect workers' marginal product, it can still have a positive effect on job creation incentives. If the advantage that employers gain from the presence of immigrants in the labour market is large, a positive job creation effect is possible, even when the immigration influx lowers workers' marginal product. In terms of Eqs. (5.1) and (5.2), an inflow of immigrants in market *i* will decrease p_{it}, but also shift weights in the right-hand side of (5.1) from J_{iN} to J_{iI}, where subscripts *N* and *I* denote 'immigrant' and 'native', respectively. If $J_{iI}>J_{iN}$ then the right-hand side of Eq. (5.1) may increase, despite the decrease in p_{it}, leading to higher job creation in market *i* that benefits also the natives participating in that market.

One way of employers benefiting is by using immigrant labour to cut on labour costs. Immigrants, and especially undocumented immigrants, may be willing to accept lower wages than their similar natives because they have a worse outside option. There are many reasons why immigrants' outside option is smaller than that of natives with similar skills. Being in a foreign country, immigrants may have more difficulty finding a job due to lack of social networks, for instance. But, in addition, immigrants' unemployment income may be lower, since they do not qualify for the same unemployment insurance benefits as natives. Undocumented immigrants are often not eligible for any unemployment insurance benefits, but even legal immigrants may qualify for significantly fewer benefits than natives.[2] These differences in outside option may be a key factor explaining the observed wage gaps between seemingly identical native and legal or illegal immigrant workers. Borjas and Friedberg (2009) estimate a 20% wage gap between legal immigrants and natives in the US for the year 2000, after controlling for observed abilities such as education and age.[3]

This feature generates also the possibility that immigration improves the employment and wages of competing natives. An immigration influx of immigrants of skill type *i* in market *i* will lower the average wage that firms expect to pay, will increase the expected profits from a new job (right-hand-side of Eq. (5.1)) and will induce more job entry and consequently lower unemployment and a better bargaining position for native workers. This advantage that employers gain from having access to the cheaper labour provided by immigrants may be especially important in labour-intensive industries in which jobs are mainly manual and productivity depends less on the type of skills that immigrants may have a disadvantage on, such as language proficiency.

The labour cost effect of immigration has been emphasized in Chassamboulli and Palivos (2014). They develop a search and matching model of a labour market with differential search costs between natives and immigrants, reflecting the lower outside option of the latter due to the difficulties mentioned above. In their set up, an immigration influx has the standard effects on the productivity of skilled and unskilled native workers, also present in the canonical model, owned to complementarity and substitutability effects, but lowers in addition the average wage that firms expect to pay, leading to more job entry and consequently a better bargaining position for native workers. They calibrate the model to the US economy and find that the impact of the skill-biased increase in immigration that took place between 2000 and 2009 is positive on the overall net income to natives. They find that it lowered the unemployment and raised the wage rate of unskilled native workers, because, as expected, it increased the marginal product of unskilled labour, but also because it lowered employers' labour costs due to the lower wages paid to immigrants, inducing unskilled job entry. However, what is less expected is that they also find that it encouraged skilled job entry. Despite being skill-biased, meaning that it lowered the marginal product of skilled labour, the 2000–2009 immigration influx, had a positive impact on the employment of not only unskilled but also skilled natives. The increase in skilled job entry is again due to firms anticipating that, with a higher number of skilled immigrants searching for jobs, they will have to pay lower wages on average, which dominated over the negative productivity effect.

But the advantage that employers gain from the presence of immigrants in the labour market is sometimes more than just access to cheaper labour. Immigrants are sometimes more productive than natives especially in cases where their admission into a country is based on skills and merit. In such cases, with more immigrants in the labour force employers may anticipate higher productivity on average. This can drive the growth of jobs and increase the employment of also natives. The H-1B programme in the US, for instance, admits only skilled foreigners with exceptional abilities and skills. Admissions through this programme are employment-based meaning that all individuals applying for an H-1B visa must already have a job and an employer who is willing to sponsor their immigration to the US. It is meant to fill skill-specific gaps and unlike other immigration programmes and entry channels, foreigners entering on an H-1B visa are screened for their qualifications and are selected based on productivity. There is evidence of a positive impact of high-skilled employment-based admissions on US productivity. Kerr and Lincoln (2010) find that increasing H-1B admissions in the US increases the amount of US patenting, especially for firms and cities that depend highly on the programme. Similar results are also found in Hunt and Gauthier-Loiselle (2010) for immigrants who are college graduates. Peri et al. (2015) attribute their finding of a positive effect of foreign-born STEM workers on wages of native college-educated workers across US metropolitan areas to a higher total factor productivity growth driven by these workers. Hunt (2011) shows that immigrants who first entered into the US on a student trainee or a work visa outperform natives in wages, patenting, publishing and other innovative activities, while those who arrived as permanent residents (mainly through the family unification programme) perform similar to natives. The high productivity of H-1B workers is also supported by evidence in Lofstrom and Hayes (2011) that this group of workers earns more than natives. Chassamboulli and Peri (2019) also find that immigrants on employment visas earn significantly more than skilled immigrants on family visas or skilled natives.

Another advantage that employers may gain from immigration is access to a larger supply of workers, readily available to work, which helps keep recruitment costs down, especially in sectors where the supply of native labour is relatively low. Enabling employers to hire foreign workers when they have difficulty finding native workers, helps them avoid long and costly search periods, keep hiring costs low and preserve their jobs or even expand. The main goal of the US temporary employment-based immigration system is exactly that. The H-1B programme, mentioned above, admits highly skilled foreigners to work in specialty occupations, in which supply of workers is low. Foreigners are admitted through the H-1B programme on the basis of employers' demand for their skills. Two other programmes, the H-2A and H-2B for agricultural and non-agricultural workers, respectively, allow less educated foreigners, again on the basis of employers' needs.

5.2.2 The Labour Market Effects of Immigration Policies

As mentioned above, the government cannot directly control the total number of immigrants. A change in immigration can be achieved through policies that either restrict immigrant entry (e.g. visa quotas) or increase immigrant exit (e.g. deportations). We show here that the various policies that can be used to reduce a certain group of immigrant workers can have different effects on labour markets, even if they produce exactly the same decrease in the number of immigrants.

A restrictive immigration policy can be direct, such as tighter visa quotas, enforcement of deportations or shorter visa durations, or indirect, affecting immigrant entry or exit through its impact on foreigners' incentives to enter or remain in the country. Such indirect policies could be, for instance, restricting immigrants' access to welfare benefits, restricting their right to employment in certain sectors and so on. Such policies can reduce the migration benefit and discourage foreigners from entering into the country or encourage those already in the country to return.

In a labour market with search frictions in which wages are the outcome of bargaining, the latter indirect policies are likely to have less negative (or more positive) effects on job creation, compared to direct policies. In particular, policies that reduce immigrants' value from staying in the country, especially while unemployed, will put downward pressure on their wage. They will make it costlier for immigrants to be unemployed and induce them to accept lower wages by worsening their bargaining position in wage setting. As shown in Eq. (5.2), and as discussed above, lower wages mean more profits for firms. Such indirect policies that reduce the migration incentive by putting downward pressure on immigrants' wages, reduce immigrant entry (and increase exit), but increase also the employers' surplus from employing immigrants with a positive impact on incentives to post vacancies and create jobs. Direct policies, on the other hand, such as shorter visa durations or deportations, are more likely to have a negative effect on employers' profits. What such policies effectively do is to increase the discount factor used to evaluate the value of a job that is occupied by an immigrant worker. In terms of Eq. (5.2), shorter visa durations or a higher return probability (for instance, due to enforcement of deportations) can be captured by an increase in the rate of separation s_{it}, which affects the value of a match negatively, since a higher separation rate means that the match is expected to last less. By reducing the presence of immigrants in the labour force all types of restrictive policies reduce the weight $\frac{u_{iI}}{u_i}$ put on the value of matching with immigrant worker, but direct policies may also decrease that value of a match with an immigrant worker J_{iI}, while indirect policies may increase it. If for the reasons discussed above firms generate more surplus from employing immigrants than natives $J_{iI} > J_{iN}$, then shifting weights in Eq. (5.1) from J_{iI} to J_{iN} will lower employers' profits and in turn job creation. But this negative job creation effect is likely to be smaller if this shift is achieved through indirect, instead of direct, policies.

The effects of immigration policies on job creation have been explored in Chassamboulli and Peri (2015). The question they ask is how to deal with the presence of a large number of illegal immigrants in the US. In particular, what policy should be used to reduce the presence of illegal immigrants in the US and how would this affect the US labour market. They develop a search model of two countries linked by migration flows representing the US and Mexico. In the model, unskilled workers from Mexico can find both legal and illegal opportunities to migrate to the US. The decision to take up such an opportunity depends on the benefit from migrating to the US, which in turn, depends on labour market conditions and immigration policies in the US. They analyse both direct policies, such as increasing border enforcement and increasing the frequency of deportations, and indirect policies, such as increasing illegal immigrant's cost of searching for a job, which could reflect for instance, limited access to benefits. However, they consider in addition, the alternative option of reducing illegal immigration through legalization. In line with Chassamboulli and Palivos (2014), in this study also immigration benefits US firms by allowing them to pay a lower cost. More illegal immigrants actually encourage firms to create more unskilled jobs per unemployed worker, and increase the employment of unskilled natives. The skilled natives also benefit in terms of job creation and employment through complementarities in production. The relevant question then is which policy can reduce illegal immigration with the least negative effect on native workers. They find that the legalization of illegal immigrants is the only policy among those considered that does not have a depressing effect on the employment of native workers. This is because this policy, unlike the other policies, does not decrease total immigration. It decreases illegal immigration, but at the same time provides higher incentives for new immigrants to enter as their chances of becoming legal increase, and as a result, the total number of immigrants increases. The increased presence of legal immigrants helps firms maintain lower labour costs and create new jobs. It dominates over the depressing effect of fewer illegal immigrants in the market.

We see here the importance of allowing in our analysis for immigration to be an equilibrium outcome, instead of treating it as an exogenous policy variable. To a large extent, the positive effect of a legalization programme comes from its positive impact on entry incentives, which helps increase the inflow of new immigrants as the number of illegal immigrants decreases. Such effects are overlooked when considering exogenous decreases in the number of immigrants.

5.2.3 The US Immigration System

Studies of the effects of immigration in the US have typically focused on the two major entry channels, legal and illegal, or have focused mainly on unskilled immigration. But there are two main channels of legal entry into the US, family-based and employment-based, that admit not only unskilled but also skilled immigrants. The family-based immigration system, introduced in 1965, was based on reuniting immigrant families while abolishing national-origins quota. While admission on a family visa is not skill selective, skilled foreigners are also admitted through this route. Employment visas, on the other hand, are targeted towards highly skilled foreigners who are in high demand for US firms. Legal immigrants admitted on family visas can stay and work in the country indefinitely while most of the employment immigrants are initially admitted on temporary work permits and may transition to a permanent residence status subsequently. Moreover, while family entries are not conditional on having a job in the US, all immigrants entering with a work permit must already have a job in the US, and unless they transition to permanent residency, their stay in the US is conditional on having job. There are therefore reasons to expect that immigrants admitted through these two channels, although all legal, may influence the US labour market differently.

When it comes to their labour market effects, the employment-based system has two main advantages over the family-unification system. First, through the employment-based system US employers can gain access to a highly skilled labour force, readily available to work, without having to engage in time-consuming search in the US labour market. Second, admissions through the employment-based system are based on the demand for skills by US employers; workers entering on work permits are petitioned by their employers whereas those entering on family visas are petitioned by their relatives. Thus, employment immigrants are more selected on the productivity dimension, as supported by the evidence mentioned above that they receive higher wages and contribute more to innovation and productivity growth. Thus, considering only immigrants' skill characteristics or only their legal status and not differentiating between family and employment immigrants may leave out important aspects for how immigration affects the US labour market.

Another distinctive characteristic of the US immigration system is its strong network dependence. It allows, in a sense, for legal migration to the US to be a "self-sustained" process, since opportunities for new entries through each of the two legal routes depend strongly on networks, which means incumbent immigrants. To be eligible for a family visa, a foreigner must have a relative who is a legal permanent resident of the US. This effectively means that admitting more immigrants generates more opportunities for future entries through the family unification route. A foreigner can apply for a permit to enter and work in the US only if he has already been offered a job in the US Such job offers are presumably made available to workers abroad through referrals from their network of co-ethnics who are legal residents of the US. This also means that as the network of legal immigrants expands, opportunities for entry through each of the two legal routes become more frequent. This feature of the US immigration system implies that small changes in immigration policies can have unintended long-run equilibrium effects, since networks and family linkage effects may increase substantially the immigration opportunities in the future. For instance, the introduction of the family-based immigration system in 1965 allowed over time the largest increase in immigrants in the US.

The only study that differentiates among the two most relevant channels of legal entry to the US and in addition accounts explicitly for the role of immigrant networks in generating opportunities for legal entry is Chassamboulli and Peri (2019). They develop a two-country economy that represents the US and the rest of the world and model in detail the three main immigrant entry routes to the US: illegal, family-based and employment-based. They also use a search and matching model to describe the labour market in which firms post vacancies for skilled and unskilled workers and unemployed workers search for jobs. An innovation of their approach is that they allow for immigration from each entry route to be an equilibrium outcome reflecting entry incentives and network effects. For instance, they can increase border enforcement to decrease illegal immigration, while leaving all other immigrant entry routes unchanged, and then examine what would happen in equilibrium to the other groups of immigrants. Similarly, they can decrease the approval rate of petitions for family unification entries and then analyse what would happen to employment-based entries and illegal entries. Hence, in their model immigration policies targeting one immigrant group will also affect natives' outcomes through their impact on entry incentives and entry opportunities for other immigrant groups.

Chassamboulli and Peri (2019) find that the job creation effects of policies restricting any of the three entry routes are negative, but for different reasons. Unskilled family and undocumented immigrants allow firms to cut on labour costs by accepting lower wages than natives due to their worse outside options. Employment immigrants, on the other hand, receive higher wages than natives, but still generate larger surplus to firms because their productivity per unit of wage is higher than that of skilled natives or family immigrants. Their higher productivity is owed to the fact that, unlike natives and other immigrants, they are selected based on ability. Interestingly, they find that although firms are almost indifferent between hiring skilled natives or skilled family immigrants, decreasing the approval rate of family admissions can have a depressing effect on job creation mainly because it reduces also employment-based admissions. With fewer family immigrants there are also fewer opportunities for highly skilled individuals to enter through on the job referrals. In fact, because the two legal routes depend strongly on networks, restricting any of the two routes turns out to have very similar negative job creation effects and very similar effects on the skill composition of immigrant labour force. Given that the job creation effects of all types of immigrants benefit natives, their analysis suggests that policy combinations that restrict one entry route but relax the other will be more beneficial to natives compared to purely restrictive policies that restrict one entry channel only.

5.3 Reducing Illegal Immigration Via a Temporary Visa Programme

The decreasing supply of native workers in low-skill sectors as they are becoming older and choosing to become more educated, together with the high demand for these low-skill labour services (e.g. in construction, landscaping, housekeeping etc.), may have resulted in recent decades in stronger pressures to hire undocumented immigrants, thereby also creating incentives for unskilled foreigners to seek entry into the US though illegal channels. By implementing policies that reduce illegal immigration while shifting toward a "merit-based" immigration system that grants permanent residency to more skilled and highly educated foreigners, a number of sectors in the US economy that rely mainly on low-cost labour from low-skill and undocumented immigrants are expected to shrink, hurting this way the employment of also natives in these sectors. The low-skilled and undocumented immigrants provide, in addition, important services that complement the work of more skilled natives. They also support the growth of sectors that employ mostly native workers in jobs that require more skills and education. Thus, reducing their presence will also hurt the employment of natives in jobs requiring more skills. While the common perception is that some of the low-skill manual jobs freed up will be taken by native workers, as shown in Chassamboulli and Peri (2015), the negative job creation effects in low-skill sectors due to increasing labour costs and the negative impact on job creation in complementing sectors will dominate over this small positive effect.

Based on the studies discussed above, which explore the positive labour cost and productivity effects of different types of immigrants, the immigration policies that benefit natives the most are not those that decrease immigration, but instead, those that change the composition of immigrants towards the types of immigrants that are most beneficial to natives. Chassamboulli and Peri (2015) show that the legalization of undocumented immigrants provides the best alternative solution to the problem of reducing illegal immigration, because it maintains the supply of important low-skill and relatively cheaper labour services to US firms. Based on the results shown in Chassamboulli and Peri (2019), the employment-based visa programme is particularly valuable to US firms, so that a programme that replaces family-based with employment-based immigration is more beneficial to natives compared to a programme that reduces immigration overall.

In what follows, we explore an alternative policy combination that aims to reduce illegal immigration while avoiding the negative job creation effects. The policy that we explore attempts to offset the negative job creation effects of fewer illegal immigrants in the market by maintaining the supply of low-skill foreign labour through a temporary employment programme. That is, we analyse a policy combination that eliminates illegal immigration, but introduces, at the same time, the possibility of hiring unskilled foreigners directly from abroad on temporary work permits. With the introduction of temporary work permits employers gain access to a large pool of low-skill foreigners who are available to work, presumably at a lower wage than natives, since their outside option—the option of searching for a job in their home country—yields a much lower return. The temporary visa programme helps to maintain the advantage that employers gain from having access to cheaper labour, it maintains the supply of low-skill labour in the market and allows employers to save on recruitment costs. We examine whether these effects are strong enough to outweigh the negative job creation effects of reducing illegal immigration. We quantify these effects by simulating these policy changes in a two-country search model that represents the US and the rest of the world and accounts for the two main types of immigrant entry: illegal and legal. The model developed here borrows elements from Chassamboulli and Peri (2015, 2019).

5.3.1 The General Set-up

We describe here the main features of the model. Details of the equilibrium conditions and Bellman equations are described in the Appendix. The model consists of two countries: country 1 and country 2. Country 1, which represents the US, offers better labour market prospects (wages and employment opportunities) than country 2, thus workers have incentive to migrate from country 2 (the rest of the world) to country 1 (the US). Each period some of the individuals born in country 2 will migrate to country 1. The labour force of country 1 thus consists of both natives and immigrants. The size of the native labour force of country 1 is normalized to 1 and it is divided into skilled workers of measure S and unskilled workers of measure $1 - S$. The size of the native labour force in country 2 is of measure F and is also divided into skilled and unskilled workers of measures F_s and F_u, respectively. We keep the overall size of the labour force (native of country 1 and 2) constant by assuming that individuals from either country enter and exit the labour force at a common rate τ. New individuals enter the labour force as unemployed, all agents are risk neutral and discount the future at a common rate r equal to the interest rate, and time is continuous.

Migration to country 1 can be legal or illegal, and such opportunities arise as random events occurring at rates x_L and x_I, respectively. Opportunities for legal migration arise for both skilled and unskilled natives of country 2 at equal rates.[4] Opportunities for illegal migration arise only for the unskilled natives of country 2, in line with evidence that most of the undocumented immigrants in the US are unskilled.[5] There are two labour markets in country 1, one for skilled and one for unskilled workers, each producing a different labour input. Skilled and unskilled immigrants (documented or not) enter the corresponding market and search for jobs. Illegal immigrants face the risk of deportation, while legal immigrants have the right to stay and work in country 1 indefinitely. Legal immigrants still have a positive probability of returning home for personal idiosyncratic reasons. Illegal immigrants face, in addition, the risk of deportation. Let d_L and d_I denote the instant return rate of legal and illegal immigrants, respectively. We set $d_I > d_L$ and the difference between the two is the deportation risk.

Besides migrating to country 1 in order to search for a job, an unskilled native of country 2 can also apply for a permit to enter and work in country 1 temporarily, provided that he has found an employer in country 1 who is willing to offer him a job. To be qualified for a work permit an individual must have a job in country 1. Thus, all individuals entering on work permits enter with a job and do not have to search for a job in the market. We assume that a firm in the unskilled sector of country 1 hires a temporary worker from country 2 at rate x_T. This may reflect both the rate at which opportunities to hire a temporary worker arise, but also the rate at which petitions for temporary work permits are approved. To hire a temporary worker from abroad the firm does not have to post a vacancy and search for a worker. Instead, it just expands, by hiring the new temporary worker and creating a new temporary job. The advantage of temporary work permits is that firms can expand by gaining access to unskilled workers from abroad, who are readily available to work, without having to engage in time-consuming search for such workers in the local labour market. For workers on temporary work permits, stay in country 1 is conditional on having a job in country 1. They return home at rate d_T, reflecting the end of their employment contract, the expiration of their work permit or other personal reasons.

The total labour force of country 1 thus consists of natives (N) and immigrants, legal (L) and illegal (I) and temporary workers (T) and is of size $1 + N + L + T$. The total number of workers who are natives of country 2 that remain in country 2 is of measure $F - I - L - T$. All illegal immigrants and temporary workers are unskilled, while legal immigrants can be skilled (L_S) or unskilled (L_S) so that $L = L_S + L_u$.

5.3.2 Workers and Firms

There are three sectors in country 1: two intermediate sectors that produce intermediate goods Y_u and Y_s using "unskilled" and "skilled" labour, respectively, and the final sector. The production technology in the intermediate sector is linear so that the number of units produced equals the number of respective workers employed. The two intermediate inputs are non-storable. Once produced, they are sold in competitive markets and are assembled for the production of country 1's final good (Y), the numeraire. The production of the final good is given by:

$$Y = \left[xY_s^{\rho} + (1-x)Y_u^{\rho} \right]^{\frac{1}{\rho}} \tag{5.3}$$

where x is a positive parameter that governs income shares and ρ determines the elasticity of substitution between the two inputs. It implies diminishing marginal products and complementarity between the two inputs. Since the two intermediate inputs are sold in competitive markets, their prices, p_s and p_u will be equal to their marginal products, that is:

$$p_s = x\left(\frac{Y}{Y_s}\right)^{1-\rho} \tag{5.4}$$

$$p_u = (1-x)\left(\frac{Y}{Y_u}\right)^{1-\rho} \tag{5.5}$$

For simplicity, and since our focus here is on illegal immigration, we do not differentiate between the two main legal avenues for skilled immigration to the US, the family and the employment. We do, however, take into account that some of the skilled legal immigrants of country 1 (the US) are admitted on employment visas, meaning that they are screened for their occupational qualifications and abilities and thus are selected more on the productivity dimension, compared to skilled natives. We account for this by assuming that each skilled native produces one unit of the intermediate input, while each skilled immigrant produces $\lambda > 1$ units. In the numerical experiments that follow, we calibrate the value of λ by matching the wage difference between skilled legal immigrants and skilled natives and this parameter turns out to be larger than one. Unskilled workers, on the other hand, are all equally productive. They all produce one unit of the intermediate input. Given a linear production technology for each of the two intermediate inputs, we can write, $Y_u = e_{uL} + e_{uN} + e_{uI} + T$ and $Y_s = \lambda e_{sL} + e_{sN}$, where e_{ij} denotes the number of employed workers of skill type $i = [s, u]$ with s = skilled, u = unskilled and status $j = [N, L, T]$ with N = native, L = legal and I = illegal.

5.3.3 Search and Matching

In each of the two labour markets (skilled and unskilled), unemployed workers and job vacancies are matched via a stochastic technology $M(u_i, v_i)$; where u_i and v_i denote, respectively, the number of unemployed workers and vacancies of skill i. We can write the job finding and job filling rates in each market i as $\frac{M(u_i, v_i);}{u_i} = m(\theta_i)$ and $\frac{M(u_i, v_i);}{v_i} = q(\theta_i)$ where $\theta_i = \frac{v_i}{u_i}$ is tightness in market i and $m'(\theta_i) > 0$ while $q'(\theta_i) < 0$.[6] In each market there is free entry of firms that drives the value of posting a vacancy to zero. That is, firms post vacancies until all rents are exhausted. Each firm opens one vacancy and hires one worker. Vacancies of each skill type are open to both natives and immigrant workers with those skills. Hence, natives and immigrants in market i all find jobs at the common rate $m(\theta_i)$.

Unemployed workers receive a flow of income b_i, representing the opportunity cost of employment. In addition, unemployed legal and illegal immigrant workers pay a search cost π_L and π_I, respectively and $\pi_I > \pi_L$. This means that immigrants' and especially illegal immigrants' flow value while unemployed is lower than that of natives. We account for the fact that legal immigrants have access to significantly fewer benefits than US citizens, especially when unemployed. Undocumented immigrants' flow value while unemployed is even lower (i.e. their search cost is even higher) because they cannot access any unemployment insurance. The cost of maintaining a job vacancy is c_i, representing the recruitment cost.

The flow revenue to an unskilled firm from matching with an unskilled worker (native or immigrant) is p_u (given in Eq. (5.5)). A skilled firm generates revenue p_s (given in Eq. (5.4)) when matched with a skilled native worker and λp_s when matched with a skilled immigrant worker. When a vacancy and a worker are matched, they bargain over the division of the match surplus. The worker's type as well as the revenue that results from a match are known to both parties. The wages, denoted as w_{ij}, differ by skill type i and status $j = [N, L, I, T]$ (native, legal, illegal, and temporary worker), and are determined by Nash bargaining between the two parties over the match surplus. Once the wage is agreed, production commences immediately. Matches dissolve at rate s_i. In the event of a separation, the worker joins the pool of unemployed, the job becomes vacant, and both start searching for a new match.

5.3.4 Optimality Conditions and Free Entry

At each point in time, a worker is either employed (E) or unemployed (U), while a vacancy may be either filled (J) or empty (V). We use the notation E_{ij}; U_{ij}; J_{ij} and V_{ij} to denote the present discounted value associated with the state where a worker is employed, a worker is unemployed, a job is filled and a job is vacant, where $i = [s; u]$ and $j = [N; I; L; T]$. Note that we can drop the subscript j from V_{ij}, since a type$-i$ vacancy is open to any worker of skill type i, immigrant or native and is therefore described by the same Bellman equation. We can also drop the subscript i whenever $j = [I, T]$, since all illegal immigrants and temporary workers are unskilled. The full set of Bellman equations that describe the optimal behaviour of workers and firms in country 1 is in the Appendix.

A second set of equilibrium conditions is that of free-entry of firms in each of the two labour markets. Firms open vacancies up to the point that an additional one has zero expected value. In equilibrium this implies the following two conditions:

$$V_i = 0 \; i = [s;u] \tag{5.6}$$

Wages are then determined by Nash bargain between the firm and the worker. The outside options of the firm and the worker are the value of a vacancy (i.e. of searching for a worker) and the value of being unemployed (i.e. of searching for a job), respectively. Let S_{ij} denote the surplus of a match between a vacancy of skill type i and a worker of status j. With Nash-bargaining the wage is set to a level such that the worker gets a share β of the surplus, where β represents the relative bargaining power of workers, and the share $1-\beta$ goes to the firm. This implies the following six equilibrium conditions:

$$\beta S_{i\kappa} = E_{i\kappa} - U_{i\kappa}, (1-\beta) S_{i\kappa} = J_{i\kappa} - V_i, i = [s;u], \kappa = [N;L] \quad (5.7)$$

$$\beta S_I = E_I - U_I, (1-\beta) S_I = J_I - V_u \quad (5.8)$$

$$\beta S_T = E_T - U_u^2, (1-\beta) S_T = J_T - V_u \quad (5.9)$$

Notice that for workers on temporary work permits the outside option is the value of searching for a job in country 2, U_u^2 (and not in country 1), because these workers' stay (or entry) in country 1 is conditional upon having a job in country 1. If an agreement is not reached and they are not offered a job in country 1, they will be denied a work permit and they will have to search for a job in country 2. For the rest of the workers, whose stay in country 1 is unconditional, the outside option is the respective value of searching for a job in country 1.

5.3.5 The Immigration Decision and Inflows

A worker will take up an opportunity to migrate to country 1 if the benefit exceeds the cost. Each time an immigration opportunity arises the worker draws a migration cost, z, from a distribution with CDF $F(z)$ and support $[\underline{z}, \bar{\bar{z}}]$. We assume that only the unemployed natives of country 2 are actively searching for opportunities to migrate illegally, so such opportunities arise only for the unskilled natives of country 2 who are unemployed. We also assume that only unemployed workers are willing to act upon opportunities to migrate legally. Since all workers deciding whether to migrate or not, either legally or illegally, are unemployed, their benefit from migrating is the difference between their value of searching for a job in country 1 and their value of being unemployed (searching for a job) in their home country. Note that all new immigrants (legal or illegal) enter without a job and must search for a job in the market. An unskilled individual whose migration cost is z will take advantage of an opportunity to enter illegally into country 1 only if $U_I - U_u^2 > z$. Likewise, a type-i native of country 2 will migrate legally only if $U_{iL} - U_i^2 > z$. The threshold costs, denoted as $\tilde{z}_I$ and $\tilde{z}_{iL}$ and representing the highest cost a worker is willing to pay in order to obtain illegal or legal entry into country 1, are defined by the following conditions:

$$\tilde{z}_I = U_I - U_u^2 \tag{5.10}$$

$$\tilde{z}_{iL} = U_{iL} - U_i^2, i = [s;u] \tag{5.11}$$

These threshold immigration costs give the three rates $F(\tilde{z}_I)$, $F(\tilde{z}_{uL})$ and $F(\tilde{z}_{sL})$ at which natives of country 2 take up opportunities to migrate, illegally or legally. Changes in wage and unemployment conditions, as well as changes in immigration policies in country 1, will affect these threshold costs and in turn the inflows of legal and illegal immigrants. Let u_i^2 denote the number of unemployed workers of skill type $i = [s; u]$ in country 2. Inflows of illegal immigrants are given by $x_I u_u^2 F(\tilde{z}_I)$ and inflows of legal immigrants of skill type i by $x_L u_i^2 F(\tilde{z}_{iL})$.

Notice that all the conditions of country 2 that can influence the decision to migrate and the flow of migrants from country 2 to country 1 are summarized in only two values: the value of searching for a job U_i^2 and the number of unemployed individuals u_i^2. The value of searching for a job reflects all home-country labour market conditions that may influence the benefit of migrating, such as wages, employment opportunities and so on, while the number of unemployed gives the pool of potential migrants to country 1. A detailed description of the labour market of country 2 is therefore not necessary. Since our focus is on the impact of immigration policies in country 1, we can simply focus on only these two values. Further, for simplicity we take these two values as given. The underlying assumption is that labour market conditions in country 2 are independent of immigration and labour market conditions in country 1.

5.3.6 Immigrant Stocks and Unemployment Rates

The last set of equilibrium conditions are the steady-state conditions for the numbers of legal immigrants, skilled (L_s) and unskilled (L_u), the number of illegal immigrants (I), the number of temporary workers (T) and the numbers of unemployed workers of each type in country 1: u_{sN} and u_{uN} are skilled and unskilled natives in country 1, u_{sL} and u_{uL} are skilled and unskilled legal immigrants and u_I are illegal immigrants. The formal conditions defining these steady-state variables (by equating flows in to flows out of each state) are given in the Appendix. We can write the steady-state conditions for unemployed and immigrants as follows:

$$\tilde{u}_{sN} = \frac{u_{sN}}{S} = \frac{s_s + \tau}{s_s + \tau + m(\theta_s)} \tag{5.12}$$

$$\tilde{u}_{uN} = \frac{u_{uN}}{1-S} = \frac{s_u + \tau}{s_u + \tau + m(\theta_s)} \tag{5.13}$$

$$\tilde{u}_{iL} = \frac{u_{iL}}{L_i} = \frac{s_i + \tau + d_L}{s_i + \tau + d_L + m(\theta_i)}, i = [s;u] \tag{5.14}$$

$$\tilde{u}_I = \frac{u_I}{I} = \frac{s_u + \tau + d_I}{s_u + \tau + d_I + m(\theta_u)} \tag{5.15}$$

$$L_s = \left[\frac{x_L \tilde{u}_s^2 F(\tilde{z}_{sL})}{\tau + d_L + x_L \tilde{u}_s^2 F(\tilde{z}_{sL})} \right] F_s \tag{5.16}$$

$$L_u = \left[\frac{x_L \tilde{u}_u^2 F(\tilde{z}_{uL})}{\tau + d_L + x_L \tilde{u}_u^2 F(\tilde{z}_{uL})} \right] (F_u - T - I) \tag{5.17}$$

$$I = \left[\frac{x_I \tilde{u}_u^2 F(\tilde{z}_I)}{\tau + d_I + x_I \tilde{u}_u^2 F(\tilde{z}_I)} \right] (F_u - T - L_u) \tag{5.18}$$

$$T = \left[\frac{x_T \left[(1 - \tilde{u}_{uN})(1 - S) + (1 - \tilde{u}_I) I + (1 - \tilde{u}_{uL}) L_u \right]}{\tau + d_T} \right] \tag{5.19}$$

We see from Eqs. (5.12)–(5.15) that the unemployment rates decrease with the matching probability $m(\theta_i)$. A policy that decreases θ_i, and in turn, the matching probability $m(\theta_i)$, will increase natives' unemployment rate. Also it can be easily verified by inspecting expressions (5.16)–(5.19) that the equilibrium numbers of workers of each type depend negatively on the return probabilities (d_I, d_L and d_T), positively on the rates of entry opportunities (x_I, x_L and x_T), and in the case of legal and illegal immigrants also positively on the threshold migration costs ($\tilde{z}_I$ and $\tilde{z}_{iL}$). Any economic and policy factor that increases the value of searching for a job in country 1 relative to country 2 (i.e. increases the threshold migration costs) encourages immigration and increases the equilibrium numbers of immigrants in country 1.

5.3.7 Key Conditions and Mechanisms

The job creation condition in the unskilled market can be written as:

$$\frac{c_i}{q(\theta_i)} = \frac{u_I}{u_u} J_I + \frac{u_{uL}}{u_u} J_{uL} + \frac{u_{uN}}{u_u} J_{uN} \tag{5.20}$$

Where $u_u = u_{uN} + u_{uL} + u_I$ is the total number of unemployed workers searching for unskilled jobs. Given $\pi_I > \pi_L > 0$ there is reason to expect that $J_I > J_{uL} > J_{uN}$. In fact, as can be verified by inspecting Eqs. (5.57),

(5.59) and (5.60) in the Appendix, this will be the case as long as the deportation risk of illegal immigrants and the return probability of legal immigrants are small enough. On the one hand, the higher search cost of immigrants implies that their wages are lower, which increases the firm's surplus from employing them. On the other hand, the expected duration of a match with an immigrant worker is shorter, due to returns and deportations. Firms benefit more from employing immigrants when their outside option is smaller, but also when the probability of a match break due to returns is smaller.

If $J_I > J_{uL} > J_{uN}$, then removing illegal immigrants from the market will shift weights in the right-hand-side of Eq. (5.20) from J_I to J_{uL} and J_{uN} with a negative impact on the expected profits of a new unskilled job. However, it will also reduce the relative supply of unskilled labour and thus increase the price of the unskilled input p_u, with a positive impact on the expected profits of firms. This is the standard channel present also in the canonical model. Hence, the overall impact on unskilled job creation is in general ambiguous and depends on which of the two effects dominates. But the skilled workers will be definitely hurt, in terms of both employment and wages, by the removal of undocumented immigrants from the market, because their marginal product, and thus the price p_s will decrease. Again, this is the complementarity effect present also in the canonical model. Firms in the skilled market will react to the decrease in p_s by opening fewer vacancies per unemployed worker, that is by decreasing θ_i. This will in turn lower the matching probability $m(\theta_i)$, will increase the unemployment rate of skilled natives and will force them to accept lower wages as their outside option worsens due to their lower job finding probability.

A policy combination that replaces illegal immigrants with legal unskilled immigrants or temporary workers prevents the relative supply of unskilled labour and thus the price of the skilled labour input p_s from falling. It thus helps repress the negative effects on skilled native workers. When it comes to unskilled natives, however, it is not clear cut that they will be better off when the supply of competing foreign workers remains unchanged. They will be better off only when the unskilled foreigners replacing illegal immigrants generate a significantly larger positive job creation effect, large enough to outweigh the negative effect on the price of the unskilled labour input.

As discussed above, allowing for the option to hire unskilled foreign workers directly from abroad, without having to go through costly search in the market, increases the expected profits of firms. To see this more clearly, consider the case where $d_I = d_L = 0$ so that immigrants legal and illegal and natives differ only with respect to search costs. Substituting the expressions for J_I, J_{uL} and J_{uN} (given by Eqs. (5.57), (5.59) and (5.60) in the Appendix) in (5.20) we get:

$$\frac{c_i}{q(\theta_i)} = \frac{(1-\beta)\left(p_u - b_u + \frac{u_I}{u_u}\pi_I + \frac{u_{uL}}{u_u}\pi_L\right) + x_T J_T}{r + s_u + \tau + \beta m(\theta_u)} \tag{5.21}$$

Evidently, when $x_T > 0$ the expected surplus from a new job increases, since firms anticipate that they will be able to expand by hiring a temporary worker from abroad, which yields surplus J_T without having to pay additional recruitment costs. If this benefit is large enough to dominate over the negative competitive pressure from the new temporary workers on p_u, then unskilled natives also will be better off when the policy implemented is not purely restrictive, but replaces instead illegal immigrants with temporary workers. It should also be noted that the firms' surplus from employing temporary workers, J_T, is higher the longer the duration of temporary work permits, and the lower the wage of temporary workers. The latter depends, in turn, on the value of searching for a job in country 2, which as mentioned above, reflects the outside option of temporary workers (see Eq. (5.61) in the Appendix). Given that some unskilled natives of country 2 are willing to pay the migration cost in order to enter illegally into country 1 and search for a job there (i.e. given $\tilde{z}_I > 0$), then from Eq. (5.10) it must be the case that $U_I > U_u^2$, which ensures that illegal immigrants have a better outside option and thus can bargain for higher wages than temporary workers. This points to significant gains from employing temporary workers for unskilled firms. But still, we need to take into account the negative competitive pressure on p_u before reaching any conclusion.

5.3.8 Policy Experiments

In this section, we simulate the effects on natives' labour market outcomes (wages, unemployment rate and net income) of different immigration policies aiming to reduce illegal immigration. The parameter choice is summarized in Table 5.2 in the Appendix. Our parameter choice follows closely the parameterization in Chassamboulli and Peri (2019), which aims to match as closely as possible moments of the data for the 2010–2015 average. Country 1 represents the US and we consider Mexico as the main country supplying low skilled immigrants and China and India as the two main countries supplying high skilled immigrants. Our measures of F_u and F_s, are therefore the unskilled Mexican labour force and the skilled Indian and Chinese labour force, respectively. Likewise, to calculate our measures of u_u^2 and u_s^2 we use the unemployment rate of unskilled workers in Mexico and the unemployment rates of skilled workers in India and China. We define as skilled a worker who has at least some college education and unskilled workers are those with no college education. We assume that the CDF of the immigration cost, $F(z)$, is uniform. Finally, we use a Cobb-Douglas matching function, $M_i = \xi v_i^{\varepsilon} u_i^{1-\varepsilon}$, $i = [s,u]$, where ξ is the matching efficiency parameter.

We consider first a "restrictive" policy that eliminates all undocumented immigrants from the unskilled market (i.e. 100% decrease in I). Notice that because we eliminate all illegal immigrants from the market, the policy used, that is, whether increased deportations (increase in d_I), reduced benefits (decrease in π_I) or border enforcement (decrease in x_I), is not important for the results obtained; any policy has the same impact because there are no illegal immigrants left behind, so whether their wages are lower or their return probability higher does not matter for the firms' profits. We then consider a combination of policies that reduce illegal immigration, on the one hand, but allow entry of unskilled foreigners through temporary work permits, on the other hand, so that the total number of unskilled foreigners remains unchanged. In the baseline parameterization we set $x_T = 0$, meaning that there are no temporary work permits for unskilled foreigners. We then examine what happens when we eliminate illegal immigration, but increase x_T so that the total supply of unskilled foreign labour remains the same. We also explore an alternative policy combination of reducing illegal immigration but increasing opportunities for unskilled foreigners to enter through the legal route (i.e. increasing x_L but only for the unskilled foreigners) so that total unskilled immigration remains the same.

The results are shown in Table 5.1. Removing all illegal immigrants from the US labour market has a depressing effect on both skilled and unskilled natives in terms of job creation. The unemployment rate of both types of native workers increases. The marginal product of unskilled natives increases as the supply of low-skill labour decreases. This means a higher price for the unskilled labour input, which raises firms' profits. But at the same time, without the undocumented immigrants in the market, firms expect to pay higher wages on average. This depressing effect dominates over the positive price effect and firms react by reducing job openings per unemployed worker. The resulting decrease in the production of the unskilled labour input, which complements the production of the skilled labour input, lowers also the price of the skilled labour input. As a result, firms in the skilled sector also open fewer vacancies per

Table 5.1 Results of policy experiments

	Eliminate illegal immigrants	Replace illegal with legal immigrants	Replace illegal immigrants with temporary workers
Tightness			
θ_s	−6.43	−1.07	3.18
θ_u	−17.88	−16.54	7.73
Unempl. rates			
$\tilde{u}_{sN}$	2.82	0.45	−1.31
$\tilde{u}_{uN}$	6.71	6.15	−2.48
Wages			
w_{sN}	−1.82	−0.30	0.90
w_{uN}	4.93	0.35	8.95
Net income			
$\tilde{Y}$	−1.48	−0.70	1.08
$\tilde{Y}_1$	−2.47	−1.29	1.55

The entries in the Table represent the percentage effects of three policy experiments on market tightness (first 2 rows), natives' unemployment rates (next 2 rows), natives' wages (next 2 rows) and natives' net income (last 2 rows). Column 1 shows the effects of eliminating illegal immigrants, column 2 shows the effects of replacing illegal immigrants with legal unskilled immigrants, and column 3 shows the effects of replacing illegal immigrants with temporary workers unemployed worker. The impact on wages follows that on prices. The wage of skilled natives decreases because their marginal product decreases but that of unskilled natives increases because their marginal product increases. But the positive effect on unskilled wages is not enough to outweigh the negative employment effects on both types of natives. The net income of natives decreases.

Replacing illegal immigrants with legal unskilled immigrants does little to improve the effects on natives' labour market outcomes, and especially the effects on unskilled natives. This policy combination helps to maintain the supply of unskilled labour which keeps the marginal product of skilled labour from falling too much. The negative impact on skilled job creation is smaller in this case, which implies also a smaller increase and decrease, respectively, in the unemployment and wage rate of skilled natives. The unskilled natives, on the other hand, benefit much less from this shift in the composition of low-skill immigrants towards legal immigrants. It helps to keep the expected labour cost for firms in the unskilled sector lower, since unskilled legal immigrants also receive lower wages than natives. But it also prevents the price of the unskilled labour input from increasing. The negative labour cost effect is smaller in this case, but so is the positive price effect, implying almost the same negative effect on unskilled job creation as a purely restrictive policy that eliminates illegal immigration only.[7]

Among the three policies considered, the only one generating positive job creation effects for both types of native workers is the one that replaces illegal immigrants with temporary workers. Allowing for the option to hire unskilled foreigners to replace the undocumented in the market increases the profits of firms in the unskilled market considerably. Unskilled jobs generate a significantly larger surplus, which also explains why unskilled natives' wages increase significantly. As the match surplus expands, the share of surplus that goes to the worker also expands. Expected profits from opening vacancies in the unskilled market increase and firms open more vacancies per unemployed worker. The unskilled unemployment rate also decreases. As the unskilled sector expands, and the production of the unskilled labour input increases, the price of the skilled labour input also increases. Job creation in the skilled market also expands, and skilled natives benefit both in terms of wages and employment.

Appendix

Model Details

Bellman Equations

The Bellman equations describing the values of job vacancies for unskilled and skilled workers in country 1 are as follows:

$$rV_u = -c_u + q(\theta_u)\left[\frac{u_I}{u_u}J_I + \frac{u_{uL}}{u_u}J_{uL} + \frac{u_{uN}}{u_u}J_{uN}\right] \quad (5.22)$$

$$rV_s = -c_s + q(\theta_s)\left[\frac{u_{sL}}{u_s}J_{sL} + \frac{u_{sN}}{u_s}J_{sN}\right] \quad (5.23)$$

Next, the value of a job depends on the type of worker filling the job:

$$rJ_{sN} = p_s - w_{sN} + (s_s + \tau)[V_s - J_{sN}] \quad (5.24)$$

$$rJ_{uN} = p_u - w_{uN} + x_T J_T + (s_u + \tau)[V_u - J_{uN}] \quad (5.25)$$

$$rJ_{sL} = \lambda p_s - w_{sL} + (s_s + d_L + \tau)[V_s - J_{sL}] \quad (5.26)$$

$$rJ_{uL} = p_u - w_{uL} + x_T J_T + (s_u + d_L + \tau)[V_u - J_{uL}] \quad (5.27)$$

$$rJ_T = p_u - w_T + (d_T + \tau)[V_u - J_T] \quad (5.28)$$

$$rJ_I = p_u - w_I + x_T J_T + (s_u + d_I + \tau)[V_u - J_I] \quad (5.29)$$

The value of unemployment for each worker type satisfies:

$$(r+\tau)U_{iN} = b_i - m(\theta_i) + [E_{iN} - U_{iN}],\ i = [s,u] \tag{5.30}$$

$$(r+\tau)U_{iL} = b_i - \pi_L + m(\theta_s)[E_{iL} - U_{iL}] + d_L\left[U_i^2 - U_{iL}\right] \tag{5.31}$$

$$(r+\tau)U_I = b_u - \pi_I + m(\theta_u)[E_I - U_I] + d_I\left[U_u^2 - U_I\right] \tag{5.32}$$

There is no value of being unemployed in country 1 for an immigrant on temporary work permit, since, as already mentioned, stay in country 1, in this case, is conditional on having a job. All immigrants on temporary work permits are employed, otherwise they must return home.

Finally, the value of being employed in steady state is given by the following five conditions relative to each country and worker type:

$$(r+\tau)E_{iN} = w_{iN} + s_i\left[U_{iN} - E_{iN}\right],\ i = [s,u] \tag{5.33}$$

$$(r+\tau)E_{iL} = w_{iL} + s_i\left[U_{iL} - E_{iL}\right] + d_L\left[U_i^2 - E_{iL}\right] \tag{5.34}$$

$$(r+\tau)E_I = w_I + s_u\left[U_I - E_I\right] + d_I\left[U_u^2 - E_I\right] \tag{5.35}$$

$$(r+\tau)E_T = w_T + d_T\left[U_s^2 - E_T\right] \tag{5.36}$$

Steady-State Conditions

By equating the outflow of immigrants of each type, which includes returns to the home country and labour force exits, to the inflow of new immigrants into each group we obtain the steady-state conditions for the number of legal immigrants, skilled and unskilled, L_s and L_u, respectively, the number of temporary workers, T, and the number of illegal immigrants, I:

$$\left(d_L+\tau\right)L_i = x_L u_i^2 F\left(\tilde{z}_{iL}\right) \tag{5.37}$$

$$\left(d_T+\tau\right)T = x_T\left(e_{uN}+e_{uL}+e_I\right) \tag{5.38}$$

$$\left(d_I+\tau\right)I = x_I u_u^2 F\left(\tilde{z}_I\right) \tag{5.39}$$

where $e_{uL} = L_u - u_{uL}$ is the number of unskilled legal immigrants that are employed, $e_I = I - u_I$ is the number of unskilled illegal immigrants that are employed and $e_{uN} = 1 - S - u_{uN}$ is the number of unskilled natives that are employed.

The conditions for the steady-state unemployment of natives (u_{sN} and u_{uN}), legal immigrants (u_{sL} and u_{uL}) and illegal immigrants (u_I) are as follows

$$\tau S + s_s\left(S-u_{sN}\right) = \left(m\left(\theta_s\right)+\tau\right)u_{sN} \tag{5.40}$$

$$\tau\left(1-S\right)+s_u\left(1-S-u_{uN}\right) = \left(m\left(\theta_u\right)+\tau\right)u_{uN} \tag{5.41}$$

$$s_i\left(L_{iL}-u_{iL}\right)+x_L u_i^2 F\left(\tilde{z}_{iL}\right) = \left(m\left(\theta_i\right)+d_L+\tau\right)u_{iL} \tag{5.42}$$

$$s_u\left(I-u_I\right)+x_I u_u^2 F\left(\tilde{z}_I\right) = \left(m\left(\theta_u\right)+d_I+\tau\right)u_I \tag{5.43}$$

Wages

Using the Bellman Eqs. (5.22)–(5.36), the free-entry conditions (5.6), the Nash bargaining conditions (5.7)–(5.9) and the immigration conditions in (5.10) and (5.11), we can solve for the equilibrium wage rates:

$$w_{sN} = \beta p_s + \left(1-\beta\right)\left[b_s + \beta m\left(\theta_s\right)S_{sN}\right] \tag{5.44}$$

$$w_{uN} = \beta\left[p_u + x_T J_T\right] + \left(1-\beta\right)\left[b_u + \beta m\left(\theta_u\right)S_{uN}\right] \tag{5.45}$$

$$w_{sL} = \beta\lambda p_s + (1-\beta)\left[b_s - \pi_L + \beta m(\theta_s)S_{sN}\right] \tag{5.46}$$

$$w_{uL} = \beta\left[p_u + x_T J_T\right] + (1-\beta)\left[b_u - \pi_L + \beta m(\theta_u)S_{uN}\right] \tag{5.47}$$

$$w_I = \beta\left[p_u + x_T J_T\right] + (1-\beta)\left[b_u - \pi_I + \beta m(\theta_u)S_I\right] \tag{5.48}$$

$$w_T = \beta p_u + (1-\beta)(r+\tau)U_u^2 \tag{5.49}$$

Value of a Job

Setting $V_i = 0$ in (5.24)–(5.29), we get:

$$J_{sN} = \frac{p_s - w_{sN}}{r + s_s + \tau} \tag{5.50}$$

$$J_{uN} = \frac{p_u + x_T J_T - w_{uN}}{r + s_u + \tau} \tag{5.51}$$

$$J_{sL} = \frac{\lambda p_s - w_{sL}}{r + s_s + d_L + \tau} \tag{5.52}$$

$$J_{uL} = \frac{p_u + x_T J_T - w_{uL}}{r + s_u + d_L + \tau} \tag{5.53}$$

$$J_I = \frac{p_u + x_T J_T - w_I}{r + s_u + d_I + \tau} \tag{5.54}$$

$$J_T = \frac{p_u - w_T}{r + d_T + \tau} \tag{5.55}$$

Apparently, the values of jobs to the firms increase with the worker's productivity and decrease with the worker's break up probability and wage, while the possibility of hiring a temporary worker increases the value of unskilled jobs.

Substituting the equilibrium wages (given in Eqs. (5.44)–(5.49)) into the equations above and using the Nash bargaining conditions in (5.7)–(5.9) we can write:

$$J_{sN} = (1-\beta)S_{sN} = \frac{(1-\beta)(p_s - b_s)}{r + s_s + \tau + \beta m(\theta_s)} \tag{5.56}$$

$$J_{uN} = (1-\beta)S_{uN} = \frac{(1-\beta)(p_u - b_u) + x_T J_T}{r + s_u + \tau + \beta m(\theta_u)} \tag{5.57}$$

$$J_{sL} = (1-\beta)S_{sL} = \frac{(1-\beta)(\lambda p_s - b_s + \pi_L)}{r + s_s + d_L + \tau + \beta m(\theta_s)} \tag{5.58}$$

$$J_{uL} = (1-\beta)S_{uL} = \frac{(1-\beta)(p_u - b_u + \pi_L) + x_T J_T}{r + s_u + d_L + \tau + \beta m(\theta_u)} \tag{5.59}$$

$$J_I = (1-\beta)S_I = \frac{(1-\beta)(p_u - b_u + \pi_I) + x_T J_T}{r + s_u + d_I + \tau + \beta m(\theta_u)} \tag{5.60}$$

$$J_T = (1-\beta)S_I = \frac{(1-\beta)(p_u - (r+\tau)U_s^2)}{r + d_T + \tau} \tag{5.61}$$

Net Income

The net income of natives is given by the following expression:

$$\tilde{Y} = Y + b_s u_{sN} + b_u u_{uN} - c_s v_s - c_u v_u - w_{sL} e_{sL} - w_{uL} e_{uL} - w_I e_I - w_T T$$

The expression above assumes that employers are natives and it shows that net income to natives includes total wage income to natives plus unemployment income to natives minus the cost of vacancy posting and the wages paid to immigrants. An alternative definition can be obtained by omitting the natives' unemployment income.

$$\tilde{Y}_1 = \tilde{Y} - b_s u_{sN} + b_u u_{uN}$$

Parameterization of the Model

Table 5.2 Parameterization and matched moments

	From the literature
$\epsilon = 0.5$	Petrongolo and Pissarides (2001)
$\beta = 0.5$	Satisfies the Hosios (1990) condition
$\varrho = 0.5$	Ottaviano and Peri (2012)
$\underline{z} = 0$	Normalization
$d_L = 0.0023$	Chassamboulli and Peri (2015)
$d_I = 0.0039$	Chassamboulli and Peri (2015)
$s_s = 0.032$	Chassamboulli and Peri (2015)
$s_u = 0.024$	Chassamboulli and Peri (2015)
$x_T = 0$	Benchmark case
	Measured from the data
$r = 0.004$	The monthly interest rate
$\tau = 0.00072$	The growth rate of the population
$S = 0.604$	The share of skilled labour force in the US
$\tilde{u}_s^2 = 0.067$	Average skilled unemployment rate in China and India
$\tilde{u}_s^2 = 0.036$	Unskilled unemployment rate in Mexico
$F_s = 0.562$	Skilled labour force of India and China/US native labour force
$F_u = 0.323$	Unskilled labour force of Mexico/US native labour force
	Jointly calibrated to match moments of the data
$\alpha = 0.699$	The skilled wage premium in the US of 78%

(continued)

Table 5.2 (continued)

$\xi = 0.125$	The vacancy to unemployment ratio in the US of 0.62
$b_s = 0.439$	The ratio of unemployment to employment income of 0.71 for
$b_u = 0.231$	both skill types (Hall and Milgrom 2008)
	The US wage ratio between:
$\lambda = 1.16$	1. Skilled natives and skilled immigrants of 0.92
$\pi_L = 0.183$	2. Unskilled natives and legal-unskilled immigrants of 1.173
$\pi_I = 0.389$	3. Illegal (unskilled) immigrants and unskilled natives of 0.8
$c_s = 0.0165$	The employment rates of skilled and unskilled native workers
$c_u = 0.0440$	In the US: 0.84 and 0.67
$\frac{x_I}{\bar{\bar{z}}} = 0.0065$ ¥	The ratio of illegal immigrants to the US native labour force of 0.07
$\frac{x_L}{\bar{\bar{z}}} = 0.0016$	The ratio of legal immigrants to the US native labour force of 0.12
$d_T = 0.0833$	Average duration of a temporary worker visa is 12 months (benchmark case)
$U_u^2 = 7.83$	$U_{sF} = 4U_s^2$
$U_s^2 = 22.66$	$U_{uF} = 4U_u^2$

From Chassamboulli and Peri (2019)

¥ Under the assumption that the distribution of immigration cost if uniform over $[0, \bar{\bar{z}}]$, the individual values of x_I, x_L, and $\bar{\bar{z}}$ do not matter. What only matters is the values of $\frac{x_I}{\bar{\bar{z}}}$ and $\frac{x_L}{\bar{\bar{z}}}$. We therefore match those

Sensitivity Checks

In the benchmark parameterization we set the duration of work permits to 12 months. In Table 5.3 below we examine how the results of the policy combination of replacing illegal immigrants with temporary workers change when the duration of work permits changes. The effects are robust to changes in the duration of work permits, since in all cases considered, both types of natives benefit in terms of job creation. We see that the positive job creation effect on unskilled workers decreases as the duration increases, mainly because with longer duration of work permits the inflow of temporary workers necessary to replace illegal immigrants is smaller. This means that opportunities to hire temporary workers are less frequent (i.e. x_T is smaller), which implies, in turn, that firms' benefit less from the introduction of the temporary-worker programme.

Table 5.3 Sensitivity analysis with respect to the duration of work permits

	Duration 6 months	Duration 12 months (benchmark)	Duration 36 months
Tightness			
θ_s	3.18	3.22	3.03
θ_u	7.73	8.67	4.40
Unempl. rates			
$\tilde{u}_{sN}$	−1.31	−1.32	−1.25
$\tilde{u}_{uN}$	−2.48	−2.77	−1.44
Wages			
w_{sN}	0.90	0.91	0.86
w_{uN}	8.95	9.17	8.14
Net income			
$\tilde{Y}s$	1.08	1.08	1.06
$\tilde{Y}_1$	1.55	1.58	1.45

Notes

1. Firms produce labour inputs by employing workers. The inputs they produce are then sold in competitive markets. Because markets are competitive, the price of the labour input, which represents the firm's revenue from operating the job is the worker's marginal product.
2. In the United States, for example, not all legal immigrants qualify for unemployment benefits extending beyond the period of 26 weeks and are paid during recessions by the federal government. Moreover, since the Personal Responsibility and Work Opportunity Reconciliation Act (PRWORA) of 1996 many federal government benefits (Food stamps, TANF, AFDC and others) were restricted to US citizens only. In some states some of these benefits were reinstated in the 2000s, but not all of them. Overall, immigrants in the US, even the legal ones, either on temporary visas or permanent residency, have access to significantly fewer benefits than US citizens, especially when unemployed.
3. Several other papers (e.g. LaLonde and Topel 1991; Kerr and Kerr 2011) show that immigrants are paid less than natives even after controlling for other observable productivity determinants such as education and language.
4. Most legal immigrants in the US are on family unification visas. A foreigner, irrespective of his skill level, can apply for a family visa as long as a member of his family is a legal permanent resident of the US and those

admitted are not selected based on skills. Given this, we think it is reasonable to assume that opportunities for legal entry arise at the same rate for both skilled and unskilled foreigners.

5. According to estimates reported by the Migration Policy Institute in 2012, more than 80% of undocumented immigrants in the US had at most a high school degree.
6. The function M(ui, vi) exhibits the standard properties: it is at least twice continuously differentiable, increasing in its arguments, exhibits constant returns to scale and satisfies the Inada conditions.
7. Compared to a legalization programme, this policy is less beneficial to native workers because it keeps the total number of immigrants that same. With a legalization programme, the entry of new illegal immigrants increases, and they are then legalized to keep the number of illegal immigrants low. As a result, although illegal immigration decreases, total immigration increases.

References

Battisti, Michele, Gabriel Falbermayr, Giovanni Peri. (2018), Immigration, search and redistribution: A quantitative assessment of native welfare, *Journal of the European Economic Association*, 16(4), 1137–1188.

Borjas, George, Friedberg, Rachel. (2009), Recent trends in the earnings of new immigrants to the United States. NBER Working Paper No. 1540.

Bound, John, Gaurav Khanna and Nicolas Morales. (2017), Understanding the economic impact of the H-1B Program on the US, NBER Working Paper No. 23153.

Chassamboulli, Andri and Theodore Palivos. (2013), The impact of immigration on the employment and wages of native workers, *Journal of Macroeconomics*, 38 (part A), 19–34.

Chassamboulli, Andri and Theodore Palivos. (2014), A search-equilibrium approach to the effects of immigration on labour market outcomes, *International Economic Review*, 55, 111–129.

Chassamboulli, Andri, Giovanni Peri. (2015), The labour market effects of reducing the number of illegal immigrants, *Review of Economic Dynamics,* 18, 792–821.

Chassamboulli, Andri, Giovanni Peri. (2019), The economic effect of immigration policies: Analyzing and simulating the U.S. case, NBER Working Paper No. 25074.

Hall, Robert E., and Paul R. Milgrom. "The limited influence of unemployment on the wage bargain." *American Economic Review* 98, no. 4 (2008): 1653–74.

Hosios, Arthur J. "On the efficiency of matching and related models of search and unemployment." *Review of Economic Studies* 57, no. 2 (1990): 279–298.

Hunt, Jennifer. (2011), "Which immigrants are most innovative and entrepreneurial? Distinctions by entry visa", *Journal of Labour Economics*, vol. 29(3), 417–57.

Hunt, Jennifer, Marjolaine Gauthier-Loiselle. (2010), How much does immigration boost innovation?, *American Economic Journal: Macroeconomics*, 2(2), 31–56.

Jaimovich, Nir and Henry Siu. (2017), "High-skilled immigration, STEM employment and non-routine-biased technical change," NBER Working Paper No. 23185.

Kerr, Sari Pekkala, Kerr, William. (2011), Economic impacts of immigration: a survey. *Finnish Economic Papers,* 24 (1), 1–32.

Kerr, William, and William Lincoln. (2010), The supply side of innovation: H-1B visa reforms and U.S. ethnic invention, *Journal of Labour Economics*, 28(3): 473–508.

LaLonde, Robert, Robert Topel. (1991), Immigrants in the American labour market: quality, assimilation, and distributional effects, *American Economic Review*, 81 (2), 297–302.

Lewis, Ethan, Giovanni Peri, (2015), Immigration and the economy of cities and regions, *Handbook of Regional and Urban Economics*, 5, 625–685.

Liu, Xiangbo. (2010), On the macroeconomic and welfare effects of illegal immigration. *Journal of Economic Dynamics and Control,* 34, 2547–2567.

Liu, Xiangbo, Theodore Palivos, Xiaomeng Zhang. (2017), Immigration skill heterogeneity and qualification mismatch, *Economic Inquiry*, 55(3), 1231–1264.

Lofstrom, Magnus and Hayes, Joseph. (2011), H-1Bs: how do they stack up to US born workers?, IZA Discussion Papers 6259.

Moreno-Galbis, Eva, Ahmed Tritah. (2016), *European Economic Review*, 84, 76–98.

Ottaviano, Gianmarco IP, and Giovanni Peri. "Rethinking the effect of immigration on wages." *Journal of the European Economic Association* 10, no. 1 (2012): 152–197.

Orrenius, Pia, Madeline Zavodny and Alexander Abraham (2020), The Effect of Immigration on Business Dynamics and Employment. Federal Reserve Bank of Dallas, Working Paper 2004.

Palivos, Theodore. (2009), Welfare effects of illegal immigration, *Journal of Population Economics*, 22, 131–144.
Peri, Giovanni, Kevin Shih, and Chad Sparber. (2015). STEM workers, H-1B visas, and productivity in US cities, *Journal of Labour Economics,* 33(S1, Part 2), 225–255.
Peri, Giovanni. (2016), Immigrants, productivity, and labour markets, *Journal of Economic Perspectives*, vol. 30(4), 3–30.
Petrongolo, Barbara, and Christopher A. Pissarides. "Looking into the black box: A survey of the matching function." *Journal of Economic Literature* 39, no. 2 (2001): 390–431.
Pissarides, Christopher (2000), Equilibrium unemployment theory, Second edition. Cambridge, MA: MIT Press.
Zavodny, Madeline, (2011) Immigration and American Jobs, New American Economy. Retrieved from: https://www.newamericaneconomy.org/sites/all/themes/pnae/img/NAE_Im-AmerJobs.pdf

6

Doing Business in the Shadows: Informal Firms, Irregular Immigrants and the Government

Eleni Kyrkopoulou and Theodore Palivos

6.1 Introduction

The informal sector, also known as the shadow economy, is of great importance in most economies nowadays.[1] This is so because it is thought to have a significant impact on macroeconomic factors, such as wages and unemployment. Moreover, it is related to tax evasion, which constitutes a key controversy among policy makers. Besides revisiting these issues, this chapter analyzes one more important aspect of the informal sector, its interrelation with irregular immigration.

6.1.1 Literature Review

There is a rich literature studying the size of the informal sector, the reasons for its existence and how it emerges. For example, Bosh and Pretel (2012) use data from Brazil to calibrate a two-sector search and matching

E. Kyrkopoulou • T. Palivos (✉)
Athens University of Economics and Business, Athens, Greece
e-mail: kyrkopel@aueb.gr; tpalivos@aueb.gr

E. Vella et al. (eds.), *Understanding Migration with Macroeconomics*,
https://doi.org/10.1007/978-3-030-40981-4_6

model. They suggest that policies that either reduce the cost of entry to the formal sector or increase the cost of informality raise the size of the formal sector. Fugazza and Jacques (2004) also employ a search and matching model and suggest a similar way to deal with the problem, namely, to increase incentives for participation in the formal sector, rather than employ deterrence policies. Zenou (2008) suggests a model with search frictions in the formal sector and a competitive informal sector. He finds that a wage subsidy or a hiring subsidy has a clearly positive effect on the employment in the formal sector.

Boeri and Garibaldi (2005) also develop a search and matching model with two sectors, a formal and an informal. Firms optimally choose to create jobs in either sector through a mechanism that is akin to tax evasion. Moreover, there is a positive probability that irregular employment is detected, and the match is destroyed. Workers differ in terms of productivity and sort across sectors. Workers' sorting will determine the productivity level for which a worker is indifferent between working in the formal or the informal sector. The authors experiment with various policies such as changes in taxation, regulation, the monitoring rate, and the size of the unemployment benefits. They find that the effect of a change in taxation (or regulation) on unemployment is not sharp, since there are two countervailing effects: the indirect effect on job creation, via the increase in the reservation productivity, reduces unemployment, while the direct effect of taxes on market tightness in the legal sector increases it. Furthermore, an increase in monitoring intensity or in unemployment benefits reduces the size of the informal sector and increases unemployment.

Finally, Di Porto et al. (2017) also analyze a search and matching model with an informal sector. They find that an increase in the inspection rate leads to higher destruction of informal jobs, which in turn reduces the flow of temporary workers and lowers job creation in the informal sector. Therefore, the size of the informal sector drops. Furthermore, lower taxation or firing costs induce an increase in both job destruction and job creation of permanent positions, with a prevalence of the latter, and boost the flow of workers from informal to formal positions. However, combinations of lower payroll taxes for permanent contracts and a higher inspection rate are more effective on the reduction of the shadow sector, as opposed to combinations of lower firing costs and a higher inspection rate.

Immigration and its impact on the labor market outcomes have been in the center of a lively debate among labor economists. The empirical results on the subject are often ambiguous and controversial; some, for example, Card (1990), find little or no effect of immigration on the wage of native workers, whereas others, like Borjas et al. (1997), find a strong negative effect.

Irregular immigrants can only be employed in the informal sector. In this sector, firms are unregulated and therefore cannot be directly affected by labor market policies. Nevertheless, they might be subject to indirect effects through policies applied in the formal sector, such as unemployment benefits, taxes, and severance payments.

Cuff et al. (2011) have studied irregular immigration in an economy with two sectors, a formal and an informal one. More specifically, they consider the role played by the presence of domestic and undocumented workers on *optimal* tax and enforcement policy. Domestic workers can work in either sector, but undocumented workers can only work informally. In this context, they analyze *optimal policies*. They find that enforcement may not always be decreasing in its cost and that it is not optimal for the government to enforce market segmentation if enforcement costs are too high.

6.1.2 Contribution

The present chapter contributes to the existing literature by adding a worker type with different labor market opportunities. This is important as this type cannot be formally employed; therefore, the incentive and deterrence policies cannot have a direct effect on her decisions. We develop a rich model with various types of policies that can affect the size of the informal sector, namely incentive, deterrence, and immigration policies. In contrast to Cuff et al. (2011), mentioned above, we study the effects of these policies in an *equilibrium* set-up with market frictions.

More specifically, we develop a dynamic search and matching model, with two sectors, a formal and an informal one. Workers can be either natives or irregular immigrants.[2] The former can seek employment in both sectors, whereas the latter can only be employed in the informal sector. Native workers trade off the costs and benefits of the two sectors in order to make an optimal decision. If they find a job in the formal sector, they have to pay an income tax but are also entitled to unemployment benefits and a severance payment, should they be laid off.

Firms also decide optimally the sector in which they want to post a vacancy. Firms operating in the formal sector are entitled to a subsidy for maintaining a position but are also obliged to pay a payroll tax and face a firing cost; the latter includes a severance payment, as well as some administrative costs.

On the other hand, workers and firms in the informal sector do not have to pay taxes or a firing cost but face the probability to get audited. If that happens, the match is terminated, and the firm has to pay a penalty. Moreover, the separation rate is higher in the informal sector. Search frictions exist in both sectors and wages in each sector are determined by Nash bargaining between firms and workers. Irregular immigrants have a lower outside option, and thus are in a lower bargaining position. The wage of each worker is a combination of her outside option and her productivity in that job.

There are intermediate goods produced either in the formal or in the informal sector. Subsequently, they are sold in a competitive market and are used to produce the final good.

We examine several policies, such as an immigration amnesty, a change in unemployment benefits and a change in payroll tax rates. Among others, we find that an irregular immigration influx will increase the size of the informal sector. This is the exact opposite result of that of an immigration amnesty. Finally, we show that an increase in unemployment benefits in the formal sector can possibly increase the unemployment in the same sector.

The rest of the chapter is organized as follows. Section 6.2 describes the model. Section 6.3 presents the calibration of the model to Greece in the period 2000–2007. Section 6.4 presents the simulations of various policies. Section 6.5 concludes the chapter.

6.2 The Model

Consider an economy that has two sides: a formal and an informal one. Both sides consist of two sectors, one that produces an intermediate input and one that produces the final good. Throughout the chapter, we take the final good to be the numeraire.

There is a continuum of workers who are either natives (N) or irregular immigrants (M) and are indexed by $i = N, M$.[3] The mass of native workers is normalized to one, while that of irregular immigrants is also constant and denoted by M. Native workers seek employment in any of the two intermediate sectors, whereas irregular immigrants can work only in the informal intermediate sector. The mass of jobs in each intermediate sector is determined endogenously, as specified below. Time is continuous. All agents are risk neutral and discount the future at a constant rate $r > 0$.

6.2.1 Production

We start with the formal side of the economy. An intermediate input L_F is produced using only (native) labor. More specifically, firms operate a simple linear technology

$$L_F = e_{NF} \tag{6.1}$$

where e_{NF} is the number of native (M) workers who are employed in the formal intermediate sector (F). Accordingly, a job in that sector can be filled only by a native worker and the outcome from such a pair is one unit of L_F. Moreover, there are firms of the final good operating in the formal side; they use L_F to produce the final good Y_F according to the following technology

$$Y_F = A_F L_F, A_F > 0. \tag{6.2}$$

The informal side of the economy has a similar structure. There are two intermediate inputs L_{NI} and L_{MI}, which are produced using only native and immigrant labor respectively:

$$L_{NI} = e_{NI} \text{ and } L_{MI} = e_{MI},$$

where e_{ij} is the number of workers who are employed in the intermediate informal (I) sector and are of origin $i = N, M$.

There are also informal firms that produce the final good. They do so using the technology

$$Y_I = A_I L_I,\ A_I > 0, \tag{6.3}$$

where

$$L_I = \left[x\left(L_{NI}\right)^{\rho} + \left(1-x\right)\left(L_{MI}\right)^{\rho} \right]^{\frac{1}{\rho}}. \tag{6.4}$$

The final goods Y_F and Y_I are perfect substitutes; that is, the total quantity of the final good is $Y = Y_F + Y_I$.

6.2.2 Markets

In the intermediate markets, there are search and matching frictions that prevent market clearing. More specifically, each firm possesses one vacancy and must decide first whether to open it in the formal (F) or the informal (I) sector. We use the index $j = F, I$ to distinguish between the two types of jobs. There is free-entry in both markets. After opening a vacancy, the firm starts seeking for a worker. Similarly, native workers decide first whether to seek employment in the formal or the informal sector (as mentioned above, irregular migrants have no such option).

Job seekers and vacant jobs are matched in a pair-wise fashion. The mass of successful job matches in the formal sector is determined by the matching function $M_F(v_F, u_{NF})$ where v_F is the mass of formal vacancies and u_{NF} denotes the mass of unemployed native workers in the formal sector. Similarly, the mass of matches in the informal sector is given by the matching function $M_I(v_I, u_{NI} + u_{MI})$, where v_I is the mass of informal vacancies and u_{NI} (u_{MI}) is the mass of unemployed native (immigrant) workers in the informal sector. The matching functions are assumed to be twice continuously differentiable, strictly increasing and strictly concave with respect to each of their arguments, exhibit constant returns to scale and satisfy standard Inada conditions.

We follow the literature and define the labor market tightness θ_j as the number of jobs per unemployed worker; that is, in the formal sector $\theta_F = v_F/u_{NI}$ and in the informal sector as $\theta_I = v_I/(u_{NI} + u_{MI})$. The rate at which vacancies in sector j are filled is $q_j = M_j/v_j$, where $q_j'(\theta_j) < 0$. Moreover, the rate at which unemployed workers (native or immigrant) find jobs in each sector is $m_j(\theta_j) = \theta_j q_j(\theta_j)$.

Each of the two intermediate inputs, L_F and L_I, is sold in a competitive market. Thus, their prices equal their marginal products:

$$p_F = \frac{\partial Y_F}{\partial L_F} = A_F, \tag{6.5}$$

$$p_{NI} = \frac{\partial Y_I}{\partial L_{NI}} = A_I x \left(\frac{L_I}{L_{NI}} \right)^{1-\rho}, \tag{6.6}$$

$$p_{MI} = \frac{\partial Y_I}{\partial L_{MI}} = A_I (1-x) \left(\frac{L_I}{L_{MI}} \right)^{1-\rho}. \tag{6.7}$$

6.2.3 Institutions

There are some fundamental differences between firms and workers that operate in the two intermediate sectors. First, to maintain a vacancy a firm in each sector must pay a differential cost c_j.

Second, firms that operate in the formal sector pay a payroll tax at a rate t_F, a tax on profits t_Π and face a firing cost. We consider two components of the firing cost: The first component includes various administrative costs and is captured by the parameter $f > 0$. These costs include the requirement to give the worker advance notice, procedures that the firm must follow if it wants to lay off, legal expenses in case of a trial, and so on. The second component of the firing cost is a severance payment, that is a transfer from the firm to the employee.[4] As it is the case in most countries, we assume that the severance payment is proportional to the wage, that is, it equals γw_{NF}, where w_{NF} is the wage rate of a worker who is employed in the formal sector (F) and is native (she is of origin N). On the other hand, firms that operate in the informal sector receive no subsidies and pay neither taxes nor firing costs. However, the labor market is monitored and if a firm is caught operating in the informal sector, it is forced to terminate the match and pay a penalty rate η on output.[5] Such an event occurs with a probability (arrival rate) δ. Hence, $\delta\eta$ is the expected penalty rate paid by a firm in the informal sector.

Third, native workers who work in the formal sector pay an income tax at a rate t_w. On the other hand, workers in the informal sector do not pay taxes. Nevertheless, informal jobs are less stable for the following two reasons. First, the arrival rate of negative shocks is probably higher, that is, the separation rate in the informal sector s_I is higher than that in the formal s_F. Second, as mentioned above, firms are audited at a rate δ and if they are caught operating illegally, then they have to terminate the match. Finally, during unemployment, native workers receive a flow of income b_{ij}, which captures the opportunity cost of employment, for example, the payoff from home production, leisure, and unemployment benefits. This income is net of any search cost that they incur when looking for a job. Typically, workers in the informal sector do not receive any unemployment benefits, that is, $b_{NI} = 0$. Irregular immigrants do not receive unemployment benefits; nevertheless, they also incur a cost of searching for a job, which is, in general, higher than that faced by natives.[6] Let b_{MI} denote the income of an immigrant in unemployment, which is negative. Thus, we have $b_{NF} > b_{NI} = 0 > b_{MI}$. Moreover, throughout the chapter, we assume that the output of a match between a vacancy and a worker exceeds the income of the unemployed worker of the same type, that is, $p_F > b_{NF}$, $p_{NI} > b_{NI}$ and $p_{MI} > b_{MI}$.

6.2.4 Asset Values

Let Π and V be the values associated with a filled and an unfilled vacancy, and E and U the values associated with an employed and an unemployed worker, respectively. Moreover, let Π_{ij} be the present discounted value associated with a firm in sector j that is matched with a worker of origin i. Then in steady state:

$$r\Pi_{NF} = (1 - t_{\Pi})\left[p_F - (1 + t_F) w_{NF}\right] - s_F\left(\Pi_{NF} - V_F + f + \gamma w_{NF}\right), \quad (6.8)$$

$$r\Pi_{NI} = (1 - \delta\eta) p_{NI} - w_{NI} - (s_I + \delta)(\Pi_{NI} - V_I), \quad (6.9)$$

$$r\Pi_{MI} = (1 - \delta\eta) p_{MI} - w_{MI} - (s_I + \delta)(\Pi_{MI} - V_I), \quad (6.10)$$

where w_{ij} is the wage rate of a worker who is employed in the intermediate sector j and is of origin i and V_j is the value associated with an unfilled (vacant) position inintermediate sector j. As mentioned above, the total firing cost in the formal intermediate sector is $f + \gamma w_{NF}$, where $f > 0$ is a fixed amount. Recall the assumption that jobs matched with natives in the informal sector have a higher separation rate than jobs matched with natives in the formal sector $s_I + \delta > s_F$.

The expected income streams accrued to an unfilled vacancy in the intermediate sector j are given by

$$rV_F = -c_F + q(\theta_F)(\Pi_{NF} - V_F), \quad (6.11)$$

$$rV_I = -c_I - q(\theta_I)\left[\phi_{NI}\Pi_{NI} + (1 - \phi_{NI})\Pi_{MI} - V_I\right], \quad (6.12)$$

where ϕ_{NI} represents the probability that a vacancy meets a native worker in the informal sector. More specifically,

$$\phi_{NI} = \frac{u_{NI}}{u_{NI} + u_{MI}}. \quad (6.13)$$

Next, we turn to values associated with the workers. The expected income streams accrued to employed workers are given by

$$rE_{NF} = (1 - t_w) w_{NF} - s_F (E_{NF} - U_{NF} - \gamma w_{NF}), \tag{6.14}$$

$$rE_{NI} = w_{NI} - (s_I + \delta)(E_{NI} - U_{NI}), \tag{6.15}$$

$$rE_{MI} = w_{MI} - (s_I + \delta)(E_{MI} - U_{MI}). \tag{6.16}$$

Similarly, the values associated with unemployed workers are

$$rU_{NF} = b_{NF} + m_F(\theta_F)(E_{NF} - U_{NF}), \tag{6.17}$$

$$rU_{NI} = b_{NI} + m_I(\theta_I)(E_{NI} - U_{NI}), \tag{6.18}$$

$$rU_{MI} = b_{MI} + m_I(\theta_I)(E_{MI} - U_{MI}) \tag{6.19}$$

We also assume free entry in establishing either type of vacancy. Thus, in equilibrium, the expected payoff of posting a vacancy is equal to zero that is,

$$V_j = 0, j = F, I. \tag{6.20}$$

6.2.5 Wage Determination

Once a worker meets a firm, they bargain over the wage rate. They essentially solve a generalized Nash bargaining problem given by[7]

$$max_{w_{NF}} (E_{NF} - U_{NF} - \gamma w_{NF})^{\beta} (\Pi_{NF} - V_F + f + \gamma w_{NF})^{1-\beta}$$

for the matches in the formal sector and by

$$max_{w_{ij}} (E_{ij} - U_{ij})^{\beta} (\Pi_{ij} - V_j)^{1-\beta},$$

for the matches in the informal sector, where $\beta\epsilon(0,1)$ represents the worker's bargaining strength. The solution to each of these two problems gives, respectively,

$$(1-\beta)\left[(1-t_{\Pi})(1+t_F)-r\gamma\right]\left[E_{NF}-U_{NF}-\gamma w_{NF}\right]=\beta(1-t_w-r\gamma)\left[\Pi_{NF}-V_F+f+\gamma w_{NF}\right], \tag{6.21}$$

$$(1-\beta)\left(E_{ij}-U_{ij}\right)=\beta\left(\Pi_{ij}-V_j\right). \tag{6.22}$$

The total surplus generated by a match in the formal and the informal sector is $S_{NF}=\Pi_{NF}-(V_F-f)+(E_{NF}-U_{NF})$ and $S_{iI}=\Pi_{iI}-V_i+E_{iI}-U_{iI}$, $i=N, M$, respectively. Notice that the severance payment, γw_{NF}, being a pure transfer from the firm to the worker, drops out of the definition of the surplus S_{NF}. Nevertheless, the compensation rate and the tax rates, t_F and t_w, affect the workers' and firms' shares in the formal sector. More specifically, in the case of a formal match, workers get a share

$$\beta_F=\frac{\beta(1-t_w-r\gamma)}{\beta(1-t_w-r\gamma)+(1-\beta)(1-t_{\Pi})(1+t_F)-r\gamma},$$

and firms $1-\beta_F$. In the case of an informal match, on the other hand, workers and firms get a share β and $1-\beta$, respectively, of the surplus.

Next, by using the above asset value equations, we can derive the expressions for the wage rates. Substituting for $E_{ij}-U_{ij}$ and Π_{ij}, using Eqs. (6.8), (6.9) and (6.14)–(6.19), in Eqs. (6.21) and (6.22), and noting that $V_j=0$ (Eq. 6.20), we find

$$w_{NF}=\frac{\beta(r+s_F+m_F)\Delta\left[(1-t_{\Pi})p_F+rf\right]+(1-\beta)(r+s_F)\Gamma b_{NF}}{\Phi_F}, \tag{6.23}$$

$$w_{NI} = \frac{\beta(r+s_I+m_I)(1-\delta\eta)p_{NI}+(1-\beta)(r+s_I+\delta)b_{NI}}{\Phi_I}, \quad (6.24)$$

$$w_{MI} = \frac{\beta(r+s_I+m_I)(1-\delta\eta)p_{MI}+(1-\beta)(r+s_I+\delta)b_{MI}}{\Phi_I}, \quad (6.25)$$

where $\Phi_F = \beta\Gamma\Delta m_F + (r + s_F)\Gamma[\Delta - \gamma(1 - \beta)m_F]$, $\Gamma = (1 - t_\Pi)(1 + t_F) - r\gamma$, $\Delta = 1 - t_w - r\gamma$, and $\Phi_I = r + s_I + \delta + \beta m_I$. In each case, the worker's wage when employed in a particular job is a combination of her outside option and her productivity in that job.

6.2.6 Steady-State Composition of the Labor Force

The following definitions apply regarding the different sub-groups in the labor force:

$$u_{NF} + e_{NF} = \lambda,$$

$$u_{NI} + e_{NI} = 1 - \lambda,$$

$$u_{MI} + e_{MI} = M.$$

Where $\lambda \epsilon (0, 1)$ and $1 - \lambda$ represent the share of native workers in the formal and informal sector, respectively, and M denotes the mass of irregular immigrants. The share λ is determined endogenously, as shown below. Moreover, in steady state, where the flows in and out of unemployment for each sub-group are equal to each other,

$$u_{NF} = \frac{s_F}{s_F + m_F}\lambda, \; e_{NF} = L_F = \frac{m_F}{s_F + m_F}\lambda,$$

$$u_{NI} = \frac{s_I + \delta}{s_I + \delta + m_I}(1-\lambda), e_{NI} = L_{NI} = \frac{m_I}{s_I + \delta + m_I}(1-\lambda),$$

$$u_{MI} = \frac{s_I + \delta}{s_I + \delta + m_I}M, e_{MI} = L_{MI} = \frac{m_I}{s_I + \delta + m_I}M. \tag{6.26}$$

Next, we can write the expression regarding the probability that a firm finds a native worker in the informal sector as

$$\phi_{NI} = \frac{u_{NI}}{u_{NI} + u_{MI}} = \frac{1-\lambda}{1-\lambda+M}. \tag{6.27}$$

6.2.7 Steady-State Equilibrium

As mentioned above, native workers must decide in advance whether to search in the formal or in the informal sector. In making their decision, they compare the values of being in each of the two sectors. In equilibrium, they are indifferent between entering the formal or the informal sector. Therefore, the no-arbitrage condition is given by

$$U_{NF} = U_{NI}.$$

Using Eqs. (6.8), (6.17) and (6.21) to solve U_{NF} and Eqs. (6.9), (6.18) and (6.22) to solve for U_{NI}, this equality can be written as:

$$\frac{\beta m_F (1 - t_w + s_F \gamma) \Delta \left[(1 - t_\Pi) p_F + rf \right] + \Gamma \Delta (r + s_F) b_{NF}}{\Phi_F}$$
$$= \frac{\beta m_I (1 - \delta \eta) p_{NI} + (r + s_I + \delta) b_{NI}}{\Phi_I}. \tag{6.28}$$

Definition A steady-state equilibrium is a set $\left\{\theta_j^*, e_{ij}^*, u_{ij}^*, w_{ij}^*, \lambda^*\right\}$ where $i = N, M$ and $i = F, I$ such that

1. The intermediate input markets clear (Eqs. 6.5, 6.6, and 6.7);
2. The free-entry condition for vacancies of each sector is satisfied (Eq. 6.20);
3. The Nash bargaining condition between a worker of origin i and a firm in sector j holds (Eqs. 6.21 and 6.22);
4. The numbers of employed and unemployed workers of origin i in sector j remain constant (Eq. 6.26);
5. The no-arbitrage condition regarding workers' mobility between sectors is satisfied (Eq. 6.28).

Substituting in the free-entry conditions, we derive the following two equations

$$\frac{c_F}{q_F} = \frac{\Theta_F\left[\left(1-t_{\Pi}\right)p_F + rf\right] - \left(1-\beta\right)\Psi\Gamma b_{NF}}{\Phi_F} - f, \tag{6.29}$$

$$\frac{c_I}{q_I} = \left(1-\beta\right)\frac{\phi_{NI}\left[\left(1-\delta\eta\right)p_{NI} - b_{NI}\right] + \left(1-\phi_{NI}\right)\left[\left(1-\delta\eta\right)p_{MI} - b_{MI}\right]}{\Phi_I}, \tag{6.30}$$

where $\Theta_F = (1-\beta)\Gamma\Delta - \Gamma\gamma(1-\beta)m_F - \gamma\beta(r + s_F + m_F)\Delta$, $\Psi = [(1-t_\Pi)(1 + t_F) + s_F\gamma]$ and ϕ_{NI} is defined in Eq. (6.27).

Next, substituting the steady-state values of L_F and L_I (determined by Eqs. 6.1, 6.4, and 6.26) into the price equations of p_{NI} and p_{MI} (Eqs. 6.6 and 6.7) yields

$$p_{NI} = A_I x\left[x + \left(1-x\right)\left(\frac{M}{1-\lambda}\right)^{\rho}\right]^{\frac{1-\rho}{\rho}},$$

$$p_{MI} = A_I(1-x)\left[x\left(\frac{1-\lambda}{M}\right)^{\rho} + (1-x)\right]^{\frac{1-\rho}{\rho}}.$$

Finally, substituting the expressions for p_F, p_{NI} and p_{MI} into Eqs. (6.28), (6.29) and (6.30) forms a system of three equations that describes the behavior of the three variables θ_F, θ_I and λ. Having determined the steady-state equilibrium values of them, we can obtain the equilibrium values for all the other variables by substituting in the appropriate equations.

Proposition 1 (Existence and Uniqueness). Under certain parameter restrictions, a steady-state equilibrium exists and is unique.[8]

6.3 Calibration

We calibrate the model to the Greek economy for the period 2000–2007. One period in the model represents three months, so all the parameters are interpreted quarterly. In order to perform the model calibration, we have chosen parameter values according to the relevant literature, the national legislation, and the statistics provided by various formal sources for statistics.

Recall the previous assumption that the number of new matches is given by a matching function $M(u,v)$, depending on the number of unemployed workers u and the number of vacancies v. Following common practice, see, for example, Blanchard and Diamond (1989), we assume a Cobb-Douglas function of the form with constant returns to scale: $M(u, v) = \varepsilon u^{\alpha} v^{1-\alpha}$. Following Shimer (2005), we infer the job-finding rate from the dynamic behavior of the unemployment level and short-term unemployment level. Let u_t^s denote the number of workers unemployed for under a quarter in quarter t. Then assuming all unemployed workers find a job with probability m_t in quarter t and no unemployed worker exits the labor force, we have $u_{t+1} = u_t(1-m_t) + u_{t+1}^s$. The unemployment in the next quarter is the sum of the number of unemployed workers this quarter who fail to find a job and the number of newly unemployed workers. Therefore, the job-finding rate is given by $m_t = 1 - \frac{u_{t+1} - u_{t+1}^s}{u_t}$. Given the matching function and the job-finding rate, one can compute the labor market tightness in each sector.

Next, we calculate the separation rate in the formal sector from data on employment, short-term unemployment and the hiring rate. When a worker loses her job, she becomes unemployed. The separation rate can be computed as the ratio $\frac{u_{t+1}^s}{e_t}$. In this case though, we ignore the fact that the individual can get a new job before she gets recorded as an unemployed. Assuming that during this quarter the individual has half the quarter to find a job before she gets recorded as unemployed, the short-term unemployment equals $u_{t+1}^s = s_t e_t (1 - 0.5m_t)$. The separation rate is then calculated using the formula $s_t = \frac{u_{t+1}^s}{e_t (1 - 0.5m_t)}$, where u_t^s is the number of native workers unemployed for under a quarter in quarter t, e_t denotes the number of employed workers in quarter t and m_t is the job finding rate, given by the formula $m_t = 1 - \frac{u_{t+1} - u_{t+1}^s}{u_t}$. We assume that the separation rate in the informal sector is equal to the one in the formal sector, that is $s_F = s_I$. We use data from Eurostat to obtain the value for the overall unemployment rate, u_{rate}.

Next, we obtain the size of undocumented immigrant population, M, from the European Commission's Clandestino project. Also, we turn to the value of the proportion of native workers that choose to work in the formal sector, λ. We follow Hazans (2011) who calculates the percentage of labor force employed in the formal sector in Southern Europe. We set the probability to get audit, δ, equal to 0.05, which falls in the range suggested by the literature.[9] Next, we set the production parameter $\rho = 0.85$ as in Ottaviano and Peri (2012). We also set x equal to 0.5 and $A_F = 1$. Finally, we calculate the size of the informal sector using data from Schneider and Williams (2013).

We calculate the interest rate in the following way: using data from Eurostat, we calculate the average yield to 10-year government bonds and using data from the World Bank we calculate the average growth rate of the Consumer Price Index over the period 2000–2007. Also, following the common practice, we set the elasticity of the matching function $\varepsilon = 0.5$, which satisfies the range given by Petrongolo and Pissarides (2001). We also follow the literature, setting workers' bargaining power $\beta = 0.5$. We use data from the OECD to calculate the value of the unemployment benefits of the native workers in the formal sector, b_{NFrate}. We calculate the value of the various taxes, namely t_F, t_w and t_Π using data from the OECD taxing wages. We set the penalty rate, η, as in Di Porto et al. (2017). We set the value of the administrative cost, f_{rate}, as in Mortensen and Pissarides (1999) and set the severance payment, γ, equal to 1. A summary of our calibration is presented in Table 6.1.

Table 6.1 Baseline calibration

Variable/ parameter	Value	Interpetation	Source
s_F	*0.0072*	*Separation rate in formal sector*	*Authors' calculations*
m_F	*0.082*	*Rate at which a worker finds a job in the formal sector*	*Authors' calculations*
u_{rate}	*0.1*	*Unemployment rate* $u_{rate} = (u_{NF} + u_{NI} + u_{MI}) / M + 1$	*OECD*
M	*0.0562*	*Irregular immigrants*	*Clandestino, World Bank*
λ	*0.71*	*Percentage of labor force employed informal sector in Southern Europe*	Hazans (2011)
S_I	*0.0072*	*Separation rate in informal sector*	*Assume* $S_I = S_F$
δ	*0.02*	*Probability to get audit*	Di Porto et al. (2013)
x	*0.5*	*Production function parameter*	*Set*
ρ	*0.85*	*Production function parameter*	Ottaviano and Peri (2012)
Y_I/Y_F	*0.274*	*As a % of GDP*	Schneider and Williams (2013)
A_F	*1*	*Production function parameter*	*Set*
r	*0.0035*	*Interest rate*	*World Bank*
β	*0.5*	*Worker's bargaining power*	*Standard in literature*
ε	*1*	*Matching function parameter*	*Standard in literature*
α	*0.5*	*Matching function parameter*	*Standard in literature*
b_{NFrate}	*0.21*	*Unemployment income in F sector*	*OECD*
t_Π	*0.031*	*Tax on profits*	*World Bank*
f_{rate}	*0.78*	*Administrative firing cost*	Mortensen and Pissarides (1999)
t_F	*0.28*	*Payroll tax*	*OECD wages and benefits*
t_W	*0.4*	*Income tax*	*OECD wages and benefits*
γ	*1*	*Severance payment*	*Set*
η	*0.42*	*Penalty rate*	Di Porto et al. (2017)

6.4 Simulations

There are three different type of policies that can affect the relative size of the informal sector. We start with the deterrence policies, namely increasing the probability to get audited, δ, and the severity (penalty) of the punishment when a firm gets caught operating in the informal sector, η. These policies do not affect the labor market tightness in the formal sector, and thus formal wages will remain unchanged. Deterrence policies reduce the expected value of a filled value in the informal sector and change the labor market tightness, θ_I, which in turn changes the share of workers who choose to work in the formal sector, λ.

The second type is the incentive policies, such as a tax reduction or an increase in the unemployment benefits. These directly affect the labor market tightness and the wages in the formal sector. Consequently, labor market tightness and wages in the informal sector are affected and so is the fraction of workers who chose to participate in the formal sector. Naturally, deterrence and incentive policies are combined to obtain a more desirable result.

The final type of policies we study are immigration policies. These can include an influx of (undocumented) migration and a naturalization or a deportation of a fraction of the (undocumented) migrant population. These policies do not affect the labor market tightness and the unemployment of the native workers in the formal sector, but they do affect the size of the fraction of native workers who choose to work in the formal sector, as well as, and the size of the informal sector.[10]

6.4.1 Deterrence Policies

We start with a rise in the auditing rate, δ, that does not affect θ_F as (see Eq. 6.29). Since the only influence of aggregate labor market conditions on the wage occur via θ_F, wages in the formal sector remain intact. The increase of δ leads to an increase of the job destruction in the informal sector, which in turns raises the labor market tightness in the sector, θ_I. The unemployment rate in the informal sector rises, but vacancies fall at a higher rate. More people decide to go to the formal sector and thus

Table 6.2 An increase in the auditing rate, δ

	Benchmark	(+) 1%	(+) 5%	(+) 10%
	$\delta = 0.02$	$\delta = 0.0202$	$\delta = 0.021$	$\delta = 0.022$
u_{NF}	0.0573	0.0578	0.0599	0.0620
u_{NFrate}	0.0807	0.0807	0.0807	0.0807
u_{NI}	0.0405	0.0396	0.0365	0.0332
u_{NIrate}	0.1396	0.1399	0.1415	0.1434
u_{rate}	0.1	0.0997	0.0988	0.0978
e_{NF}	0.6526	0.6589	0.6821	0.7067
e_{NI}	0.2496	0.2436	0.2215	0.1981
e_{MI}	0.0484	0.0483	0.0482	0.0481
λ	0.7099	0.7168	0.742	0.7687
w_{NF}	0.7437	0.7437	0.7437	0.7437
w_{NI}	0.4941	0.4942	0.495	0.4959
w_{MI}	0.2964	0.2938	0.2835	0.2716
Y_I/Y_F	0.2742	0.2662	0.2384	0.2109
m_F	0.0820	0.0820	0.0820	0.0820
m_I	0.1677	0.1684	0.1711	0.1744
θ_F	0.0067	0.0067	0.0067	0.0067
θ_I	0.0281	0.0284	0.0293	0.0304

λ rises. All the above lead to a decrease of the relative size of the informal sector and a subsequent rise of the formal employment, as well as, a decrease of the informal employment. Finally, the overall unemployment rate drops. The quantitative results of a decrease in the auditing rate are presented in Table 6.2.

An increase in the penalty rate η has qualitatively similar effects. In fact, in terms of reduction of the (relative) size of the informal sector, an increase in the auditing rate seems to be more effective than an increase in the penalty rate. This means that a 1% increase of the auditing rate results in a larger reduction of the informal sector than a 1% increase of the penalty rate. On the other hand, one has to consider the fact that the former policy requires more resources in its implementation than the latter. Furthermore, in the case of δ, unemployment rate in the informal sector increases, while it falls in the case of η (details are presented in the Appendix). In conclusion, an increase in η is a milder policy than an increase in δ; the labor market tightness increases less, and the job destruction is lower.

6.4.2 Incentive Policies

Moving on to incentive policies, we study a decrease of the payroll tax, t_F. This reduction induces job creation; in fact, vacancies increase more than the number of unemployed and the labor market tightness in the formal sector, θ_F, increases. More people decide to work in the formal sector. The wages of the native workers rise and the size of the informal sector falls. Finally, the informal unemployment falls and thus labor market tightness in the informal sector rises (details are given in the Appendix).

A decrease of the income tax gives an incentive to more workers to enter the formal sector, thus increasing λ (notice how it directly increases the left-hand side of Eq. 6.28). The relative size of the informal sector falls. The unemployment rate in the formal sector falls, so the formal labor market tightness increases. Similarly, the unemployment rate in the informal sector falls and the respective labor market tightness rises. As a result, the overall unemployment rate also increases. Net native wages fall in the formal sector, while they increase in the informal sector. The respective results appear in Table 6.3.

Table 6.3 A reduction in the worker's income tax, t_W

		(–) 1%	(–) 5%	(–) 10%
	Benchmark	$t_W = 0.396$	$t_W = 0.38$	$t_W = 0.36$
u_{NF}	0.0573	0.0587	0.0632	0.0666
u_{NFrate}	0.0807	0.0804	0.0794	0.0782
u_{NI}	0.0405	0.0371	0.0266	0.0182
u_{NIrate}	0.1396	0.1377	0.1306	0.1227
u_{rate}	0.1	0.0981	0.092	0.0868
e_{NF}	0.6526	0.6718	0.7328	0.7847
e_{NI}	0.2496	0.2323	0.1774	0.1304
e_{MI}	0.0484	0.0485	0.0489	0.0493
λ	0.7099	0.7306	0.796	0.8513
w_{NF}	0.7437	0.7436	0.7432	0.7427
w_{NI}	0.4941	0.4961	0.5042	0.5147
w_{MI}	0.2964	0.2958	0.2947	0.2952
Y_I/Y_F	0.2742	0.2516	0.1877	0.1407
m_F	0.0820	0.0823	0.0835	0.0849
m_I	0.1677	0.1704	0.1811	0.1945
θ_F	0.00672	0.00677	0.00697	0.00721
θ_I	0.0281	0.0290	0.0328	0.0378

An increase of the replacement rate in the formal sector increases the formal net wage, w_{NF}, and decreases the labor market tightness in the sector, θ_F. This reduction is the result of an increase in the number of unemployed u_{NF} (and a reduction in v_{NF}). Through the no arbitrage condition, a change in the labor market tightness in the informal sector, θ_I, is imposed. This is translated to a lower unemployment rate, u_{NI} (and a higher v_{NI}). More people decide to go to the formal sector and thus λ rises. Consequently, the relative size of the informal sector falls. Finally, it is interesting to note that unemployment and employment rates co-move in both sectors. The overall unemployment rises.

6.4.3 Immigration Policies

Moving on to the immigration policies, consider first an influx of the undocumented immigrant population, M. As indicated by Eq. (6.29), labor market tightness in the formal sector is not affected by a change in M, therefore θ_F remains intact. An increase in M leads λ to adjust so that θ_I remains constant. The resulting rise of 1-λ induces more native workers to participate in the informal sector. Consequently, we observe a rise of the relative size of the informal sector. Since θ_F and θ_I remain constant, unemployment in both sectors does not change, but the overall unemployment increases. Employment in the formal sector falls, but informal employment increases and so is the overall unemployment. The results are presented in the Appendix.

A naturalization or equivalently an amnesty policy decreases the size of the immigrant population and increases the native population. Now more workers have the option to work in the formal sector and thus λ rises. Naturally, we observe a reduction of the size of the informal sector. Again, since a change in M does not affect the labor market tightness in either sector, the respective unemployment rates remain unchanged. Formal employment rises, while informal employment and overall unemployment fall. Finally, we do not observe any change in wages, as all labor market changes are imposed into the wage equations through the labor market tightness. The quantitative effects of a naturalization policy are presented in Table 6.4.

Table 6.4 Naturalization

	Benchmark	1% Naturalization	10% Naturalization
u_{NF}	0.0573	0.0575	0.0592
u_{NFrate}	0.0807	0.0807	0.0807
u_{NI}	0.0405	0.0402	0.0372
u_{NIrate}	0.1396	0.1396	0.1396
u_{rate}	0.1	0.0998	0.0982
e_{NF}	0.6526	0.6552	0.6792
e_{NI}	0.2496	0.2472	0.2247
e_{MI}	0.0484	0.0479	0.0435
λ	0.7099	0.7122	0.7333
w_{NF}	0.7437	0.7437	0.7437
w_{NI}	0.4941	0.4941	0.4941
w_{MI}	0.2964	0.2964	0.2964
Y_I/Y_F	0.2742	0.2703	0.2371
m_F	0.0820	0.0820	0.0820
m_I	0.1677	0.1677	0.1677
θ_F	0.0067	0.0067	0.0067
θ_I	0.0281	0.0281	0.0281

6.4.4 Combined Policies

Finally, we present the effects of some combined policies. Scenario (I) involves a 1% increase of the auditing rate, δ, and a 1% reduction of the workers' income tax, t_W. Scenario (II) involves a 1% increase of the auditing rate, δ, and a 1% reduction of the payroll tax, t_F. Scenario (III) involves a 1% increase of the penalty rate, η, and a 1% reduction of the workers' income tax, t_W. Scenario (IV) involves a 1% increase of the auditing rate, η, and a 1% reduction of the payroll tax, t_F. In all scenarios, we have a decrease in the unemployment rate in both sectors, as well as the overall unemployment rate. However, scenario (I) is the most effective in terms of reducing the overall unemployment and unemployment in the formal sector. Furthermore, in this case the fraction of people who choose to participate in the formal sector, λ, is the highest. Also, in all scenarios the size of the informal sector falls. In scenario (IV) the drop is the highest of all cases and it is followed by scenarios (II), (III) and (I). Finally, it is worth noting that formal wages fall in scenarios (I) and (III), while they rise in (II) and (IV). The results appear in Table 6.5.

Table 6.5 Combined policies

	Benchmark	(I) $\delta = 0.0202$ $t_W = 0.396$	(II) $\delta = 0.0202$ $t_F = 0.2772$	(III) $\eta = 0.4242$ $t_W = 0.396$	(IV) $\eta = 0.4242$ $t_F = 0.2772$
u_{NFrate}	0.0807	0.0804	0.0807	0.0804	0.0807
u_{NF}	0.0573	0.0592	0.0584	0.0588	0.0579
u_{NIrate}	0.1396	0.1381	0.1393	0.1377	0.1389
u_{NI}	0.0405	0.0363	0.0385	0.0371	0.0393
u_{rate}	0.1	0.0979	0.0992	0.0981	0.0994
e_{NF}	0.6526	0.6775	0.6654	0.6721	0.6595
e_{NI}	0.2496	0.2269	0.2377	0.2321	0.2433
e_{MI}	0.0484	0.0484	0.0484	0.0485	0.0484
λ	0.7099	0.7368	0.7238	0.7309	0.7174
w_{NF}	0.7437	0.7436	0.7454	0.7436	0.7454
w_{NI}	0.4941	0.4962	0.4949	0.496	0.4947
w_{MI}	0.2964	0.2932	0.2936	0.2957	0.2961
Y_I/Y_F	0.2742	0.2448	0.2586	0.2513	0.2658
m_F	0.0820	0.0823	0.0820	0.0823	0.0820
m_I	0.1677	0.1710	0.1693	0.1704	0.1686
θ_F	0.00672	0.00677	0.00672	0.00677	0.00672
θ_I	0.0281	0.0292	0.0287	0.0290	0.0284

6.5 Conclusions

We have constructed a search and matching model with two sectors, a formal and an informal. The two sectors differ in the sense that the formal sector is regulated; firms and workers are subject to paying taxes. Firms bear some firing costs and workers are entitled to unemployment benefits. The informal sector is unregulated, but firms can get audited and if caught, they have to pay a penalty and the match is terminated. There are two types of workers; natives who can choose in which sector they want to work and irregular immigrants who can only be employed in the informal sector. We have calibrated the model for the Greek economy in the period 2000–2007 to examine the effects of three types of policies, namely deterrence, incentive, and immigration policies.

Starting with the deterrence policies, we observe that an increase in the auditing rate, δ, or the penalty rate, η, will not affect the labor market tightness or the wages in the formal sector. Increasing the auditing rate seems to be more effective in terms of reducing the size of the informal sector, while it also reduces more the overall unemployment rate and raises more the fraction of workers who choose to search for a job in the formal sector. Despite this, one should note that increasing the auditing rate requires more resources than increasing the penalty rate.

In terms of a reduction in the size of the informal sector, decreasing the workers' income tax is the most effective incentive policy. This is also the only incentive policy reducing the unemployment rate in the informal sector and the one reducing the most unemployment in the informal sector, as well as the overall unemployment. These come at the cost of a reduction of the formal wages, which rise in the case of the other two incentive policies studied. Finally, in this case the fraction of people who decide to work in the formal sector is the highest.

Immigration policies are also effective in reducing the relative size of the informal sector. For example, a naturalization policy or an immigration amnesty reduces the size of the informal sector as well as the overall unemployment rate. The opposite is true for an influx of (undocumented) immigrants.

Finally, we find that the best option is to impose a policy mix that involves a reduction in the workers' income tax, t_W, and an increase in the auditing rate, δ. Such a policy mix provides the best results in the reduction of the relative size of the informal sector.

Notes

1. Schneider et al. (2010) finds that the average size of the informal sector in southern Europe countries, during the period 1999–2007, was 25% of official GDP.
2. Previous studies that use the search and matching model, for example, Mortensen and Pissarides (1994), to analyze issues pertaining to immigration include Ortega (2000), Chassamboulli and Palivos (2013, 2014) and Liu et al. (2017).
3. We abstract from legal immigration. Alternatively, one can assume that legal immigrants are lumped together with natives.
4. In this model, there are no quits and every termination of employment is a no-fault dismissal.

5. We assume that η is the penalty rate net of any administrative cost that is necessary to enforce the law.
6. Battisti et al. (2018) cite empirical evidence in support of this assumption.
7. We assume that wages are constantly renegotiated at no cost. Hence, the relevant wage for an unemployed worker who contacts a firm in the formal sector for the first time, and hence is not entitled to a severance payment, is the same wage as the one for an already employed worker. This is so, because the unemployed worker will immediately renegotiate the wage once a contract is signed.
8. All proofs are presented in an Appendix available upon request.
9. See, for example, Boeri and Garibaldi (2005) and Pappa et al. (2015).
10. We present below some representative cases; details are available upon request.

References

Battisti, M., G. Felbermayr, G. Peri, and P. Poutvaara (2018). "Immigration, Search, and Redistribution: A Quantitative Assessment of Native Welfare", *Journal of the European Economic Association*, 16(4), pp. 1137–1188.

Blanchard, O., and P. Diamond (1989). "The Aggregate Matching Function", NBER Working Paper No. 3175.

Boeri, T., and Garibaldi, P., (2005, September). Shadow sorting. In NBER International Seminar on Macroeconomics (pp. 125–163). University of Chicago Press.

Borjas G., Friedman R., and Katz L. (1997). "How Much Do Immigration and Trade Affect Labor Market Outcomes", *Brookings Papers of Economic Activity* 28(1), pp. 1–90.

Bosh M. and Pretel J., (2012). "Job Creation and Job Destruction in the Presence of Informal Markets", *Journal of Development Economics* 98, pp. 270–286.

Card D., (1990). "The Impact of the Mariel Boatlift on the Miami Labor Market", *Industrial and Labor Relations Review* 43(2), pp. 245–257.

Chassamboulli, A., and T. Palivos (2013). "The Impact of Immigration on the Employment and Wages of Native Workers." *Journal of Macroeconomics*, 38(Part A), pp. 19–34.

Chassamboulli, A., and T. Palivos (2014). "A Search-Equilibrium Approach to the Effects of Immigration on Labor Market Outcomes." *International Economic Review*, 55(1), pp. 111–29.

Cuff K., Marceau N., Mongrain S., and Roberts J., (2011). "Optimal Policies with an Informal Sector", *Journal of Public Economics* 95, pp. 1280–1291.
Di Porto E., Elia L. and Tealdi C., (2017). "Informal work in a flexible labour market", *Oxford Economic Papers*, 69(1), 1 January 2017, pp. 143–164.
Di Porto, E., Persico, N., & Sahuguet, N. (2013). "Decentralized Deterrence, with an Application to Labor Tax Auditing", *American Economic Journal: Microeconomics*, 5(1), pp. 35–62.
Fugazza M., and Jacques J., (2004). "Labor Market Institutions, Taxation and the Underground Economy," *Journal of Public Economics* 88(1–2), pp. 395–418.
Hazans, M., (2011). "Informal Workers Across Europe: Evidence from 30 Countries". *IZA Discussion Paper*, No. 5871.
Liu, X., T. Palivos and X. Zhang (2017). "Immigration, skill heterogeneity, and qualification mismatch, *Economic Inquiry*, 55(3), pp. 1231–1264.
Mortensen, D. T., and C. A. Pissarides (1994). "Job Creation and Job Destruction in the Theory of Unemployment." *Review of Economic Studies*, 61(3), pp. 397–415.
Mortensen, D. T., and C. A. Pissarides (1999). "New developments in models of search in the labor market" in O. Ashenfelter and D. Card (Eds.) *Handbook of Labor Economics*, Amsterdam. North Holland.
Ortega, J. (2000). "Pareto-Improving Immigration in an Economy with Equilibrium Unemployment," *Economic Journal* 110(460), pp. 92–112.
Ottaviano, G. I. P. and Peri G., (2012). "Rethinking The Effect Of Immigration On Wages," *Journal of the European Economic Association*, 10(1), pp. 152–197.
Pappa, E., R. Sadeji, and E. Vella, E. (2015). "Fiscal Consolidation with Tax Evasion and Rent Seeking," *Journal of International Economics*, 96, pp. S56-S75.
Petrongolo, B., and Pissarides, C. A. (2001). "Looking into the Black Box: A Survey of the Matching Function." *Journal of Economic Literature*, 39(2): pp. 390–431.
Shimer, R., (2005). "The Cyclical Behavior of Equilibrium Unemployment and Vacancies," *American Economic Review* 95(1), pp. 25–49.
Schneider F., Buehn A. and Montenegro C., (2010), "New Estimates for the Shadow Economies all over the World", *International Economic Journal*, 24 (4), pp. 443–461.
Schneider, F. G. and C. C. Williams (2013). The Shadow Economy. Institute of Economic Affairs.
Zenou, Y. (2008). "Job Search and Mobility in Developing Countries: Theory and Policy Implications," *Journal of Development Economics* 86(2), pp. 336–355.

7

Productivity Shocks, VAT Hikes and Emigration

Guilherme Bandeira, Jordi Caballé, and Eugenia Vella

7.1 Introduction

The euro area twin crises, associated with the Great Recession and the sovereign debt crisis, resulted in unprecedented high levels of public debt. Public debt for the euro area as a whole reached an all-time peak of 94% of GDP in 2014. The projection for 2019 was a decrease to 86% of GDP, which is still around 20 percentage points above the pre-crisis level of

G. Bandeira
New South Wales Treasury, Sydney, Australia
e-mail: guilherme.bandeira@treasury.nsw.gov.au

J. Caballé
Universitat Autònoma de Barcelona, Barcelona, Spain

Barcelona GSE, Barcelona, Spain
e-mail: jordi.caballe@uab.es

E. Vella (✉)
University of Sheffield, Sheffield, UK

MOVE, Barcelona, Spain
e-mail: e.vella@sheffield.ac.uk

E. Vella et al. (eds.), *Understanding Migration with Macroeconomics*,
https://doi.org/10.1007/978-3-030-40981-4_7

2007. This high and persistent public debt triggered a strong effort of fiscal consolidation after 2009, aiming to rapidly decrease public deficits. Greece stands out as the starkest case. During the period 2010–2015, the unemployment rate rose to 25%, GDP shrank by one quarter, and the country experienced the biggest bailout in global financial history, with fiscal consolidation policies being a condition. For instance, in May 2016, seven years after the start of the European sovereign debt crisis, Greece implemented its thirteenth austerity package, featuring an increase in VAT and increased excise taxes on fuel and tobacco.

At the same time, high unemployment rates and fiscal austerity led to net emigration from many European countries that suffered a strong recession. Prior to the crisis, immigration from new European Union member states or outside the European Union contributed to migration surpluses in peripheral countries. With the onset of the crisis, not only was there a significant slowdown in immigration but also a pronounced increase in emigration, which received a lot of attention in public media. In the case of Greece, it is estimated that over the period 2010–2015, half a million of working-age residents, or equivalently, around 7% of the active population, left the country in search of employment, better pay and better social and economic prospects. Germany and the United Kingdom received more than half of the post-2010 emigration (Labrianidis and Pratsinakis 2016). In Spain, annual outflows between 2010 and 2014 exceeded 400,000, which is the highest level of emigration in Spanish history and is comparable to the average annual inflow of 485,000 during the immigration boom of 2000–2006 (Bentolila et al. 2008). For around 40% of these outflows, the destination was other European Union countries and for 30%, South America (Izquierdo et al. 2016).

This chapter is motivated by the fiscal austerity measures implemented in peripheral countries of Europe during the recent debt crisis and the surge in emigration that these countries experienced. We study a particular type of fiscal consolidation: the one carried out through the increase in consumption tax rates, which has been an important part of implemented fiscal consolidation packages. Our goal is to shed light on the macroeconomic links between VAT hikes and emigration by introducing endogenous migration decisions in a Dynamic Stochastic General Equilibrium (DGSE, henceforth) model of a small open economy (SOE, henceforth) with sticky prices and search and matching frictions. The unemployed members of the labour force have an incentive to migrate abroad where better labour market opportunities exist. Apart from supplying labour, migrants pay taxes, buy the foreign consumption goods and send remittances to the country of origin. We calibrate the model to the Greek economy, which constitutes a canonical case of study as we argued above.

We first explore the reaction of the economy to a standard business cycle shock. We find that a negative shock to Total Factor Productivity (TFP, henceforth) increases the job search abroad of the unemployed, with a positive, short-run impact on the unemployment of stayers, while it also reinforces the negative consumption effects of the shock and therefore can lead to higher unemployment costs over time. Then, we turn to the results for a tax-based consolidation. When fiscal consolidation is carried out through consumption tax hikes, the fall in private consumption demand leads to a decline in labour demand and an increase in emigration. The departure of emigrants reinforces the fall in internal demand and employment relative to an economy without labour mobility. Emigration helps to mitigate the increase of unemployment in the short-run, but over time the stronger contraction in employment and the shrinking labour force can lead to a bigger increase in unemployment relative to the no-migration scenario. A comparison with labour income tax hikes shows much stronger effects for this type of tax-based consolidation on emigration due to more adverse effects on labour market variables and investment.

The rest of the chapter is organised as follows. Section 7.2 provides a literature review, Sect. 7.3 lays out the theoretical model, Sect. 7.4 discusses our findings for a negative TFP shock and Sect. 7.5 reports the results for tax hikes. Finally, Sect. 7.6 discusses policy implications and concludes the chapter.

7.2 Literature Review

The macro-migration literature has examined the steady-state effects of immigration within search and matching models, often with a focus on welfare analysis. Ortega (2000) studies a two-country model in which unemployed workers decide where to search for a job. Chassamboulli and

Palivos (2014), Liu (2010), and Chassamboulli and Peri (2015, 2020) investigate the effects of immigration into the United States. Battisti et al. (2018) build a general equilibrium model featuring two skill types, search frictions, wage bargaining and a welfare state that redistributes income through unemployment benefits and the provision of public goods. The quantitative analysis suggests that immigration attenuates the effects of search frictions and has increased native welfare in almost all 20 OECD countries considered. Iftikhar and Zaharieva (2019) calibrate a search and matching model of the German labour market to analyse the impact of a 25% increase in immigration observed in the period 2012–2016, allowing for the possibility of vertical skill mismatch of high skill workers. Their results show that recent immigration to Germany, including refugees, has a moderate negative effect on the welfare of low skill workers in manufacturing, but all other worker groups gain from immigration, with high-skill, service employees gaining the most.

Research using dynamic general equilibrium models appears more limited (see, e.g., Lozej 2019; Kiguchi and Mountford 2019). Recently, House et al. (2018) use a multi-country DSGE model with cross-border migration and search frictions to quantify the benefits of increased labour mobility in Europe. Labour mobility and flexible exchange rates both work to reduce unemployment and per capita GDP differentials across countries provided that monetary policy is sufficiently responsive to national output. Hauser and Seneca (2019) study macroeconomic dynamics and optimal monetary policy in an economy with cyclical labour flows across two distinct regions sharing trade links and a common monetary framework. In their New Keynesian model calibrated to the United States, migration flows are driven by fluctuations in the relative labour market performance across the monetary union. While labour mobility can be an additional channel for cross-regional spillovers as well as a regional shock absorber, they find that a mobile labour force closes the efficiency gaps in the labour market and thus lessens the trade-off between inflation and labour market stabilisation. Theoretical models without labour market frictions are developed, among others, in Canova and Ravn (2000), Hauser (2017), and Smith and Thoenissen (2019). In a multi-country setting, reference should be made to the work of Mandelman and Zlate (2012), who develop a two-country model with endogenous migration decisions to study the role of remittances from the United States to

Mexico, and Farhi and Werning (2014), who study labour mobility and macroeconomic adjustment within a currency union. On the empirical front, recent work includes, for example, Dustmann and Frattini (2014), Furlanetto and Robstad (2019), and d'Albis et al. (2019).

Another body of the literature has looked at the labour market effects of emigration in source countries (see, e.g., Docquier et al. 2013; Mishra 2007; and the survey in Kapur and McHale 2012), as well as the fiscal implications of emigration in source countries. The studies in the latter group are either empirical, with a focus on developing countries, or are based on a neo-classical framework (see, e.g., Desai et al. 2009; Wilson 2008). Notably, the topic of "brain drain" has received significant attention in this literature, often using endogenous growth models (e.g., Miyagiwa 1991; Galor and Tsiddon 1997; Wong and Yip 1999) and, more recently, a search-and-matching setting (e.g., Docquier and Iftikhar 2019).

The literature on the macroeconomic effects of fiscal consolidation has so far assumed an immobile labour force (see, e.g., Erceg and Lindé 2012, 2013; Pappa et al. 2015; Philippopoulos et al. 2017; House et al. 2019; Bandeira et al. 2018). An exception is the recent study by Bandeira et al. (2019) who propose labour mobility as a new channel through which fiscal austerity affects the macroeconomy. They introduce endogenous migration both for the unemployed and the employed members of the labour force in a small open economy New Keynesian model with search and matching frictions. Their model-based simulations for the austerity mix during the Greek Depression match the total number and composition in terms of labour market status of emigrants. Fiscal austerity accounts for one third of the output drop and more than 10% of the emigration increase, whereas a counterfactual without migration underestimates the fall in output by one fifth. They also find that labour income tax hikes induce long-lasting emigration, while the effect of spending cuts is hump-shaped due to the opposite forces of the negative demand, Keynesian effect from sticky prices and the positive wealth effect from the expectation of lower future taxes. Regarding the fiscal implications of emigration, they show that emigration implies an increase in both the tax hike and time required for a given debt reduction, as the tax base erodes. Last, unemployment gains from emigration during fiscal consolidation can be reversed over time, due to the labour-reducing effect of the higher tax hikes needed and of the higher wages sustained by emigration.

7.3 The Theoretical Model

In this section, we first provide an informal description of the model setup and then present the corresponding equations. Finally, we briefly discuss the parameterisation.

7.3.1 Informal Description

The model is a simplified version of the setup in Bandeira et al. (2019).[1] We incorporate migration for the unemployed in a SOE model with search and matching frictions and price stickiness. As we model a SOE, labelled Home, we take foreign demand for goods and labour as given. The household's members can be employed or unemployed. Unemployed job seekers can search for jobs abroad where higher wages and lower unemployment exist. Apart from supplying labour, migrants pay taxes and consume part of their income abroad. Searching for foreign jobs is subject to a pecuniary cost, whereas living abroad entails a utility cost. In line with evidence about strong family ties in Southern European countries (see, e.g., Alesina and Giuliano 2014; Giuliano 2007), consumption and savings, together with supply of worked hours and migration decisions, are defined at the household level.

On the production side, there are three types of firms: (a) competitive firms that use labour, subject to search and matching frictions, and capital to produce a non-tradable intermediate good, (b) monopolistic retailers that transform the intermediate good into a tradable good (price rigidities occur here), and (c) competitive final goods producers that use domestic and foreign produced retail goods to produce a final, non-tradable good. Since employment is a state variable in the search and matching framework, it is the adjustment in the number of hours in the production function of competitive firms what allows output to react on impact to macroeconomic shocks.

Finally, the government collects taxes and issues debt to finance wasteful public expenditure, lump-sum transfers and unemployment benefits. Implementation of debt consolidation can occur through consumption tax hikes or labour income tax hikes (for comparison). The model features investment adjustment costs, which help to generate smooth responses with reasonable degrees of nominal rigidities.

7.3.2 Equations of the Model

In what follows, the asterisk ★ denotes foreign variables or parameters. We treat foreign variables as exogenous and omit the time subscript. All quantities in the model are in aggregate terms.

Nationals, Residents and Migrants

There is a continuum of identical households of mass one. The number of nationals of the representative household is equal to constant $\hat{n}$. The number of residents N_t varies depending on changes in the stock of migrants abroad $n_{e,t}$, with the latter varying over time either due to new arrivals or returns. It then follows

$$\hat{n} = N_t + n_{e,t}. \tag{7.1}$$

Residents are employed n_t or unemployed u_t,

$$N_t = n_t + u_t. \tag{7.2}$$

An endogenous share $1 - s_t$ of the unemployed u_t search in the domestic labour market, while the remaining s_t look for jobs abroad, facing an individual pecuniary cost $\varsigma(\tilde{s}_t \tilde{u}_t)$, where $\tilde{s}_t$ and $\tilde{u}_t$ are the average shares of s_t and u_t per household and the function $\varsigma(\tilde{s}_t \tilde{u}_t)$ is increasing in both arguments. This cost function links positively the cost of search abroad with the number of corresponding job seekers, helping to smooth out migration decisions in the model.

Jobs in the domestic labour market are created through a matching function,

$$m_t = \mu_1 (v_t)^{\mu_2} \left((1 - s_t) u_t\right)^{1-\mu_2}, \tag{7.3}$$

where m_t denotes matches, v_t denotes vacancies, μ_1 measures the efficiency of the matching process and μ_2 denotes the elasticity of the matching technology with respect to vacancies. We define the probabilities of a job seeker to be hired $\psi_{H,t}$ and of a vacancy to be filled $\psi_{F,t}$,

$$\psi_{H,t} \equiv \frac{m_t}{(1-s_t)u_t} \text{ and } \psi_{F,t} \equiv \frac{m_t}{v_t}.$$

The evolution of Home employed workers n_t is given by

$$n_{t+1} = (1-\sigma)n_t + \psi_{H,t}(1-s_t)u_t, \tag{7.4}$$

where σ denotes the exogenous separation rate.

The evolution of emigrant employment $n_{e,t}$ is given by

$$n_{e,t+1} = (1-\sigma^{*})n_{e,t} + \psi_H^{*} s_t u_t. \tag{7.5}$$

Households

In a representative household framework, we assume that all agents pool consumption risk perfectly. The household derives utility from a consumption bundle C_t, composed of goods purchased by residents c_t and emigrants $c_{e,t}$,

$$C_t = c_t + c_{e,t}, \tag{7.6}$$

where $c_{e,t}$ is determined through (7.9) below. The household suffers disutility from hours worked in Home h_t, which are determined below through negotiation over the joint surplus of workers and firms, and from the exogenous hours abroad h_e. Disutility is also derived from having members abroad $n_{e,t}$, which captures notions such as different culture, food, habits; distance from relatives and friends; less dense networks; difficulties experienced with bureaucracy and integration and family ties. The instantaneous utility function is given by

$$U\left(C_t, h_t, n_{e,t}\right) = \frac{C_t^{1-\eta}}{1-\eta} - \chi \frac{\left(h_t^{1+\xi} n_t + h_e^{1+\xi} n_{e,t}\right)}{1+\xi} - \Omega \frac{\left(n_{e,t}\right)^{1+\mu}}{1+\mu}, \quad (7.7)$$

where the strictly positive parameters χ, Ω, ξ, μ refer to the disutility from hours worked and living abroad.

The budget constraint, in real terms (i.e. in units of the final good), is given by

$$\left(1-\tau_t^c\right)c_t + i_t + b_{g,t} + e_t r_{f,t-1} b_{f,t-1} + \varsigma\left(\tilde{s}_t \tilde{u}_t\right) s_t u_t \leq \left(1-\tau_t^n\right) w_t h_t n_t$$
$$+\left[r_t^k - \tau^k\left(r_t^k - \delta\right)\right] k_t + r_{t-1} b_{g,t-1} + e_t b_{f,t} + e_t \Xi_t + \mathrm{b} u_t + \Pi_t^r + T_t, \quad (7.8)$$

where $\varsigma\left(\tilde{s}_t \tilde{u}_t\right) s_t u_t$ is the total costs of search abroad, w_t is the hourly wage, r_t^k is the return on capital k_t, b denotes unemployment benefits, e_t is the real exchange rate, T_t denotes lump-sum transfers, and the capital depreciation rate is δ. Profits Π_t^r from monopolistic retailers enter the budget constraint in a lump-sum fashion. We consider as fiscal instruments the labour income tax rate τ^n and the consumption tax rate τ^c, treating the capital tax rate τ^k as constant. Government bonds $b_{g,t}$ pay the return r_t, while $b_{f,t}$ denotes liabilities with the rest of the world with return $r_{f,t}$.

Migrants' labour income is spent on purchases of goods abroad $c_{e,t}$ and remittances Ξ_t,

$$\Xi_t + \left(1+\tau^{c\star}\right)c_{e,t} = \left(1-\tau^{n\star}\right) w^\star h_e n_{e,t}. \quad (7.9)$$

We follow Mandelman and Zlate (2012), where the migrant labour income is part of a unified budget constraint, allowing to model migration as an inter-temporal decision of the household in the source economy. We assume the following rule for remittances

$$\Xi_t = \varrho \left(\frac{\left(1-\tau^{n\star}\right) w^\star}{\left(1-\tau_t^n\right) w_t} \right)^{\rho_\Xi}, \quad (7.10)$$

with $\rho_{\Xi} > 0$. Therefore, under this rule, improvements in the net wage premium abroad increase remittances, which represents an altruistic compensation mechanism between migrant and domestic workers. Purchases of goods abroad $c_{e,t}$ is therefore modelled as the residual of the budget constraint of migrants once remittances are chosen.

The household owns the capital stock, which evolves according to

$$k_t = \varepsilon_{i,t}\left[1-\frac{\omega}{2}\left(\frac{i_t}{i_{t-1}}-1\right)^2\right]i_t+(1-\delta)k_t. \tag{7.11}$$

where i_t is private investment, $\varepsilon_{i,t}$ denotes an investment efficiency shock, and ω dictates the size of investment adjustment costs.

Given that h_e is exogenous, $c_{e,t}$ is determined through (7.9) and h_t is determined through negotiation over the joint surplus of workers and firms (see below), the problem of the household is to choose c_t, k_{t+1}, i_t, $b_{g,t+1}$, $b_{f,t+1}$, n_{t+1}, and s_t to maximise expected lifetime utility subject to the budget constraint, the laws of motion of resident and migrant employment, taking the probability of finding a job in Home and abroad as given, the law of motion of capital and the composition of the population. The corresponding first-order conditions are presented in the Appendix.

Intermediate Goods Firms

Intermediate goods are produced with a Cobb-Douglas technology using labour and capital,

$$y_t = A_t\left(n_t h_t\right)^{1-\alpha} k_t^{\alpha}, \tag{7.12}$$

where A_t is an exogenous stationary TFP process.

Firms maximise the discounted value of future profits. The number n_t of workers currently employed is taken as given and the employment decision concerns the number v_t of vacancies posted in the current period, so as to employ the desired number n_{t+1} of workers in the next period. For firms, the law of motion of employment is given by

$$n_{t+1} = (1-\sigma)n_t + \psi_{F,t} v_t,$$

which is equivalent to Eq. (7.4). Firms also decide the amount of capital k_t to be rented from the household at rate r_t^k. The problem of an intermediate firm can be written as

$$Q(n_t) = \max_{k_t, v_t} \left\{ p_{y,t} y_t - w_t h_t n_t - r_t^k k_t - \kappa v_t + \mathrm{E}_t \beta_{t+1} Q(n_{t+1}) \right\},$$

where $p_{y,t}$ is the relative price of intermediate goods with the final good being the numeraire, κ is the cost of posting a new vacancy, and $\beta_{t+1} = \beta\lambda_{c,t+1}/\lambda_{c,t}$ is the household's subjective discount factor. The maximization takes place subject to the law of motion of employment, where the firm takes the vacancy-filling probability as given. The first-order conditions with respect to capital and vacancies are

$$r_t^k = \alpha \frac{p_{y,t} y_t}{k_t}, \tag{7.13}$$

$$\frac{\kappa}{\psi_{F,t}} = \mathrm{E}_t \beta_{t+1} \left[(1-\alpha) \frac{p_{y,t+1} y_{t+1}}{n_{t+1}} - w_{t+1} h_{t+1} + (1-\sigma) \frac{\kappa}{\psi_{F,t+1}} \right]. \tag{7.14}$$

Wage Bargaining

Wages are determined by splitting the surplus of a match between the worker and the firm. Denoting by $\vartheta \in (0,1)$ the firms' bargaining power, the splitting rule is given by $(1-\vartheta)(1-\tau_t^n) S_t^F = \vartheta S_t^H$, where S_t^H denotes the worker's surplus and S_t^F denotes the firm's surplus. The definition of surpluses as well as the solution to the wage bargaining problem is presented in detail in the Appendix. The resulting equilibrium wage income $w_t h_t$, from the splitting rule of the Nash bargaining, is

$$w_t\ h_t = (1-\vartheta)\left[(1-\alpha)\frac{p_{y,t}y_t}{n_t} + \frac{\psi_{H,t}}{\psi_{F,t}}\kappa\right] + \frac{\vartheta}{(1-\tau_t^n)}\left[\mathrm{b} + \frac{\chi}{\lambda_{c,t}}\frac{h_t^{1+\xi}}{1+\xi}\right]. \quad (7.15)$$

The first term in brackets includes the value of the marginal product of labour and the continuation value to the firm. The second term in brackets refers to the worker and includes the outside option of the unemployment benefit and the disutility from hours.

Retailers

Following standard practice in the literature with New Keynesian models, we introduce sticky prices through monopolistic competition. There is a continuum of monopolistically competitive retailers who buy domestic intermediate goods and differentiate them with a technology that transforms one unit of intermediate goods into one unit of retail goods. Since this part is standard, we present the corresponding equations in the Appendix.

Final Goods Producers

Perfectly competitive firms produce a non-tradable final good $y_{f,\,t}$ by aggregating domestic $y_{l,\,t}$ and foreign $y_{m,\,t}$ aggregate retail goods using a CES technology

$$y_{f,t} = \left[\bar{\gamma}^{\frac{1}{\gamma}}\left(y_{l,t}\right)^{\frac{\gamma-1}{\gamma}} + (1-\bar{\gamma})^{\frac{1}{\gamma}}\left(y_{m,t}\right)^{\frac{\gamma-1}{\gamma}}\right]^{\frac{\gamma}{\gamma-1}}, \quad (7.16)$$

where $\bar{\gamma}$ denotes home bias and γ is the elasticity of substitution. Final good producers maximize profits $y_{f,t} - p_{r,t}y_{l,t} - e_t p_r^{\star} y_{m,t}$, where $p_{r,\,t} \equiv P_{r,\,t}/P_t$ and $p_r^{\star} \equiv P_r^{\star} / P^{\star}$ denote the real price of $y_{l,\,t}$ and $y_{m,\,t}$, respectively, denominated in each country's numeraire. We assume the law of one price holds, that is, $p_{r,t} = e_t p_r^{\star}$. Solving for the optimal demand functions gives

$$y_{l,t} = \bar{\gamma}\left(p_{r,t}\right)^{-\gamma} y_{f,t}, \tag{7.17}$$

$$y_{m,t} = \left(1-\bar{\gamma}\right)\left(e_t p_r^{\star}\right)^{-\gamma} y_{f,t}. \tag{7.18}$$

We substitute out (7.17) and (7.18) into (7.16) to obtain

$$1 = \bar{\gamma}\left(p_{r,t}\right)^{1-\gamma} + \left(1-\bar{\gamma}\right)\left(e_t p_r^{\star}\right)^{1-\gamma}. \tag{7.19}$$

We define the national consumer price index as the value solving (7.19) for P_t.

Government and Fiscal Consolidation

The primary deficit and the government budget constraints are given by

$$DF_t = bu_t + g_t + T_t - \tau_t^n w_t h_t n_t - \tau^k\left(r_t^k - \delta_t\right)k_t - \tau_t^c c_t, \tag{7.20}$$

$$r_{t-1} b_{g,t-1} + DF_t = b_{g,t}, \tag{7.21}$$

where g_t denotes government spending, which is modelled here as a waste. The government has two potential fiscal instruments, τ_t^n and τ_t^c. We consider each instrument separately, assuming that if one is active, the other remains fixed at its steady state value. The fiscal instruments evolve depending on the discrepancy between the debt-to-GDP ratio $\tilde{b}_{g,t} \equiv b_{g,t} / gdp_t$ and an exogenous target $b_{g,t}^T$, and the discrepancy between their changes, denoted by Δ, as shown by the rule below

$$\Psi_t = \Psi^{(1-\beta_{\Psi 0})} \Psi_{t-1}^{\beta_{\Psi 0}} \left[\left(\frac{\tilde{b}_{g,t}}{b_{g,t}^T}\right)^{\beta_{\Psi 1}} \left(\frac{\Delta \tilde{b}_{g,t+1}}{\Delta b_{g,t+1}^T}\right)^{\beta_{\Psi 2}}\right]^{(1-\beta_{\Psi 0})}, \tag{7.22}$$

where $\beta_{\Psi 1}$, $\beta_{\Psi 2} > 0$ for $\Psi = \tau^n, \tau^c$. The target debt-to-GDP ratio is given by the AR(2) process,

$$\log b^T_{g,t} - \log b^T_{g,t-1} = \rho_1\left(\log b^T_{g,t-1} - \log b^T_{g,t-2}\right) + \rho_2\left(\log \bar{b} - \log b^T_{g,t-1}\right) - \varepsilon^b_t, \tag{7.23}$$

where $\bar{b}$ is the steady-state level of the debt-to-GDP ratio, ε^b_t is a white noise process representing a fiscal consolidation shock, $0 \leq \rho_1 < 1$ and $\rho_2 > 0$. By introducing strong inertia through the AR(2) process, we model a gradual (effectively permanent) reduction in the debt target.

Closing the Model

The non-tradable final output must equal private and public demand. Costs related to vacancy posting and search for jobs abroad reduce the amount of resources available,

$$y_{f,t} = c_t + i_t + g_t + \kappa v_t + \varsigma\left(\tilde{s}_t \tilde{u}_t\right) s_t u_t. \tag{7.24}$$

Aggregating the household budget constraint using the market clearing conditions, the government budget constraint and aggregate profits, we obtain the law of motion for net foreign assets,

$$e_t\left(r_{f,t-1} b_{f,t-1} - b_{f,t}\right) = nx_t + e_t \Xi_t, \tag{7.25}$$

where net exports nx_t are defined as

$$nx_t \equiv p_{r,t} y^{\star}_{m,t} - e_t p^{\star}_r y_{m,t}. \tag{7.26}$$

Exports depend on the price exporters charge to foreigners, which corresponds to the domestic price divided by the real exchange rate,

$$y_{m,t}^{\star} = \left(\frac{p_{r,t}}{e_t} \right)^{-\gamma_x} - \overline{y_m^{\star}}, \tag{7.27}$$

where γ_x is the price elasticity and $\overline{y_m^{\star}}$ is the steady-state level of exports. In turn, real GDP is defined as

$$gdp_t = y_{f,t} + nx_t. \tag{7.28}$$

There is an independent monetary authority that sets the gross nominal interest rate according to a Taylor rule:

$$R_t = \rho_R R_{t-1} + (1 - \rho_R) \rho_\pi \pi_t, \tag{7.29}$$

where domestic consumer price inflation π_t is defined as

$$\pi_t = \frac{P_t}{P_{t-1}}, \tag{7.30}$$

With fixed nominal exchange rates, the real exchange rate equals the ratio of consumer prices

$$e_t = \frac{P^{\star}}{P_t}. \tag{7.31}$$

Finally, the risk premium depends on the deviation of the net foreign liabilities to GDP ratio from its steady state,

$$r_{f,t} = r^{\star} \exp\left\{ \Gamma \left(\frac{e_t b_{f,t+1}}{gdp_t} - \frac{\overline{eb_f}}{\overline{gdp}} \right) \right\}, \tag{7.32}$$

where Γ is the elasticity, and a bar over a variable denotes its steady-state value.

7.3.3 Parameterisation

We solve the model by linearising the equilibrium conditions around a non-stochastic, zero-inflation steady state with flexible prices, and with the price of the final good and the real exchange rate both normalised to unity. We calibrate the model annually with Greece at the onset of the crisis as our target economy.

For the analysis of fiscal consolidation, we consider a shock on the random variable ε_t^b in Eq. (7.23) that drives the exogenous debt-to-GDP target 5% below its steady state. We calibrate the debt target rule so that about half of the convergence to the new long-run target is achieved after 5 years and the full implementation occurs after 10 years (see Erceg and Lindé 2013). To ensure comparability between the two tax instruments, we calibrate the parameters of the corresponding fiscal rule so that the actual debt-to-GDP ratio meets the new lower target after 10 years in the open economy without migration. When we consider a closed economy or introduce emigration, we maintain the initial set of parameters in the fiscal rules and investigate the implications of closing the economy or introducing labour mobility for the achievement of debt reduction.

Table 7.1 reports the key parameters and steady-state values we target. To do so we follow closely the parameterisation in Bandeira et al. (2019).

In what follows, we compare results for three model variants: (i) closed economy, (ii) open economy without migration and (iii) open economy with migration. We eliminate potential steady-state differences by working with the full model (iii), setting all variables related to migration and international trade to their steady-state values when considering models (i) and (ii).

Table 7.1 Parameterisation

Description	Symbol	Value
National accounts		
Per capita GDP	gdp	1.00
Private consumption/GDP	C/gdp	0.62
Private investment/GDP	i/gdp	0.18
Imports / GDP	y_m/gdp	0.25
Public debt / GDP	b_g/gdp	1.27
Net foreign assets / GDP	b_f/gdp	0.10
Remittances / GDP	Ξ/gdp	0.03
Utility		
Discount factor	β	0.96
Intertemporal elasticity	η	1.01
Home bias in consumption	$\bar{\gamma}$	0.75
Elasticity hours worked	ξ	1.00
Weight hours worked	χ	1.8221
Production		
Capital share in production	α	0.33
Capital depreciation rate	δ	0.088
Elasticity home/imported goods	γ	1.20
Elasticity exports	γ_x	0.20
Monopolistic price elasticity	ϵ	11
Price Calvo lottery	λ_p	0.25
Policy		
Elasticity risk premium	Γ	0.001
Gov. spending / GDP	g/gdp	0.209
Labour income tax	τ^n	0.289
Capital income tax	τ^k	0.172
Consumption tax (VAT)	τ^c	0.139
Rules		
Debt target	ρ_1, ρ_2	0.6, 0.000001
τ^n	$\beta_{n0}, \beta_{n1}, \beta_{n2}$	0.75, 3.0, 6
τ^c	$\beta_{c0}, \beta_{c1}, \beta_{c2}$	0.75, 4.8, 10
Migration		
Unemployed's search cost	$\varsigma_{s,1}, \varsigma_{s,2}$	0.735, 1.1
Weight of migration in utility	Ω	1.0186
Elasticity of migrant stock	μ	1.00
Labour market		
Unemployment rate	$u/(n+u)$	0.12
Stock of migrants	$n_e / \tilde{n}$	0.10
Vacancy-filling probability	ψ_F	0.70
Job-finding probability	ψ_H	0.60
Job-finding probability abroad	$\psi_H^{\star}/\psi_H$	1.60
Firm's bargaining power	ϑ	0.383
Vacancy matching elasticity	μ_2	ϑ
Vacancy posting cost	κ	0.16
Net replacement rate	$b/[(1-\tau^n)w]$	0.41
Termination rates	$\sigma, \sigma^{\star}$	0.072

7.4 A Negative TFP Shock

We start by showing in Fig. 7.1 the impulse response functions of the model economy to a negative TFP shock. Throughout this analysis, we fix all the tax rates at their respective steady-state levels.

7.4.1 Closed Economy

Starting with the case of an economy without international trade and cross-country labour mobility, depicted by the solid lines, we see in the top panel that a negative productivity shock leads to a decrease in labour demand (vacancies) and the real wage, given the drop in the marginal product of labour. The job-finding rate falls as a result and pushes down on employment. Consequently, the unemployment rate rises persistently. Due to sticky prices, markups decrease and so the drop in profits becomes larger than the decrease in wages. Because the labour-increasing income effect for the household (i.e., owner of firms) of lower profits dominates the labour-reducing effect of lower wages, hours worked rise.

Looking at the bottom panel, we see that a negative TFP shock reduces consumption, investment and GDP in the economy. Given the drop in consumption, investment and employment, the three corresponding types of tax revenue (from VAT, capital income tax, and labour income tax) fall as well. On the other hand, given the increase in the unemployment rate, the payments of unemployment benefits increase. As it is well known, a negative supply shock raises prices and the nominal interest rate reacts positively to the increase in inflation through the Taylor policy rule.

7.4.2 Open Economy Without Labour Mobility

Extending next the previous setup with international trade, the dashed lines in the bottom panel confirm that a negative TFP shock leads to a rise in net exports, both because the decrease in domestic demand induces a decrease in imports and because the reduction of domestic wages has an internal devaluation effect. With international trade, the reduction in

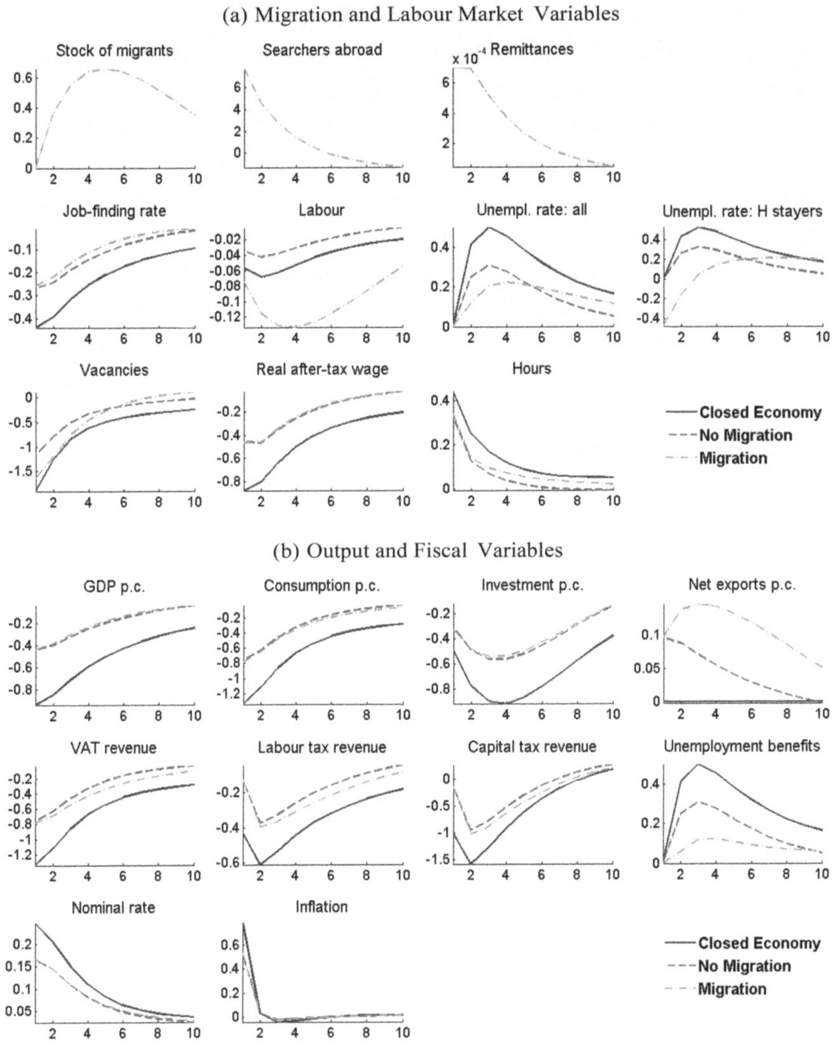

Fig. 7.1 A 1% Negative Shock to TFP. Notes: Responses for inflation and the interest rate are shown in annualised levels. Responses for the job-finding rate and net exports are in levels. All other responses are in percent deviations from steady state. Consumption refers to consumption of the domestic good. p.c. denotes per capita. Unempl. rate: all and Unempl. rate: H stayers include and exclude, respectively, the share of unemployed that target jobs abroad

consumption, investment and GDP after an adverse productivity shock is mitigated. The same holds for the decrease in VAT revenue, labour income tax revenue and capital income tax revenue.

Examining the labour market variables in the top panel, we see that the reduction in labour demand (vacancies), the real wage, the job-finding probability and employment is smaller than in the closed economy. Consequently, the increase in the unemployment rate is mitigated in the presence of international trade and the associated payments of unemployment benefits increase by less than in the case of the closed economy. Hours worked rise as in Sect. 7.4.1, but the increase is of smaller magnitude given that the labour-increasing income effect for the household (i.e., owner of firms) of lower profits is somewhat weaker when the economy is open to international trade.

7.4.3 Open Economy with Labour Mobility

Turning next to an economy with both international trade and cross-country job search for the unemployed members of the household, the dashed-dotted lines in the top panel demonstrate that after a negative TFP shock the household increases the share of searchers for jobs abroad, raising the migrants' stock. Interestingly, despite the decrease of labour supply domestically, the decrease in vacancies becomes stronger relative to the model without migration in Sect. 7.4.2. This is due to the negative demand effect from the departure of the emigrants. The reduction in labour supply and labour demand from emigration reinforces substantially the decrease in employment in comparison with the previous two model setups. For the unemployment rate we examine now two measures: *Unempl. rate: all* refers to all the unemployed residents, including those who target jobs abroad. Relative to the model in Sect. 7.4.2, migration mitigates the increase of unemployment in the short-run by reducing the total number of job seekers through successful job matches abroad. However, this is reversed in the medium-run as the reduction of job seekers is outweighed by the contraction in domestic employment. Moreover, as the impact of the shock fades out and the job-finding rate returns towards its steady-state level, we observe some (small) return migration. The second measure *Unempl. rate: H stayers* includes only those who look for jobs in the Home country. As expected, this measure reveals a reduction of unemployment in the short-run for stayers.

In the bottom panel with output and fiscal variables, we see that the responses of per capita consumption, investment and GDP hardly differ from the results in Sect. 7.4.2. This is because the higher fall in the aggregate amounts of consumption, investment and GDP, which is also reflected in the higher fall of the various types of tax revenue, is counterbalanced by the fall in resident population due to emigration. Moreover, the fact that resident population decreases due to emigration reinforces the increase in per capita net exports. Finally, it can be seen that emigration acts as a fiscal stabiliser through the smaller increase observed in the payments of unemployment benefits.

7.5 VAT Hikes

In this section, we assume that fiscal consolidation is carried out through consumption tax hikes. We present in Fig. 7.2 the impulse response functions obtained from this exercise. As explained above, the fiscal rule for VAT is calibrated so that half of the 5% reduction in the debt-to-GDP ratio is achieved after five years and the full implementation takes place after ten years.

7.5.1 Closed Economy

The solid lines show for a closed economy that when fiscal consolidation is carried out through consumption tax hikes, private consumption becomes relatively more expensive, and therefore decreases (see the bottom panel). At the same time, households anticipate the continuous increase of taxes in the mid-term (see the fiscal rule in Eq. (7.22)) and thus save more to smooth out consumption. In other words, the expectation of higher taxes tomorrow decreases the marginal utility of consumption in the future and forces the household to decrease consumption in

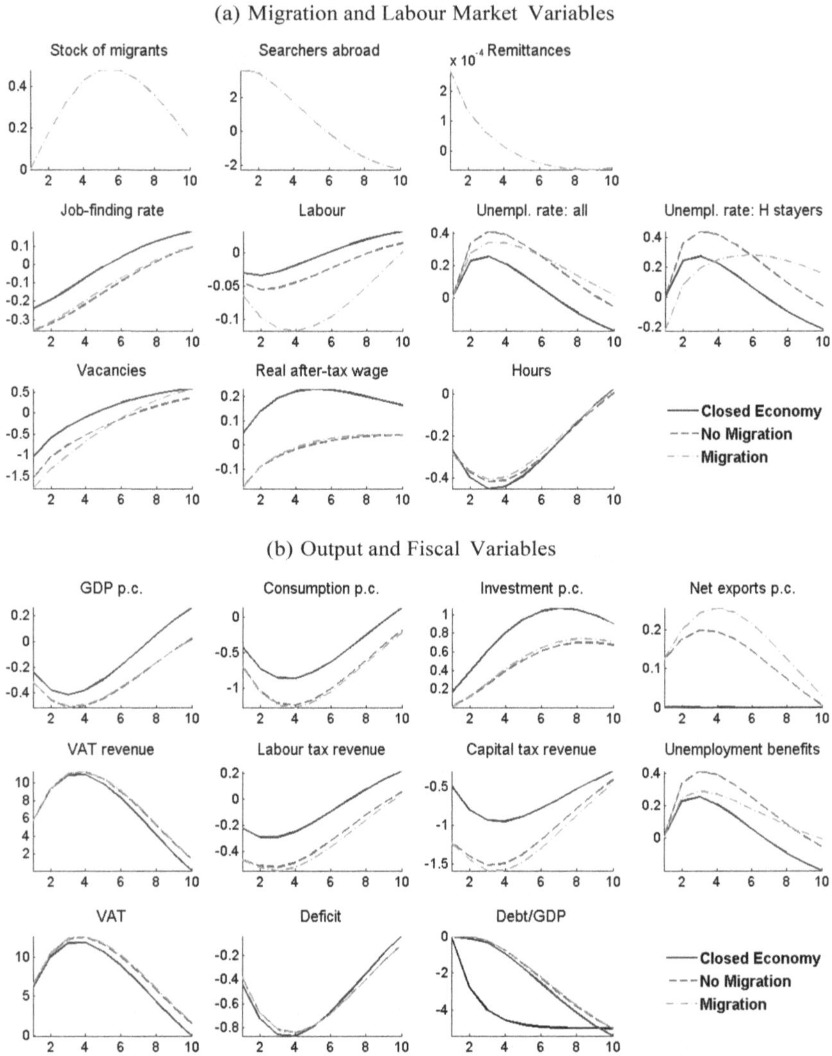

Fig. 7.2 VAT hikes in closed and open economies. Notes: Responses for the job-finding rate and net exports are in levels. All other responses are in percent deviations from steady state. Consumption refers to consumption of the domestic good. p.c. denotes per capita. Unempl. rate: all and Unempl. rate: H stayers denote measures of the unemployment rate including and excluding, respectively, the share of unemployed that target jobs abroad. The black line in the Debt/GDP panel reports the path for the debt-to-GDP target.

favour of savings today. As a result, investment increases, while GDP falls due to the fall in consumption. In terms of tax revenue, the VAT hikes lead to an increase in VAT revenue, but labour income tax revenue and capital income tax revenue both fall. On the other hand, payments of unemployment benefits rise following the increase in the unemployment rate. The deficit decreases and so does the debt-to-GDP ratio which meets the lower debt target after ten periods.

The increase in unemployment comes from the fact that the fall in private consumption demand induces a decline in labour demand, which is represented by a drop in vacancies (see the top panel). Hours and employment fall as well. The job-finding rate decreases, since vacancies decrease, while the real wage increases.

7.5.2 Open Economy Without Labour Mobility

The dashed lines refer to the case of an open economy with international trade but without labour mobility. We observe that after the VAT hike the open economy exhibits a stronger reduction in wages than the closed economy since firms reduce further labour demand and wages to generate internal devaluation. We see thus a rise in net exports, both because the decrease in domestic consumption demand induces a decrease in imports and because the reduction of domestic wages has the aforementioned internal devaluation effect. Investment increases by less and consumption falls by more relative to the case of a closed economy. In terms of GDP, the contraction seems to be mitigated due to the rise in net exports. The VAT hike required is higher than in the closed economy, since both the labour income tax revenue and the capital income tax revenue decrease by more than in Sect. 7.5.1. This is associated with the bigger fall in consumption and the smaller increase in investment relative to the closed economy.

Due to the latter effects, vacancies, the job-finding rate and employment fall by more than in the case of a closed economy (see the top panel). Consequently, the increase in the unemployment rate is more pronounced and this is translated into a higher increase in the payments of unemployment benefits.

7.5.3 Open Economy with Labour Mobility

The dashed-dotted lines refer to the case of an open economy with cross-country labour mobility. In response to consumption tax hikes, the household increases the fraction of unemployed members targeting jobs abroad to be able to purchase the foreign consumption good, which is subject to a lower consumption tax rate (see the top panel). The stock of migrants abroad therefore rises. Vacancies and employment do decrease by more now given the reduction in domestic labour supply, which also implies that hours and the job-finding probability fall by slightly less. For unemployment, we examine two measures as in Sect. 7.4, *Unempl. rate: all* refers to all unemployed residents, including those who look for jobs abroad while receiving the domestic unemployment benefit. As can be seen, emigration helps to mitigate the increase of unemployment in the short-run, but over time the stronger contraction in employment implies a bigger increase in the unemployment rate relative to the model in Sect. 7.5.2. Unemployment gains from emigration during fiscal consolidation can therefore be short-lived and reversed over time, a result also emphasised in Bandeira et al. (2019) for labour income tax hikes. The second measure *Unempl. rate: H stayers* includes only the unemployed who look for domestic jobs. As expected, this measure reveals stronger differentials in the response of unemployment between the models with and without migration.

As shown in the bottom panel, the departure of emigrants does not seem to be sufficiently strong to differentiate the effects on per capita consumption, investment and output relative to the previous model without migration (Sect. 7.5.2). In per capita terms, the differences in the responses of output and its components appear negligible. A notable exception concerns net exports, for which differences become starker. The increase in net exports is reinforced in per capita terms by the reduction in the resident population as a result of emigration.

7.5.4 VAT Hikes Versus Labour Income Tax Hikes

In this subsection, we compare our results for VAT hikes in an economy with international trade and migration with the results obtained if fiscal consolidation is carried out with labour income tax hikes. The latter case is extensively analysed in Bandeira et al. (2019). We present our findings in Fig. 7.3. Solid lines refer to consumption tax hikes, while dashed lines depict the case of labour income tax hikes.

First, we see that labour tax hikes have a much stronger effect on emigration decisions than VAT hikes (see the top panel). Given their distortionary effects, labour tax hikes also imply much more adverse effects for all labour market variables, with the exception of the unemployment rate in the short-run. The latter is largely affected by the increased emigration, which brings a short-run unemployment relief in the source country. However, after the initial periods, the response of the unemployment rate in the case of labour income tax hikes becomes positive and much bigger in magnitude than the corresponding response in the case of VAT hikes. Interestingly, this is because of the shrinking labour force due to emigration. This can be seen by looking at the negative response of the unemployment benefits in the bottom panel, which reveals that the number of unemployed is actually falling due to emigration. However, the unemployment rate increases in the later periods due to the fact that employment and the labour force are shrinking due to emigration.

The bottom panel also shows that labour tax hikes again imply much more adverse effects than VAT hikes for per capita investment and for capital income tax revenue, while the opposite is true for per capita net exports. We also see that the higher emigration induced by increases in the labour income tax rate implies a smaller fall in per capita GDP and consumption for some periods, due to the decline in resident population. As we can see, an important difference between the impulse responses after consumption tax hikes and labour tax hikes is the saving behaviour of the household. Consumption tax hikes increase investment, while labour tax hikes decrease it. In the latter case, the recession is considerably longer lasting and emigration is stronger. Per capita consumption falls by less after VAT hikes than after labour tax hikes. After a labour tax hike, emigration increases a lot and the consumption of the foreign good rises, so domestic consumption goes down by more. Finally, the desired debt reduction will require more time in the case of labour tax hikes, due to the slower improvement in public finances.

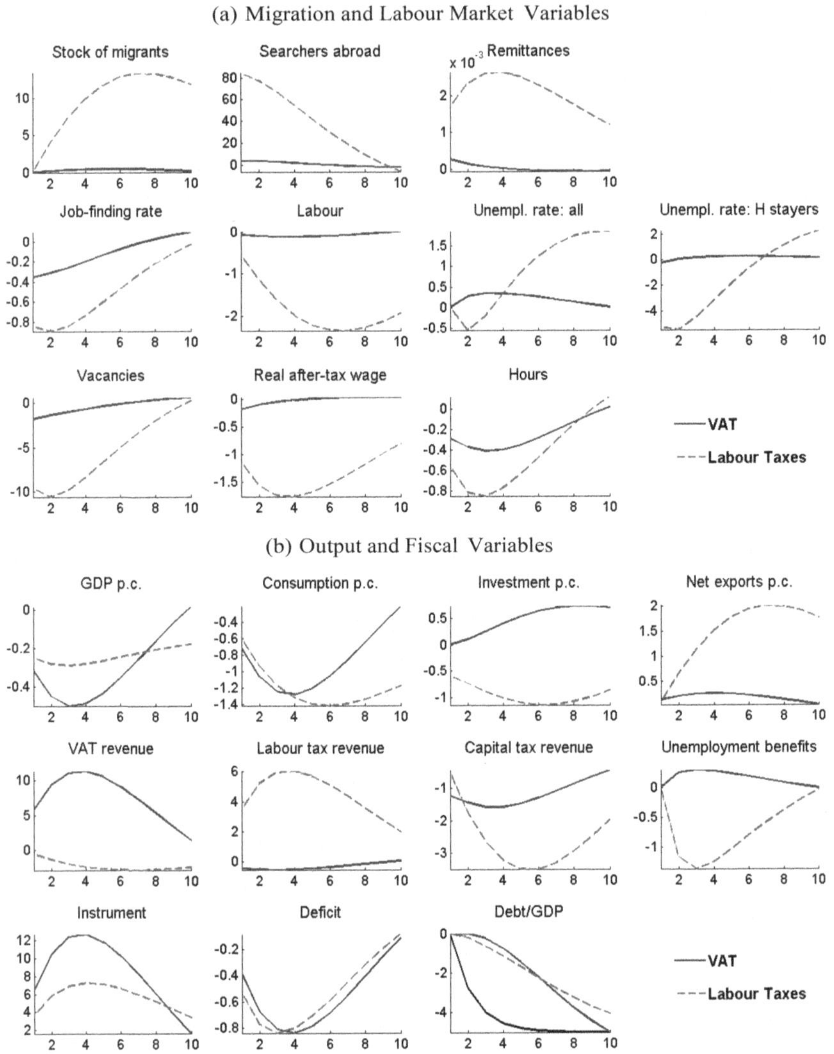

Fig. 7.3 VAT hikes vs. labour income tax hikes in an open economy with migration. Notes: Responses for the job-finding rate and net exports are in levels. All other responses are in percent deviations from steady state. Consumption refers to consumption of the domestic good. p.c. denotes per capita. Unempl. rate: all and Unempl. rate: H stayers denote measures of the unemployment rate including and excluding, respectively, the share of unemployed that target jobs abroad. The black line in the Debt/GDP panel reports the path for the debt-to-GDP target.

7.6 Policy Implications and Conclusions

This chapter has studied the macroeconomic links between consumption tax hikes and emigration using a New Keynesian model with labour market frictions. Studying first the case of negativity productivity shocks we showed that such shocks increase emigration. The departure of the emigrants has a negative demand effect, which is translated into a negative labour demand effect and reinforces the contraction in employment, despite the decrease of labour supply from the exodus of the unemployed abroad. The latter brings some unemployment relief in the short-run, but is reversed in the medium-run as the reduction of job seekers is outweighed by the contraction in domestic employment. Emigration acts as a fiscal stabiliser by mitigating the increase of unemployment benefit payments.

When fiscal consolidation is carried out through consumption tax hikes, the fall in private consumption demand leads to a decline in labour demand and an increase in emigration. The departure of emigrants reinforces the fall in internal demand and employment relative to an economy without labour mobility. Emigration helps to mitigate the increase of unemployment in the short-run, but over time the stronger contraction in employment implies a bigger increase in unemployment. A comparison with labour tax hikes shows much stronger effects for labour tax-based consolidation on emigration due to more adverse effects on labour market variables and investment. The implications of the migration channel have not received enough attention in the policy debates on fiscal austerity until now, despite the increased interest in topics such as the effects of brain drain in the countries that suffer from emigration of their workforce. Our analysis has shown that tax-based consolidation clearly increases emigration, which reinforces the negative demand effects of fiscal consolidation and can affect significantly various types of tax revenue. A careful consideration of labour mobility aspects is therefore needed in the design of fiscal policy.

Our model is relatively rich when it comes to the labour market and the incentives to migrate. However, because of the way we model consumption between residents and migrants, without internalising specifically some kind of arbitrage between the cost of consumption goods in the domestic and foreign economies, we might be underestimating the effect of VAT tax hikes on the decision to migrate. A more elaborate model could therefore be developed to shed additional light on these effects. We leave this topic for future research.

Acknowledgements Caballé acknowledges financial support through the MICINN/FEDER grant PGC2018-094364-B-I00, and the grant 2017SGR1765 from the Generalitat de Catalunya. Vella acknowledges financial support through the EU Horizon 2020 Marie Sklodowska-Curie Grant 798015 (EuroCrisisMove). The views expressed here in no way reflect those of the NSW Treasury.

Appendix

First-Order Conditions of the Household's Problem

Denoting by $\lambda_{c,t}$, $\lambda_{u,t}$, $\lambda_{n,t}$, $\lambda_{e,t}$ and $\lambda_{k,t}$ the Lagrange multipliers on the budget constraint (7.8), employment status (7.2), the laws of motion of domestic and migrant employment, (7.4) and (7.5), and the capital law of motion (7.11), the first-order conditions (FOC) are given by.

n_{t+1}:

$$\frac{\lambda_{n,t}}{\beta}=\mathrm{E}_t\lambda_{c,t+1}\left(1-\tau_{t+1}^{n}\right)w_{t+1}h_{t+1}-\mathrm{E}_t\lambda_{u,t+1}-\mathrm{E}_t\chi\frac{h_{t+1}^{1+\xi}}{1+\xi}+\left(1-\sigma\right)\mathrm{E}_t\lambda_{n,t+1}$$

$n_{e,t+1}$:

$$\begin{aligned}\frac{\lambda_{e,t}}{\beta}&=\mathrm{E}_t\lambda_{c,t+1}\left(1-\tau^{n\star}\right)e_{t+1}w^{\star}\,h_e-\mathrm{E}_t\lambda_{u,t+1}\\&-\chi\frac{h_e^{1+\xi}}{1+\xi}-\Omega E_t\left(n_{e,t+1}\right)^{\mu}+\left(1-\sigma\right)\mathrm{E}_t\lambda_{e,t+1}\end{aligned}$$

u_t:

$$\lambda_{u,t}=\lambda_{c,t}\left(b-\varsigma\left(\tilde{s}_t\;\tilde{u}_t\right)s_t\right)+\lambda_{n,t}\psi_{H,t}\left(1-s_t\right)+\lambda_{e,t}s_t\psi_H^{\star}$$

c_t:

$$\lambda_{c,t}\left(1+\tau_t^c\right)=\left(C_t\right)^{-\eta}$$

k_{t+1}:

$$\frac{\lambda_{k,t}}{\beta}=\mathrm{E}_t\lambda_{c,t+1}\left[r_{t+1}^k-\tau^k\left(r_{t+1}^k-\delta\right)\right]+\mathrm{E}_t\lambda_{k,t+1}\left(1-\delta\right)$$

i_t:

$$\lambda_{c,t}-\lambda_{k,t}\left[1-\frac{\omega}{2}\left(\frac{i_t}{i_{t-1}}-1\right)^2-\omega\left(\frac{i_t}{i_{t-1}}-1\right)\frac{i_t}{i_{t-1}}\right]=\beta\mathrm{E}_t\lambda_{k,t+1}\omega\left(\frac{i_{t+1}}{i_t}-1\right)\left(\frac{i_{t+1}}{i_t}\right)^2$$

$b_{g,t+1}$:

$$1/\beta=\mathrm{E}_t\frac{\lambda_{c,t+1}}{\lambda_{c,t}}r_t$$

$b_{f,t+1}$:

$$1/\beta=\mathrm{E}_t\frac{\lambda_{c,t+1}e_{t+1}}{\lambda_{c,t}e_t}r_{f,t}$$

where β is the household's discount factor.

Wage Bargaining

Denoting by $\vartheta \in (0, 1)$ the firms' bargaining power, the splitting rule is given by $\left(1-\vartheta\right)\left(1-\tau_t^n\right)S_t^F=\vartheta S_t^H$, where S_t^H denotes the worker's surplus and S_t^F denotes the firm's surplus. The surplus for workers consists of the asset value of employment net of the outside option (value of being unemployed), $S_t^H \equiv V_t^{E_H} - V_t^{U_H}$. The asset value of employment $V_t^{E_H}$ is given by

$$V_t^{E_H} \equiv \left(1-\tau_t^n\right)w_t h_t - \frac{\chi}{\lambda_{c,t}}\frac{h_t^{1+\xi}}{1+\xi} + \mathrm{E}_t\beta_{t+1}\left\{\left(1-\sigma\right)V_{t+1}^{E_H} + \sigma V_{t+1}^{U_H}\right\},$$

where the value of being unemployed at Home $V_t^{U_H}$ is given by

$$V_{t+1}^{U_H} \equiv \mathrm{b} + \mathrm{E}_t\beta_{t+1}\left\{\psi_{H,t}V_{t+1}^{E_H} + \left(1-\psi_{H,t}\right)V_{t+1}^{U_H}\right\}.$$

Hence, the worker's surplus S_t^H is

$$S_t^H = \left(1-\tau_t^n\right)w_t h_t - \mathrm{b} - \frac{\chi}{\lambda_{c,t}}\frac{h_t^{1+\xi}}{1+\xi} + \left(1-\sigma-\psi_{H,t}\right)\mathrm{E}_t\beta_{t+1}S_{t+1}^H.$$

The value of job seeking abroad $V_t^{U_F}$ is given by

$$V_t^{U_F} = \mathrm{b} - \varsigma\left(\tilde{s}_t\tilde{u}_t\right) + \mathrm{E}_t\beta_{t+1}\left\{\psi_H^\star V_{t+1}^{E_F} + \left(1-\psi_H^\star\right)V_{t+1}^{U_F}\right\}.$$

In the previous expression, $V_t^{E_F}$ marks the value of being employed abroad,

$$V_t^{E_F} = e_t\left(1-\tau^{n\star}\right)w^\star h_e - \frac{\chi}{\lambda_{c,t}}\frac{h_e^{1+\xi}}{1+\xi} - \frac{\Omega}{\lambda_{c,t}}\left(n_{e,t}\right)^\mu +$$
$$\mathrm{E}_t\beta_{t+1}\left\{\left(1-\sigma^\star\right)V_{t+1}^{E_F} + \sigma^\star V_{t+1}^{U_F}\right\},$$

where we assume that emigrants losing their jobs continue to look for jobs abroad. Hence, migrant worker's surplus $S_{h,t}^F \equiv V_t^{E_F} - V_t^{U_F}$ is given by

$$S_{h,t}^{H}=e_{t}\left(1-\tau^{n\star}\right)w^{\star}h_{e}-\text{b}-\varsigma\left(\tilde{s}_{t}\ \tilde{u}_{t}\right)-\frac{\chi}{\lambda_{c,t}}\frac{h_{e}^{1+\xi}}{1+\xi}-$$

$$\frac{\Omega}{\lambda_{c,t}}\left(n_{e,t}\right)^{\mu}+\left(1-\sigma^{\star}-\psi_{H}^{\star}\right)\text{E}_{t}\beta_{t+1}S_{h,t+1}^{H}.$$

Optimality implies that the value of job seeking at home or abroad must be equal (see the FOC with respect to u_t in the household's problem). Hence, $V_t^{U_H}=V_t^{U_F}$ implies

$$\psi_{H,t}\text{E}_{t}\beta_{t+1}S_{t+1}^{H}=\psi_{H}^{\star}\text{E}_{t}\beta_{t+1}S_{h,t+1}^{H}-\varsigma\left(\tilde{s}_{t}\ \tilde{u}_{t}\right).$$

For the firm, the surplus from a match is given by

$$S_{t}^{F}=p_{y,t}\left(1-\alpha\right)\frac{y_{t}}{n_{t}}-w_{t}h_{t}+\left(1-\sigma\right)\text{E}_{t}\beta_{t+1}S_{t+1}^{F},$$

which, using the FOC with respect to v_t can be written as

$$S_{t}^{F}=p_{y,t}\left(1-\alpha\right)\frac{y_{t}}{n_{t}}-w_{t}h_{t}+\left(1-\sigma\right)\frac{\kappa}{\psi_{F,t}}.$$

The resulting equilibrium wage income $w_t h_t$ arising from the splitting rule of the Nash bargaining is then obtained by using the above surpluses and is given by expression (7.15).

Hours Worked in Equilibrium

Hours worked are determined through negotiation over the joint surplus of workers and firms,

$$\max_{h_t}\left(S_{t}^{H}\right)^{1-\vartheta}\left(S_{t}^{F}\right)^{\vartheta}.$$

Using the expressions for S_t^H and S_t^F derived above, together with the wage's splitting rule, the solution to the negotiation problem over hours worked is given by

$$\frac{\partial S_t^H}{\partial h_t} = -\left(1-\tau_t^n\right)\frac{\partial S_t^F}{\partial h_t},$$

which yields

$$\chi\frac{h_t^\xi}{\lambda_{c,t}} = \left(1-\tau_t^n\right)\left(1-\alpha\right)^2\frac{p_{y,t}y_t}{n_t}.$$

Retailers

The real marginal cost faced by retailers is the relative price $p_{y,t}$ of intermediate goods. Let $y_{i,t}$ be the quantity of output produced by retailer i. These goods are aggregated into a tradable good,

$$y_{r,t} = \left[\int_0^1\left(y_{i,t}\right)^{\frac{\varepsilon-1}{\varepsilon}}di\right]^{\frac{\varepsilon}{\varepsilon-1}}.$$

where $\varepsilon > 1$ is the constant elasticity of demand for each variety. The aggregate tradable good is sold at the nominal price $P_{r,t} = \left(\int_0^1\left(P_{i,t}\right)^{\varepsilon-1}di\right)^{\frac{1}{\varepsilon-1}}$, where $P_{i,t}$ is the price of variety i. The demand for each intermediate good depends on its relative price and on aggregate demand,

$$y_{i,t} = \left(\frac{P_{i,t}}{P_{r,t}}\right)^{-\varepsilon}y_{r,t}.$$

In any period, each retailer can reset its price with a probability $1 - \lambda_p$, choosing $P^*_{i,t}$ to maximize expected real profits,

$$\Pi_t(i) = \mathrm{E}_t \sum_{s=0}^{\infty} (\beta\lambda_p)^s \frac{\lambda_{c,t+1}}{\lambda_{c,t}} \left(\left[\frac{P_{i,t}}{P_{t+s}} - p_{y,t+s} \right] y_{i,t+s} \right)$$

subject to the demand schedule, where P_t is the price of the final good and used as the numeraire. Since all firms are ex-ante identical (except for the variety they produce), $P^*_{i,t} = P^*_{r,t}$ for all i. taking into account that $p_{r,t} \equiv P_{r,t}/P_t$, the resulting expression for the reset price in real terms $p^*_{r,t} \equiv P^*_{r,t} / P_t$ is

$$\frac{p^*_{r,t}}{p_{r,t}} = \frac{\varepsilon}{\varepsilon - 1} \frac{\mathcal{N}_t}{\mathcal{D}_t}$$

with

$$\mathcal{N}_t = p_{y,t} y_{r,t} + \lambda_p \mathrm{E}_t \beta_{t+1} (\pi_{r,t+1})^{\varepsilon} \mathcal{N}_{t+1},$$

$$\mathcal{D}_t = p_{r,t} y_{r,t} + \lambda_p \mathrm{E}_t \beta_{t+1} (\pi_{r,t+1})^{\varepsilon-1} \mathcal{D}_{t+1},$$

where $\pi_{r,t} \equiv P_{r,t}/P_{r,t-1}$ is the producer price inflation. With Calvo pricing, the nominal price index is

$$(P_{r,t})^{1-\epsilon} = \lambda_p (P_{r,t-1})^{1-\epsilon} + (1 - \lambda_p)(P^*_{r,t})^{1-\epsilon}.$$

The aggregate tradable good is sold domestically and abroad

$$y_{r,t} = y_{l,t} + y^{\star}_{m,t},$$

where $y_{l,t}$ and $y^{\star}_{m,t}$ are the quantities sold locally and abroad. Note that $y^{\star}_{m,t}$ is the only variable with an asterisk ★ that is time dependent.

Note

1. Differently from this chapter, Bandeira et al. (2019) include in their model emigration of both the unemployed and employed members of the labour force, consumption habits, capital utilisation, government spending in the utility and production functions, and cuts in wasteful, productive and utility-enhancing components of government spending as fiscal consolidation instruments. Finally, Bandeira et al. (2019) do not use a Taylor rule for monetary policy and do not compare their results with the ones obtained in a closed economy framework, as we do here.

References

Alesina, Alberto, and Paola Giuliano. "Family ties." In *Handbook of Economic Growth*, vol. 2, pp. 177–215. Elsevier, 2014.

Bandeira, Guilherme, Jordi Caballé, and Eugenia Vella. Fiscal austerity and Greek emigration: A missing link. *Barcelona GSE Working Papers Series No 1075,* 2019.

Bandeira, Guilherme, Evi Pappa, Rana Sajedi, and Eugenia Vella. "Fiscal consolidation in a low-inflation environment: Pay cuts versus lost jobs." *International Journal of Central Banking* 14 (2018): 7–53.

Battisti, Michele, Gabriel Felbermayr, Giovanni Peri, and Panu Poutvaara. "Immigration, search and redistribution: A quantitative assessment of native welfare." *Journal of the European Economic Association* 16, no. 4 (2018): 1137–1188.

Bentolila, Samuel, Juan J. Dolado, and Juan F. Jimeno. "Does immigration affect the Phillips curve? Some evidence for Spain." *European Economic Review* 52, no. 8 (2008): 1398–1423.

Canova, Fabio, and Morten O. Ravn. "The macroeconomic effects of German unification: Real adjustments and the welfare state." *Review of Economic Dynamics* 3, no. 3 (2000): 423–460.

Chassamboulli, Andri, and Theodore Palivos. "A search-equilibrium approach to the effects of immigration on labor market outcomes." *International Economic Review* 55, no. 1 (2014): 111–129.

Chassamboulli, Andri, and Giovanni Peri. "The labor market effects of reducing the number of illegal immigrants." *Review of Economic Dynamics* 18, no. 4 (2015): 792–821.

Chassamboulli, Andri, and Giovanni Peri. "The economic effect of immigration policies: Analyzing and simulating the US case." *Journal of Economic Dynamics and Control* 114 (2020): 103898.

d'Albis, Hippolyte, Ekrame Boubtane, and Dramane Coulibaly. "Immigration and public finances in OECD countries." *Journal of Economic Dynamics and Control* 99 (2019): 116–151.

Desai, Mihir A., Devesh Kapur, John McHale, and Keith Rogers. "The fiscal impact of high-skilled emigration: Flows of Indians to the US." *Journal of Development Economics* 88, no. 1 (2009): 32–44.

Docquier, Frédéric, and Zainab Iftikhar. "Brain drain, informality and inequality: a search-and-matching model for sub-Saharan Africa." *Journal of International Economics* 120 (2019): 109–125.

Docquier, Frédéric, Çağlar Ozden, and Giovanni Peri. "The labour market effects of immigration and emigration in OECD countries." *The Economic Journal* 124, no. 579 (2013): 1106–1145.

Dustmann, C. and Frattini, T., 2014. "The fiscal effects of immigration to the UK." *The Economic Journal, 124*(580), pp.F593-F643.

Erceg, Christopher J., and Jesper Lindé. "Fiscal consolidation in an open economy." *American Economic Review* 102, no. 3 (2012): 186–91.

Erceg, Christopher J., and Jesper Lindé. "Fiscal consolidation in a currency union: Spending cuts vs. tax hikes." *Journal of Economic Dynamics and Control* 37, no. 2 (2013): 422–445.

Farhi, Emmanuel, and Iván Werning. Labor mobility within currency unions. No. w20105. National Bureau of Economic Research, 2014.

Furlanetto, Francesco, and Ørjan Robstad. "Immigration and the macroeconomy: Some new empirical evidence." *Review of Economic Dynamics* 34 (2019): 1–19.

Galor, Oded, and Daniel Tsiddon. "Technological progress, mobility, and economic growth." *The American Economic Review* (1997): 363–382.

Giuliano, Paola. "Living arrangements in western Europe: Does cultural origin matter?." *Journal of the European Economic Association* 5, no. 5 (2007): 927–952.

Hauser, Daniela. "Technology shocks, labor mobility and business-cycle fluctuations." No 4. Bank of Canada, 2017.

Hauser, Daniela, and Martin Seneca. Labor Mobility in a Monetary Union. No. 19–15. Bank of Canada, 2019.

House, Christopher L., Christian Proebsting, and Linda L. Tesar. "Austerity in the Aftermath of the Great Recession." *Journal of Monetary Economics* (2019).

House, Christopher L., Christian Proebsting, and Linda L. Tesar. Quantifying the benefits of labor mobility in a currency union. No. w25347. National Bureau of Economic Research, 2018.

Iftikhar, Zainab, and Anna Zaharieva. "General equilibrium effects of immigration in Germany: Search and matching approach." *Review of Economic Dynamics* 31 (2019): 245–276.

Izquierdo, Mario, Juan F. Jimeno, and Aitor Lacuesta. "Spain: from massive immigration to vast emigration?." *IZA Journal of Migration* 5, no. 1 (2016): 10.

Kapur, Devesh, and John McHale. "Economic effects of emigration on sending countries." In *Oxford Handbook of the Politics of International Migration*. 2012.

Kiguchi, Takehiro, and Andrew Mountford. "Immigration and unemployment: A macroeconomic approach." *Macroeconomic Dynamics* 23, no. 4 (2019): 1313–1339.

Labrianidis, Lois, and Manolis Pratsinakis. "Greece's new emigration at times of crisis." *Technical report*, Hellenic Observatory, LSE, 2016.

Liu, Xiangbo. "On the macroeconomic and welfare effects of illegal immigration." *Journal of Economic Dynamics and Control* 34, no. 12 (2010): 2547–2567.

Lozej, Matija. "Economic migration and business cycles in a small open economy with matching frictions." *Economic Modelling* 81 (2019): 604–620.

Mandelman, Federico S., and Andrei Zlate. "Immigration, remittances and business cycles." *Journal of Monetary Economics* 59, no. 2 (2012): 196–213.

Mishra, Prachi. "Emigration and wages in source countries: Evidence from Mexico." *Journal of Development Economics* 82, no. 1 (2007): 180–199.

Miyagiwa, Kaz. "Scale economies in education and the brain drain problem." *International Economic Review* (1991): 743–759.

Ortega, Javier. "Pareto-improving immigration in an economy with equilibrium unemployment." *The Economic Journal* 110, no. 460 (2000): 92–112.

Pappa, Evi, Rana Sajedi, and Eugenia Vella. "Fiscal consolidation with tax evasion and corruption." *Journal of International Economics* 96 (2015): S56-S75.

Philippopoulos, Apostolis, Petros Varthalitis, and Vanghelis Vassilatos. "Fiscal consolidation in an open economy with sovereign premia and without monetary policy independence." *International Journal of Central Banking* 13, no. 4 (2017): 259–306.

Smith, Christie, and Christoph Thoenissen. "Skilled migration and business cycle dynamics." *Journal of Economic Dynamics and Control* 109 (2019): 103781.

Wilson, John Douglas. "A voluntary brain-drain tax." *Journal of Public Economics* 92, no. 12 (2008): 2385–2391.

Wong, Kar-yiu, and Chong Kee Yip. "Education, economic growth, and brain drain." *Journal of Economic Dynamics and Control* 23, no. 5–6 (1999): 699–726.

8

Economic Migration with Matching Frictions and Business Cycle Amplification

Matija Lozej

8.1 Introduction

Migration has only quite recently found the way to dynamic general equilibrium models of business cycles. Part of the reason is that migration has typically not been viewed as something that is changing at business cycle frequencies. Yet, especially in Europe with the free movement of labour, and in countries that were more open to migration, there is evidence that migration is cyclical. Moreover, there is evidence that migration is substantial relative to domestic population, and this may not be the case only in countries that are among the most concerned about migration. To lend some support to such statements, Fig. 8.1 uses a very simple statistic. It shows deviations of net migration as a share of population from its trend, in percentage points (i.e., the cyclical component of net migration, expressed as per cent of a country's population).

M. Lozej (✉)
Irish Economic Analysis, Macroeconomic Modelling, Central Bank of Ireland, Dublin, Ireland

E. Vella et al. (eds.), *Understanding Migration with Macroeconomics*,
https://doi.org/10.1007/978-3-030-40981-4_8

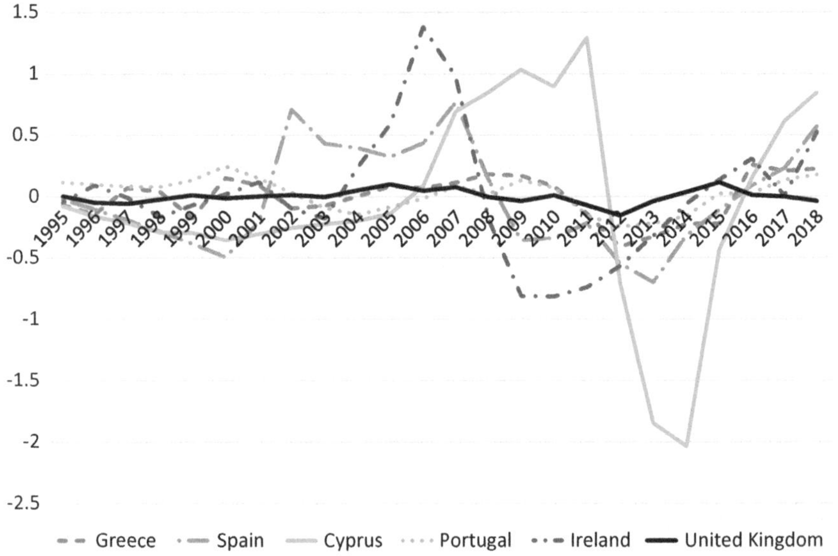

Fig. 8.1 Migration over the business cycle in selected countries. Notes: The figure shows deviations of net migration as a share of population from its trend, in percentage points. The trend was obtained from annual data using the HP filter with the smoothing constant 100. (Source of the data: Eurostat)

In all countries shown in Fig. 8.1, there is a clear pattern that coincides with strong immigration during the pre-crisis boom in Europe and the subsequent emigration during the sovereign debt crisis that followed. This pattern is seen even in countries that have not been affected by the sovereign debt crisis, like the UK or Sweden (the latter is not plotted to avoid clutter). In addition to this boom-bust pattern that seems to be aligned with the business cycle, note also that migration flows are large and that they are not large only in small countries. For instance, in Ireland cyclical immigration during the boom increased by almost 1.5% of population, and then turned to a protracted period of emigration with a trough at around −0.8% of population, resulting in a peak-to-trough difference of about 2.3% of population. Fluctuations in Cyprus are of even larger magnitude. As both countries are small and open, this should not be too surprising. However, also in Spain, a relatively large country, the peak-to-trough difference in the cyclical component of migration is just a little shy of 1.5% of population. It therefore seems warranted to study migration at business cycle frequencies, as it has become a quantitatively important determinant of labour supply over the business cycle.

What Fig. 8.1 also implies is that migration is not independent of economic conditions. There tends to be immigration during the upturn in an economy and emigration during the downturn. It is important that this endogeneity is taken into account when modelling migration.[1]

There are broadly two approaches to modelling migration. One is based on frictionless labour markets. For examples of the approach with a frictionless labour market, see, for example, Mandelman and Zlate (2012) for the case with a real model and Chortareas et al. (2008) or Farhi and Werning (2014) for a New Keynesian model. An interesting recent application is Smith and Thoenissen (2019). In their paper, immigrant workers bring human capital into the country, which means that the human capital stock is not diluted in per-capita terms when there is immigration. If the human capital of a typical immigrant is higher than the average human capital of a typical native, overall human capital in the economy increases, which provides an additional stimulus to output.

The other approach is to rely on frictional labour markets. This chapter proceeds along this line and presents a simple dynamic stochastic general equilibrium (DSGE) model of migration using the Diamond-Mortensen-Pissarides search and matching framework (see Mortensen 1970; Diamond 1982; and Pissarides 1985). This approach has several advantages over the modelling approach where labour markets are frictionless. First, there is unemployment in equilibrium that co-exists with unfilled vacancies. Second, it allows for a more detailed micro-founded modelling of the labour market, which allows for features such as wage bargaining. Third, there are externalities and congestion effects that are relevant for model dynamics, as will be shown later in the chapter.

There have been recently several papers that analyse migration and its effects on the labour market in a theoretical Diamond-Mortensen-Pissarides framework. Part of this literature focuses on the interaction of skilled and unskilled workers (see Chassamboulli and Palivos 2013, 2014; Chassamboulli and Peri 2015), or on welfare issues (Liu 2010; Battisti et al. 2018). These papers focus mostly on equilibria instead of on the dynamics at business cycle frequencies. Much of the more recent literature has been more focused on business cycles. Examples are Braun and Weber (2016), Clemens and Hart (2016), Kiguchi and Mountford (2019), Bandeira et al. (2019) and Hauser and Seneca (2019).[2]

The main characteristics of this chapter that distinguish it from the above papers are four. First, all agents in the model are equal, that is, there is no assumption that migrants are either more or less skilled than native workers, or have come into the country illegally. This may not be the case in every economy, but it is very likely to be the case in a developed country in a monetary union, such as for instance Ireland. There are several reasons why it makes sense to assume that native and immigrant workers are equal. Apart from the added simplicity, the focus of the chapter is on economic migration, that is migration due to economic reasons over the business cycle. While wars, climate change, political persecution and so on that often lead to illegal migration may also be considered as economic reasons, it is more difficult to claim that they have anything to do with business cycles. Another reason is that cyclical migration can reverse when the economy enters into a downturn, as has been observed in Fig. 8.1. In Ireland, much of emigration during the downturn has concerned native workers. Similar seems to be the case in Greece (Bandeira et al. 2019). Also, there is little evidence that firms discriminate in terms of origin when posting vacancies. Second, the migration decision is endogenous and based on the directed search approach, as in (Afonso and Gomes 2014). Third, the focus is on a small open economy and the effects of migration on its labour market. Finally, the model is kept as simple as possible in order to illustrate the main mechanisms at work in the model. In this way it differs significantly from Lozej (2019), who uses a full-fledged New Keynesian model.

8.2 Model Description

This chapter uses a very simple small open economy model, where the economy is open to the rest of the world in terms of labour flows.[3] The model is similar to the standard small open economy model of Schmitt-Grohé and Uribe (2003), with two differences. First, the mobile factor is labour (instead of capital), and second, there are search frictions in the labour market.

8.2.1 The Matching Process

The matching process is modelled using the standard matching function, where m_t denotes the number of new matches, v_t is the number of vacancies posted by firms, s_t is the number of searching workers, φ is the matching efficiency, and μ is the elasticity of the matching function. The functional form of the matching function is:

$$m_t = \exp\left(z_{M,t}\right)\varphi s_t^{\mu} v_t^{1-\mu}, \tag{8.1}$$

where $\exp(z_{M,t})$ is an exogenous shock process to the efficiency of the matching function. It follows an AR(1) process in logs, that is, $z_{M,\,t} = \rho_M z_{M,t-1} + e_{M,t}$, where ρ_M is the persistence of the shock process and e_M is the shock, which is assumed to be i.i.d.

From the matching function one can derive two probabilities, namely the probability of a worker to find a job, $p_{W,t}$, and the probability of a firm to find the worker, $p_{F,t}$. These two probabilities are given by:

$$p_{W,t} = \frac{m_t}{s_t} = \exp\left(z_{M,t}\right)\varphi\left(\frac{v_t}{s_t}\right)^{1-\mu}, \tag{8.2}$$

and

$$p_{F,t} = \frac{m_t}{v_t} = \exp\left(z_{M,t}\right)\varphi\left(\frac{v_t}{s_t}\right)^{-\mu}. \tag{8.3}$$

8.2.2 Labour Market Flows and Migration

A typical approach in standard models is to assume that there is a continuum of households with mass one. However, with migration population varies over the business cycle. Therefore, this chapter assumes throughout that *domestic* population is a continuum of households with mass one, as in standard models, but that there is a mass of *immigrant* households that varies over the business cycle. In the steady state, this fraction of immigrant population will equal 10% of total population, but this proportion is allowed to vary.

Total population in the economy at the end of each period, $P_{op,t}$, is defined as follows:

$$P_{op,t} = n_{H,t} + n_{F,t} + u_{H,t} + u_{F,t}, \tag{8.4}$$

where $n_{H,t}$ is the number of employed natives, $n_{F,t}$ is the number of employed immigrants, $u_{H,t}$ is the number of unemployed natives and $u_{F,t}$ is the number of unemployed immigrants.

A worker who is employed can either stay employed or separates with an exogenous probability δ_X. An unemployed worker who searches for a job, s_t, can find a job with the probability $p_{W,t}$. This gives the following law of motion for the total number of employed workers in the economy[4]:

$$n_t = (1 - \delta_X) n_{t-1} + p_{W,t} s_t, \tag{8.5}$$

Searching workers in the home economy consist of searching natives, $s_{H,t}$, and searching foreigners, $s_{F,t}$, so that $s_t = s_{H,t} + s_{F,t}$. Assuming identical separation rates for native and immigrant workers and equal job-finding probabilities for native and foreign searching workers (no discrimination) gives the same form of the law of motion for native and immigrant workers[5]:

$$n_{H,t} = (1 - \delta_X) n_{H,t-1} + p_{W,t} s_{H,t}. \tag{8.6}$$

$$n_{F,t} = (1 - \delta_X) n_{F,t-1} + p_{W,t} s_{F,t}. \tag{8.7}$$

All workers without a job are assumed to search for work. Native job searchers are all those who have not been employed at the end of the previous period, $1 - n_{H,t-1}$ (where 1 comes from the fact that total native population is standardised to 1), augmented by those who have lost their job in the beginning of the period. This gives the following law of motion for native searchers:

$$s_{H,t} = 1 - n_{H,t-1} + \delta_X n_{H,t-1}. \tag{8.8}$$

A similar set-up is used for foreign searching workers, but here one also needs to take account of any immigration or emigration. Foreign workers searching for a job are those foreign workers who have remained unemployed in the previous period (and have not emigrated), those foreign workers who have lost the job at the beginning of the period (and have not emigrated), plus all those who have migrated in the beginning of the period. We denote these workers by mig_t. Importantly, mig_t can be either positive (immigration) or negative (emigration), and is equal to zero in the steady state. mig_t can be interpreted as fresh migrants, who add (if immigrants) or subtract (if emigrants) from the stock of foreign workers in the domestic economy. The number of searching immigrants is therefore:

$$s_{F,t-1} = u_{F,t-1} + \delta_X n_{F,t-1} + mig_t. \tag{8.9}$$

All new immigrants come to the country without a job, but because the matching process is contemporaneous, a fraction of them obtains a job in the same period as they immigrated. Because workers can match contemporaneously, the actually unemployed workers at the end of the period are those searching workers who have not obtained a job. This is equal to the number of searching workers (native or foreign) in the beginning of the period, minus those who have found work during the period. This gives the following equation for the number of unemployed, where $i \in [H, F]$:

$$u_{i,t} = \left(1 - p_{W,t}\right) s_{i,t}. \tag{8.10}$$

The total number of unemployed is then $u_t = u_{H,t} + u_{F,t}$.

8.2.3 Value Functions and Vacancy Posting

A worker can be either employed, in which case she receives wage w_t, or unemployed, in which case she receives unemployment benefits b. In the case of separation, a worker is allowed to search for the job immediately. If the search is not successful, it ends with a worker having the value of being unemployed, U_t. Without breakup, a worker continues the employment relationship and receives the value of being employed, W_t. The value of being employed is:

$$W_t = w_t + \beta \mathbb{E}_t \frac{\lambda_{t+1}}{\lambda_t}\left(\delta_x\left(1-p_{W,t+1}\right)U_{t+1} + \left(1-\delta_x\left(1-p_{W,t+1}\right)\right)W_{t+1}\right), \tag{8.11}$$

and the value of being unemployed is:

$$U_t = b + \beta \mathbb{E}_t \frac{\lambda_{t+1}}{\lambda_t}\left(p_{W,t+1}W_{t+1} + \left(1-p_{W,t+1}\right)U_{t+1}\right). \tag{8.12}$$

In Eqs. (8.11) and (8.12), $\lambda_t = c_t^{-\sigma}$ is the marginal utility of the household and $\beta \frac{\lambda_{t+1}}{\lambda_t}$ is the stochastic discount factor of the household. Equation (8.11) states that the value for a worker of being employed is equal to the wage income in the current period, w_t, plus the discounted value of either continuing being employed or becoming unemployed. If separation occurs in the beginning of the next period, a worker still has a chance to find a job and keep the value of being employed. Similarly, Eq. (8.12) states that the value of being unemployed is the sum of unemployment benefits received during the period, b, plus the discounted value of the value of either employment in the next period, which occurs with the probability of finding a job, $p_{W,t}$, or unemployment, if no job is found.

Similarly, a firm also has a value function, denoted by J_t, which represents the value to a firm of having a worker. This value depends on a firm's profits and on the continuation value of the employment relationship. The profit, in per-worker terms, is equal to the average output per worker (after the share of capital used per worker, $\exp(z_t)\alpha K_{t-1}^{\alpha}N_t^{-\alpha}$, has been paid, where K_t is aggregate capital, N_t is aggregate labour, and $\exp(z_t)$ is aggregate productivity, which evolves according to an AR(1) process, $z_t = \rho z_{t-1} + e_t$, where e_t is a productivity shock) minus the wage.[6] The continuation value is the value of keeping the worker in the next period, which occurs with the probability $(1 - \delta_x)$.

$$J_t = \exp(z_t)(1-\alpha)K_{t-1}^{\alpha}N_t^{-\alpha} - w_t + \beta \mathbb{E}_t \frac{\lambda_{t+1}}{\lambda_t}(1-\delta_x)J_{t+1}, \tag{8.13}$$

A firm also has the value of having a vacancy. Having a vacancy open costs ψ in every period in which a vacancy is open. The value of having a vacancy, V_t, is defined as:

$$V_t = -\psi + p_{F,t}J_t + \beta \mathbb{E}_t \frac{\lambda_{t+1}}{\lambda_t}(1-p_{F,t})V_{t+1}, \tag{8.14}$$

Equation (8.14) specifies the value of having a vacancy open as the per-period cost, plus the value of getting a worker if there is a match (which occurs with the probability $p_{F,t}$). Workers become productive immediately. A firm posts vacancies as long as the prospect of obtaining a worker exceeds the costs of having the vacancy open. In equilibrium, the value of having a vacancy is $V_t = 0$ in every period, which leads to the following condition, which determines how many vacancies will be posted:

$$\psi = p_{F,t}J_t. \tag{8.15}$$

8.2.4 Migration Decision

The decision to migrate is based on the directed search approach (see Afonso and Gomes 2014; Gomes 2015). Workers who search can decide in the beginning of every period in which labour market they will search. Suppose that a foreign worker decides to migrate and search in the labour market of our home economy. She can either end up unemployed with probability $(1 - p_{W,t})$, in which case she receives the value of being unemployed, or, if the job search is successful, which occurs with probability $p_{W,t}$, she receives the value of being employed. If the searching worker stays in her own country, then the situation is analogous, just that probabilities and values are those that apply in the foreign labour market. The searching workers will therefore relocate as long as the expected value of being in the home labour market is not the same as the expected value of being in the foreign labour market.

I assume that the foreign economy is large, so that the values of being employed, unemployed, the job finding probability and wages abroad, are all unaffected by those who decide to emigrate. Therefore, the expected value of a worker staying in the large foreign country is a constant, denoted by X. This gives the following condition for directed search that determines new migration:

$$\left(p_{W,t}W_t + \left(1 - p_{W,t}\right)U_t\right) = \varepsilon_{MIG,t}\xi_{L,t}\mathrm{X}. \tag{8.16}$$

The variable $\varepsilon_{MIG,t}$ can be viewed as an exogenous shock to migration. To see how Eq. (8.16) determines migration, consider the case when labour market conditions in the home economy become better than abroad (for any reason). The value functions on the left-hand side of the equation increase (in particular the value of being employed increases by more than the value of being unemployed), while the right-hand side of the equation remains constant. To bring Eq. (8.16) back in equilibrium, the matching probability of the worker at home has to decrease (or to increase by less than it otherwise would), which would typically happen through the increased migration to the home economy and the resulting congestion of the labour market.

However, it turns out that immigration also makes it more likely that firms will find workers, which induces firms to post more vacancies, which in turn keeps the probability that workers will find jobs high (there is no congestion of the labour market from immigrant workers). This mechanism creates a problem when the foreign economy is large so that X is constant, because then the inflow of labour into the home economy can be infinitely large and the model becomes explosive. The term $\xi_{L,t}$ ensures that this does not happen. It is defined as $\xi_{L,t} \equiv \left(1-\xi_L\left(P_{op,t}-\overline{P_{op}}\right)/\overline{P_{op}}\right)$, where $\overline{P_{op}}$ is steady-state population. Its role is to create a wedge between the value of being abroad and the value of being in the home economy when home population increases due to immigration.[7] Essentially, this term has the same role as the elasticity of the interest rate premium in Schmitt-Grohé and Uribe (2003). Moreover, it has the advantage that as $\xi_L \to \infty$, the migration channel can be shut down without affecting the steady state of the economy. The model becomes simply a standard search and matching model without migration, in our case with somewhat higher but constant population (1.1 instead of 1). The approach used here is reduced form and is used for simplicity.[8]

8.2.5 Wage Setting

With search frictions in the labour market, the wage ceases to be equal to the marginal product of labour. This happens because search entails a cost: it takes time to find a worker (or a job), and posting vacancies is costly. When a worker and a firm match, a surplus is created. This surplus is split between a worker and a firm, and there are many ways in which this surplus can be split into firm profits and wages. This chapter uses Nash bargaining for splitting the surplus, which is typically found in the literature. However, a wage norm such as that in Hall (2005) could also be used.[9]

If η_B is the bargaining power of workers, wages are determined by solving the following Nash bargaining problem:

$$\max_{w_t}\left(W_t-U_t\right)^{\eta_B} J_t^{1-\eta_B}. \tag{8.17}$$

Here, $W_t - U_t$ is the surplus of the worker who finds a job (the difference between the newly-obtained value of working and the lost value of being unemployed), while the surplus of the firm is equal to $J_t - V_t$ (the value of having a worker minus the value of having a vacancy). Because the value of having a vacancy is equal to zero, the surplus of the firm is equal to the value of having a worker, J_t.

The solution of the bargaining problem results in:

$$\eta_B J_t = (1-\eta_B)(W_t - U_t). \tag{8.18}$$

This equation states that workers are able to get a share of the firm's surplus and firms are able to get a share of the worker's surplus, where the shares depend on the bargaining power of each party. The equation implicitly determines wages paid to workers.

8.2.6 Households

This chapter follows Merz (1995) and Andolfatto (1996) and assumes that there is one representative household that consists of many members, native and immigrants. The resources of all household members are pooled and the household as a whole takes the decision on how much to save and to invest. This assumption is necessary for the model to remain tractable.[10] New immigrants join the household and "become native" when they immigrate. This too is a simplifying assumption and one could adopt a different approach (Mandelman and Zlate (2012), for instance, assume that consumption of immigrant workers is determined by the foreign household). However, in many small open economies a typical immigrant is not very different from a native (e.g., a lot of immigration in Ireland and Luxembourg is from the neighbouring countries). Also, in some countries immigrant workers quickly obtain most of the rights, including voting rights (see Smith and Thoenissen 2019). Note that in the model presented here, the arrival of new immigrants dilutes the existing capital stock in per-capita terms.

Household maximises the following utility function:

$$\max_{c_{t+j}, i_{t+j}, k_{t+j}} \mathbb{E}_t \sum_{j=0}^{\infty} \left(\frac{\left(C_{t+j}\right)^{1-\sigma} - 1}{(1-\sigma)} \right) Pop_t, \tag{8.19}$$

subject to

$$Pop_t c_t + Pop_t i_t \leq Y_t - \psi V_t, \tag{8.20}$$

$$Pop_t k_t = (1-\delta) Pop_{t-1} k_{t-1} + Pop_t i_t, \tag{8.21}$$

where c_t is consumption per capita, $Y_t = \exp(z_t) K_{t-1}^{\alpha} N_t^{1-\alpha}$ is aggregate output and $K_t \equiv Pop_t k_t$ is aggregate capital and $N_t = n_{H,t} + n_{F,t}$ is aggregate employment. All household members without a job are searching for one. For simplicity, there is no choice of hours worked (i.e., labour supply is passive in terms of the extensive and intensive margin).

Household optimisation results in the standard Euler equation:

$$c_t^{-\sigma} = \beta \mathbb{E}_t c_{t+1}^{-\sigma} \left(r_{t+1} + 1 - \delta \right), \tag{8.22}$$

where $r_t = \exp(z_t) \alpha K_{t-1}^{\alpha} N_t^{-\alpha}$ is the marginal product of capital. The model assumes that all capital income is received by capital-owning household members, who bring any revenue from capital to the household budget. The same assumption is made for entrepreneur households, who operate firms that post vacancies. Any profits received are returned to the household in a lump-sum manner.

8.3 Calibration

The model is calibrated using standard values from the literature for models at a quarterly frequency. Household's discount factor β is set to 0.98, and for the (inverse of) the coefficient of relative risk aversion we set $\sigma = 2$, as is standard in the RBC literature. Capital share α is set to 0.33, and the quarterly depreciation rate takes the value $\delta = 0.025$. The elasticity of the matching function with respect to the number of searching workers μ has been set to 0.5, in line with the estimates in Petrongolo and Pissarides (2001). The separation rate ρ_x is set to 0.027, which yields the steady-state unemployment rate of about 4.5%. The bargaining power of workers is set to 0.5, which is the same as the elasticity of the matching function and therefore satisfies the Hosios condition (Hosios 1990). The efficiency of the matching function, φ, and the per-period vacancy posting cost, ψ, are obtained as follows. First, the steady-state matching probability for firms, p_F, is set to 0.7, and the matching probability for searching workers, p_W, is set to 0.6. Empirical estimates of the matching probability for firms are relatively rare and the number used here is based on the estimates for the Netherlands in van Ours and Ridder (1992). This estimate is somewhat lower than the number used in den Haan et al. (2000). The matching probability for the worker follows den Haan et al. (2000) and is within the range reported by Elsby et al. (2013) for a number of countries. Based on these values, the matching efficiency is backed out to be $\varphi = 0.65$ and the vacancy posting cost $\psi = 1.88$. For simplicity, and to reflect the fact that new immigrants come to the country into unemployment and are not eligible for unemployment benefits, these benefits are set to zero. To regulate the strength of migration flows, the parameter ξ_L is set to 0.5, such that a 1 percentage point increase in output results in about 0.2 percentage points increase in immigration on impact. These numbers are roughly in line with the estimates in Fitzgerald and Kearney (1999) for Ireland. The value of being in the foreign labour market, X, is set such that in the steady state there is no incentive to migrate. One still has to set the number of immigrants (employed or unemployed) in the home economy in the steady state. The assumption here is that the share of immigrants in the home economy is equal to 10% of the native population, in line with the Irish data (see Byrne and O'Brien 2017). The persistence of the productivity shock is set to $\rho = 0.9$, and the persistence of the matching efficiency shock is also set to $\rho_M = 0.9$.

8.4 Simulations

Two shocks are simulated to illustrate how the model works and investigate the effects on migration. The first is the productivity shock, which is a standard shock used in RBC models, and is useful to compare the model results with those from the literature. The second shock considered is a shock to the matching efficiency, and is more specific to search-and-matching models.

8.4.1 Productivity Shock With and Without Migration

Figures 8.2 and 8.3 show the responses of the variables in the model to a productivity shock, without migration (solid black line) and with migration (dashed red line). The shock is calibrated so that it raises output by approximately one per cent on impact if there is no migration.

The main result is that, after a productivity shock, all aggregate variables are more volatile and more persistent when there is migration than where there is no migration. This holds for aggregate output, consumption and

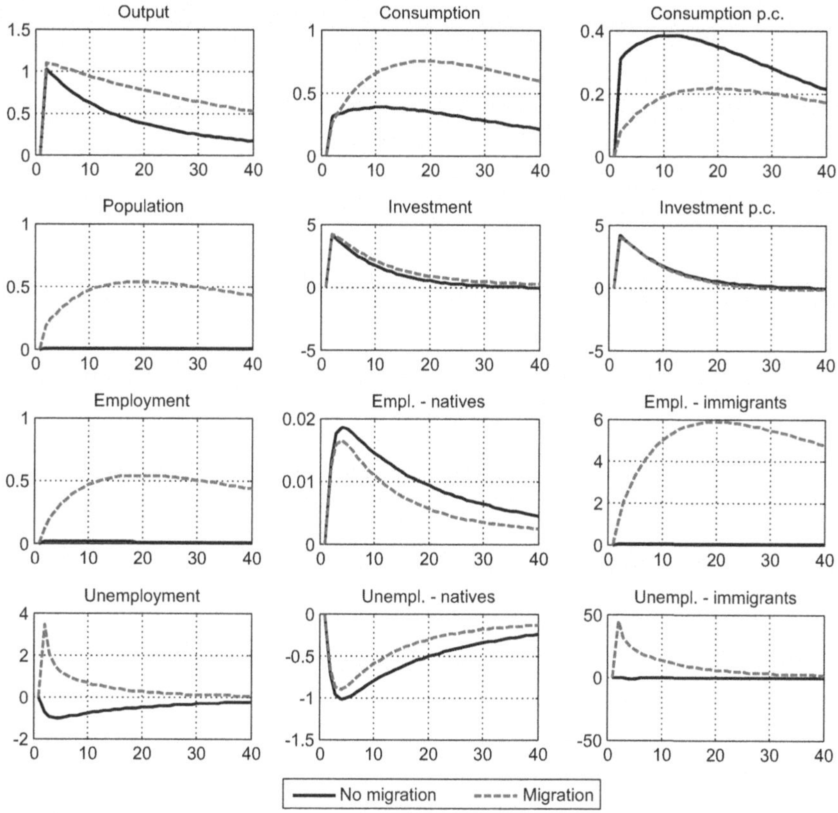

Fig. 8.2 Productivity shock raising on impact output by 1% in the no-migration case: Output and employment variables. Notes: All responses are in per cent deviations from the steady state. Units on the x-axis are quarters

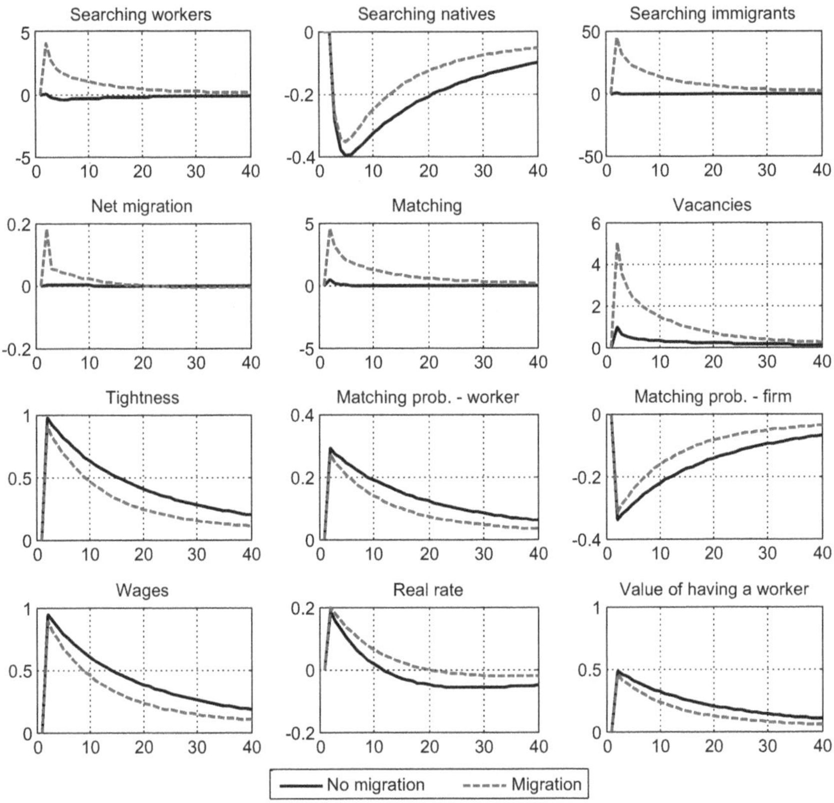

Fig. 8.3 Productivity shock raising on impact output by 1% in the no-migration case: Other labour market variables. Notes: All responses are in per cent deviations from the steady state, except matching probabilities, and the real rate, which are in per cent. Units on the x-axis are quarters

investment. At the same time, consumption per capita increases, but less so if there is immigration. The reason for this is that while the productivity shock increases the available resources in the economy, immigration leads to a population increase and this dilutes available resources in per-capita terms. The stronger are migration flows, the stronger will be the dilution.

However, despite diluting the resources in per-capita terms, immigration also increases aggregate resources by increasing employment by more than the case without immigration. This can clearly be seen in Fig. 8.2, where, after a short period of time, the difference between aggregate output with and without migration is of roughly similar magnitude as the increase in employment when there is migration (about 0.5 percentage point).

To understand the reason for the increase in resources due to higher employment in the presence of migration, it is helpful to first consider what happens after a productivity increase when there is no migration. To benefit from the higher productivity, firms post vacancies, there is an increase in new matches and unemployment decreases. However, a higher number of vacancies and a decreasing pool of searching (and unemployed) workers increase labour market tightness and workers' probability of finding a job. This increases the outside option of workers (it is less costly to wait in unemployment for a job offer if the labour market is tight), and leads to an increase in wages in the bargaining process. Higher wages dampen the increase in firms' profits and their value of having a worker, so vacancies increase by less.

Now consider what happens if workers can immigrate from abroad. The productivity increase again induces firms to increase vacancies in order to benefit from higher productivity. There is again an increase in matches and a decrease in unemployment that leads to an increase in wages. However, a higher job-finding probability and higher wages attract workers from abroad who immigrate into the country (see Fig. 8.3). This increases the number of searching workers and the number of unemployed, which prevents the pool of unemployed to decrease (for native workers, unemployment still decreases). As a result, labour market tightness increases by less and there is less upward wage pressure.

Note that with migration there is a lower increase in labour market tightness compared to the no-migration case *despite* a sharper increase in the number of vacancies. This happens even though the value of having a worker for a firm does not increase as much as in the no-migration case. The reason for such a seemingly odd result is that the inflow of labour through immigration improves the matching probability for firms and firms save on vacancy posting costs, which induces them to post more vacancies than they would have posted otherwise.

To see this more clearly, consider the free entry condition (Eq. (8.15)). After a productivity increase, the value for a firm of having a worker increases and firms post more vacancies. When there is no migration (and there is no labour supply decision), the number of searching workers and the number of vacancies move in the opposite direction (solid black lines in Fig. 8.3). The probability of finding a worker has to decrease as much as the value of having a worker increases, because the per-period vacancy posting cost is fixed. The only way the probability of finding a worker can decrease is if vacancies increase (more vacancies also means that more people will find jobs and the number of searching and unemployed workers will necessarily decrease).

With migration, the pool of searching workers does not have to decrease if vacancies increase. If immigration is strong, the pool of searching workers even increases. As long as the value of having a worker increases after a productivity shock (even if it does so by less than in the case of no migration), vacancies have to increase by more than the inflow of immigrant searching workers in order to push down the firm's probability of finding a worker, so that Eq. (8.15) remains satisfied. This is exactly the case that is shown in Fig. 8.3 with dashed red lines. As a result, one can have a simultaneous increase in vacancies and the number of searching workers.

When there is migration, the stronger increase in vacancies after the productivity shock increases the probability that a worker finds a job, which further stimulates immigration, and this in turn further stimulates vacancy posting and so on. This mutual reinforcement is the main reason why there is need to add some cost to immigration, or the model would have no stable equilibrium (as explained above, the model presented here links it to the population increase through the parameter ξ_L).

Interestingly, the simultaneous increase in the number of searching workers and in the number of vacancies is at odds with the typical Beveridge curve relationship, according to which there is a strong negative correlation between searching workers and the number of vacancies. This indicates that in small economies that are open to migration, one might expect a weaker Beveridge curve relationship if migration flows are more responsive to differences in economic conditions.

The simultaneous increase in the number of searching workers and the number of vacancies when there is migration also leads to a strong increase in employment observed in Fig. 8.2. While the discussion of distributional effects is irrelevant, because all immigrants become members of the same household as the natives, it is nevertheless interesting that the employment increase among the immigrants is larger than the increase among the natives. This is not unexpected, as the number of immigrants in the pool of searching workers increases, while the number of native searching workers decreases. Because of the strong increase in aggregate labour and because more resources are available due to the increase in productivity, households also increase investment (investment per capita responds almost the same with and without migration) to supplement the increase in labour.

Finally, note that the responses of all aggregate variables in Figs. 8.2 and 8.3 are substantially more persistent when there is migration. This happens because the population increase is persistent. However, there is also more persistence in consumption per capita. The reason is that immigration and vacancy posting reinforce each other, as described above, which leads to a more persistent increase in employment and therefore in resources available for consumption.

8.4.2 Matching Efficiency Shock With and Without Migration

The matching efficiency shock is interesting because it does not automatically increase the per-capita resources available in the economy, yet still induces immigration, because it improves job prospects and hiring prospects. Moreover, it is a shock that has been less frequently explored in the literature, yet there is evidence that it has sometimes played a non-negligible role (see, e.g., Furlanetto and Groshenny 2016). This subsection analyses the effects of such a shock in the presence of migration and compares the result with the no migration case. The shock is calibrated to increase the matching efficiency by one per cent. Figures 8.4 and 8.5 show the responses of model variables to the shock.

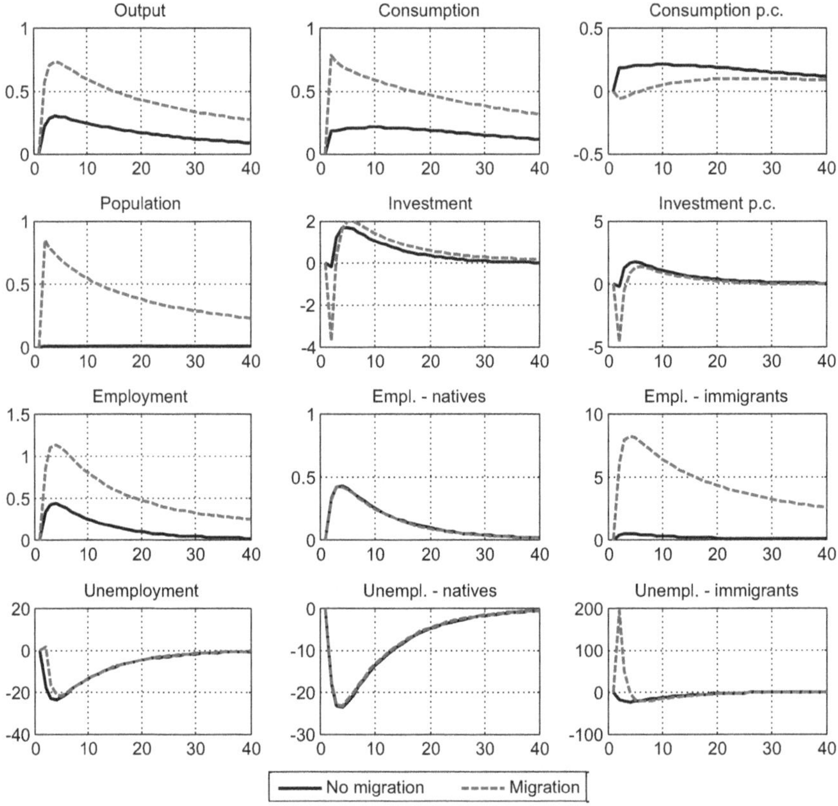

Fig. 8.4 Matching efficiency shock raising on impact matching efficiency by 1% in the no-migration case: Output and employment variables. Notes: All responses are in per cent deviations from the steady state. Units on the x-axis are quarters

Consider first what happens after an increase of matching efficiency in an economy without migration, that is when migration cost ξ_L is very high (solid black lines in Figs. 8.4 and 8.5). Higher matching efficiency directly increases probabilities of firms to find a worker and of workers to find a job. As a result, employment increases for native workers and for immigrants present in the economy (though there is no new immigration), resulting in an increase in output. The increase in output provides additional resources for consumption and investment, which increase (in both per-capita and aggregate terms, as there is no distinction between

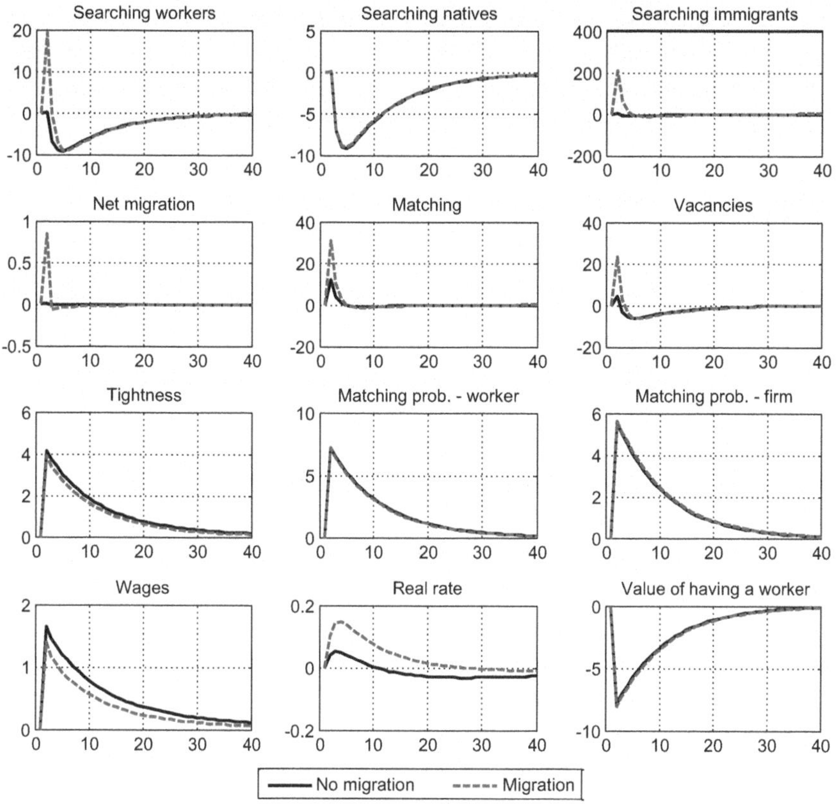

Fig. 8.5 Matching efficiency shock raising on impact matching efficiency by 1% in the no-migration case: Other labour market variables. Notes: All responses are in per cent deviations from the steady state, except matching probabilities, and the real rate, which are in per cent. Units on the x-axis are quarters

them in an economy without migration). There is a small initial decrease in investment, which happens because the available resource increase is initially not sufficient to finance an increase in both investment and consumption, and part of resources is used to pay for the increase in vacancy posting.

When additional migration is allowed (dashed red lines in Figs. 8.4 and 8.5), all aggregate responses are substantially stronger than with no migration, but this does not hold in per-capita terms. Similar to the productivity shock, strong immigration dilutes the amount of resources available in per-capita terms, especially in the short run before employment has increased sufficiently (note that after a few periods, employment increases by more than population). However, after six quarters, there are sufficient resources from new employment so that both consumption and investment can increase also in per-capita terms. This is in part due to the fact that population starts gradually returning to the initial level, because new migration turns negative after the strong initial positive burst. The initial burst of immigration happens because the increase in matching efficiency directly increases the value of being employed, the value of being unemployed, and the job finding probability, which leads to immigration through Eq. (8.16).

Similar to the positive productivity shock, one can observe the simultaneous increase in vacancies and the number of searching workers (Fig. 8.5), due to incoming immigrants. Note that the responses in Fig. 8.5 are per cent deviations from the steady state, and that the number of searching immigrants in the steady state is very small, which is why even a relatively small immigration compared to population implies a substantial increase. Again, this is something that is at odds with the conventional Beveridge curve relation that does not take migration into account. There is again a reinforcing mechanism between the simultaneous increase in the number of searching workers and the number of vacancies (the latter increase substantially more than without migration). The power of this reinforcement can be observed here even more clearly than after a productivity shock, because the value for a firm of having a worker moves almost identically with and without migration (it declines because the increase in the matching efficiency increases the probability that firms will find workers, which drives a wedge in Eq. (8.16)). Despite this almost identical path of the value of having a worker, there is a much sharper increase in the number of vacancies when there is migration than when there is not, showing clearly the strength of reinforcement.

Wages react to immigration in the same way as after a productivity shock, but for different reasons. While increased labour supply and lower market tightness dampened the wage increase in the case of a productivity shock, the wage increase is dampened after a matching efficiency shock by the difference in the values of being employed and unemployed.

The value of being unemployed follows the path of the job finding probability more closely and decreases faster than the value of being employed (which is more persistent due to the constant separation rate). The workers' outside option is therefore falling faster and this results in lower negotiated wages.

As was the case for the productivity shock, the responses of many variables (all aggregate variables, but also per-capita consumption and investment) tend to be more persistent when there is migration. Again, the reason for more persistence is the increase in population and the persistent increase in employment, which generates more resources that can be used for consumption and investment.

8.5 Conclusions

This chapter has illustrated how migration interacts with the domestic labour market. Three main findings are of interest. First, migration can lead to a substantial amplification of business cycle fluctuations. These fluctuations become not only stronger, but also more persistent. Second, there is a new amplification mechanism that arises from mutual reinforcement of vacancy posting and the increase of searching workers due to immigration. This mechanism tends to push labour supply and vacancies in the same direction, which is not something one would find in a closed economy, where vacancies and unemployment (or search) are strongly negatively correlated absent labour supply choice. Third, immigration tends to dilute the amount of resources available in per-capita terms. Unless there is a shock that increases resources directly (like a productivity shock) or some other improvement that leads to strong job creation, it is likely that available resources in per-capita terms will fall after immigration.

There are at least two important issues this chapter leaves open. The first is that it is possible that domestic labour market is inefficient. In all simulations in this chapter, the Hosios condition is satisfied, so that the steady state is not inefficient (absent migration). However, if there were inefficiencies (e.g., there could be too many vacancies and low unemployment in the steady state), one could expect that a pure immigration shock could generate enough resources that one would observe an increase also in per-capita terms. This issue is left for future research.

The second issue that is left open is that there might be externalities from migration. For example, people often migrate to countries where there are jobs that match their particular profile. This means that such migrants are more likely to land a job—perhaps they already arrive in the country with a job offer. This would show in the data as an increase in the number of matches without an increase in the number of searching workers, that is, as an increase in matching efficiency. This has implications for empirical work, but it may also signal that other shocks that give rise to migration are coupled with something that could be interpreted as a matching efficiency shock. Finally, to the extent that migrants bring in either additional resources or skills, there may be other externalities related to migration.

Notes

1. To properly study the dependence of migration between two countries on economic conditions, one should of course take into account economic conditions in both countries. This is because there could be economic migration from country A to country B even if both countries are in a recession, but the recession in country A is deeper.
2. For recent empirical research on migration, at business cycle frequencies, see Smith and Thoenissen (2019) and Furlanetto and Robstad (2019).
3. The chapter is very loosely based on Lozej (2019), with a real instead of New Keynesian model.
4. Dynare notation is used throughout the chapter, that is, predetermined variables have a time subscript t-1.
5. Admittedly, no-discrimination is a strong assumption, but not unrealistic. In many small open economies (Ireland is one), it is not obvious that immigrant workforce is either more or less skilled than domestic workforce, or that the job prospects of immigrants are different than those of the natives.
6. The assumption here is that there is one firm that posts vacancies. The profit per worker is the average profit per worker. However, because the production function is Cobb-Douglas with constant returns to scale,

this is the same as marginal product of a worker minus marginal product of capital used per worker.

7. This term could for instance be interpreted as an increasing tension in the economy if immigration becomes too large relative to the size of the initial population.
8. This reduced-form can be easily replaced by a more micro-founded approach. See Moretti (2011) for an overview and Braun and Weber (2016) or Clemens and Hart (2016).
9. In fact, there is a wage norm that gives exactly the same steady state as the model with Nash bargaining presented here (and also quite similar results outside the steady state). This wage norm assumes that entrepreneurs receive 7% of firm profits after capital has been paid off, while the remainder goes to workers.
10. Without this assumption, one would have to track employment histories of all native and immigrant workers.

References

Afonso, A., Gomes, P. (2014). Interactions between private and public sector wages. Journal of Macroeconomics 39, 97–112.

Andolfatto, D. (1996). Business cycles and labour-market search. American Economic Review 86, 112–132.

Bandeira, G., & Caballé, J., & Vella, E. (2019). Fiscal Austerity and Migration: A Missing Link. Barcelona GSE Working Paper No. 1075.

Battisti, M., Felbermayr, G., Peri, G., Poutvaara, P. (2018). Immigration, search and redistribution: A quantitative assessment of native welfare. Journal of the European Economic Association 16, 1137–1188.

Braun, S., Weber, H. (2016). How do regional labour markets adjust to immigration? A dynamic analysis for post-war Germany. Discussion Paper, Deutsche Bundesbank.

Byrne, S., O'Brien, M. (2017). Understanding Irish labour force participation. Economic and Social Review 48, 27–60.

Chassamboulli, A. & Palivos, T. (2013). The impact of immigration on the employment and wages of native workers. Journal of Macroeconomics 38, 19–34.

Chassamboulli, A. & Palivos, T. (2014). A search-equilibrium approach to the effects of immigration on labor market outcomes. International Economic Review 55, 111–129.

Chassamboulli, A. & Peri, G. (2015). The labour market effects of reducing the number of illegal immigrants. Review of Economic Dynamics 18, 792–821.
Chortareas, G., Katirtzidis, K., Tsoukalas, J. (2008). Macroeconomic effects of immigration in a New Keynesian model, in: Migration, Labour Market and Economic Growth in Europe after Enlargement, Conference hosted by the National Bank of Poland, pp. 8–9.
Clemens, M., Hart, J. (2016). A search and matching approach to business-cycle migration in the euro area. Mimeo, University of Potsdam.
den Haan, W.J., Ramey, G., Watson, J. (2000). Job destruction and propagation of shocks. American Economic Review 90, 482–498.
Diamond, P. (1982). Aggregate demand management in search equilibrium. Journal of Political Economy, 90(51), 881–894.
Elsby, M., Hobijn, B., Sahin, A. (2013). Unemployment dynamics in the OECD. Review of Economics and Statistics 95, 530–548.
Farhi, E., Werning, I. (2014). Labor mobility within currency unions. Technical Report. National Bureau of Economic Research.
Fitzgerald, J., Kearney, I. (1999). Migration and the Irish labour market. Technical Report 113. Economic and Social Research Institute.
Furlanetto, F., & Groshenny, N. (2016). Mismatch shocks and unemployment during the Great Recession. Journal of Applied Econometrics, 31(7), 1197–1214.
Furlanetto, F., and Robstad, Ø. (2019). Immigration and the Macroeconomy: Some New Empirical Evidence. Review of Economc Dynamics, 34, 1–19.
Gomes, P. (2015). Optimal public sector wages. The Economic Journal 125, 1425–1451.
Hall, R.E. (2005). Employment fluctuations with equilibrium wage stickiness. American Economic Review 95, 50–65.
Hauser, D. & Seneca, M. (2019). Labour Mobility in a Monetary Union. Bank of England Working Paper No. 786.
Hosios, A. (1990). On the efficiency of matching and related models of search and unemployment. Review of Economic Studies, 57(2), 279–298.
Kiguchi, T., Mountford, A. (2019). Immigration and unemployment: A macro-economic approach. Macroeconomic Dynamics 23(4), 1313–1339.
Liu, X. (2010). On the macroeconomic and welfare effects of illegal immigration. Journal of Economic Dynamics and Control 34, 2547–2567.
Lozej, M. (2019). Economic migration and business cycles in a small open economy with matching frictions. Economic Modelling, 81, 604–620.
Mandelman, F.S. & Zlate, A. (2012). Immigration, remittances and business cycles. Journal of Monetary Economics 59, 196–213.

Merz, M. (1995). Search in the labour market and the real business cycle. Journal of Monetary Economics 36, 269–300.
Moretti, E. (2011). Local labour markets, in: Handbook of Labor Economics. Elsevier. volume 4, 1237–1313.
Mortensen, D. (1970). A theory of wage and employment dynamics. In Phelps, E. S. (editor): Microeconomic Foundations of Employment and Inflation Theory. Macmillan.
Petrongolo, B. & Pissarides, C.A. (2001). Looking into the black box: A survey of the matching function. Journal of Economic Literature 39, 390–431.
Pissarides, C. (1985). Short-run equilibrium dynamics of unemployment, vacancies, and real wages. American Economic Review, 75(4), 676–690.
Schmitt-Grohé, S. & Uribe, M. (2003). Closing Small Open Economy Models. Journal of International Economics, 61, 163–185.
Smith, C. & Thoenissen, C. (2019). Skilled migration and business cycle dynamics. Journal of Economic Dynamics and Control, 109(2019), 103781.
van Ours, Jan, and Geert Ridder. (1992). Vacancies and the recruitment of new employees. Journal of Labor Economics, 10(2), 138–155.

Part III

Interdisciplinary Insights

9

Insights into Migration with Macroeconomics: An Interdisciplinary Assessment

Emmanuel Comte and Anna Kyriazi

9.1 Introduction

In a time of low economic growth, migration is a contentious issue in Europe. Social science research has an important role to play in this context by shedding light on the drivers and impacts of international migration to provide input for the design and implementation of effective policies. Growing academic literature on migration comes from a variety of disciplines—including sociology, demography, political science, history, anthropology, law, geography, and economics. This collection of chapters is a prime example of the increasing level of details with which macroeconomists have written about migration (see also: Radu 2008). The authors of this volume highlight the impact of immigration on

E. Comte
Barcelona Centre for International Affairs, Barcelona, Spain
e-mail: ecomte@cidob.org

A. Kyriazi (✉)
Department of Social and Political Sciences, University of Milan, Milan, Italy
e-mail: Anna.Kyriazi@unimi.it

E. Vella et al. (eds.), *Understanding Migration with Macroeconomics*,
https://doi.org/10.1007/978-3-030-40981-4_9

developed countries, with a particular focus on the labour market (Chaps. 2 and 3). They contribute to a major debate in macroeconomics concerning the impact of immigration on the labour market (Chap. 5). They also work on more recent research questions, such as immigrants' participation in the informal economy (Chap. 6). They take the perspective of sending states (Chap. 7) and review global migration trends (Chap. 4). Last, they investigate the interactions between productivity changes and migration flows (Chaps. 7 and 8). In this chapter, we capitalise on these various essays to highlight productive cross-fertilisation opportunities between macroeconomics and other disciplines in migration studies. In particular, this chapter explores the potential for interdisciplinary exchange between macroeconomics and history, on the one hand, and between macroeconomics and political science, on the other hand.

9.2 Migration at the Crossroads of History and Macroeconomics

At first sight, little would suggest that historians and macroeconomists have much to learn from each other in the field of migration. The differences in methodology and presentation of research outputs between the two disciplines do not foster dialogue. Historians have a pronounced taste for a straightforward writing style, devoid of concepts and abstraction. Macroeconomists make extensive use of theoretical models and mathematics. They seem to have a taste for universal demonstrations and build models to establish propositions true across time and space. Historians look for complexity and singularity. As a result, macroeconomists' results are typically too general to be re-inserted in historical narratives. A finding, for instance, that overall immigration could have a positive contribution to the human capital in the host country would find little room as such in a historical narrative. Until recently therefore, few historians would have considered that they should follow economists' latest research and the opposite was also true. The revival of economic history in the last decade has partly reconnected both approaches, but mostly around the study of financial history. With a focus on the study of migration and on the basis of the collection of essays in this volume, we show here the other fruitful collaboration opportunities that exist between the two disciplines. We will first review what historians can learn from macroeconomics before turning to what macroeconomists can learn from historical research for the study of migration.

9.2.1 What Historians Can Learn from Macroeconomics

In three historiographical fields connected to migration, historians can learn from the macroeconomic essays collected in this volume. They include the economic history of migration, the history of the European Union, and the history of immigration in developed countries.

The economic history of migration remains little developed—as previously stated, the field of economic history has mostly focused in the past decade on financial history. Familiarity with the macroeconomics of migration offers fertile resources to expand this historiographical field. The essays collected here provide a range of statistical information regarding migration in recent decades. There are more than 250 million migrants worldwide and their number has increased by nearly 20% since the turn of the millennium (United Nations, Department of Economic and Social Affairs, Population Division 2017). In developed countries, the recent period has been one of large immigration. Developed countries in the OECD currently host more than 40% of all migrants worldwide. The share of immigrants in those countries has steadily increased in the last 30 years, climbing from 7% in 1990 to 14% in 2019. Since the turn of the millennium, a country like Canada has admitted between 200,000 and 250,000 immigrants per year on average and this figure has increased to 300,000 in recent years. This amounts to nearly 1% of the Canadian population every year. With emigration averaging only 50,000 yearly, net migration numbers closely resemble immigration numbers in Canada. As highlighted by d'Albis and Boubtane in this volume, 80% of immigrants in developed countries are of working age—between 15 and 64 (Albis et al. 2019). The economic integration of those migrants in destination countries is a major issue. Not all find employment in the formal sector and they can fuel the informal economy. Kyrkopoulou and Palivos indicate in this volume that the informal sector in Southern European countries may have amounted to one quarter of official GDP at the time of the immigration boom in the first decade of this century (Schneider et al. 2010). What these various figures reveal is a period of migratory globalisation about which historians should soon start writing. For this purpose, macroeconomic literature provides useful information.

Admittedly, current macroeconomic essays are likely to be helpful mostly for historians working on the most contemporary period. Yet, the essays collected in this volume also include information on longer-term trends—suggesting explanations for the origins of recent migratory globalisation. On the supply side of migration flows, the chapter by Emily Barker emphasises the role of emigration from Asia in recent migratory globalisation. Whereas 80% of immigrants in Canada originated in Europe in the mid 1950s, nearly 60% have come from Asia in recent years. Chinese migrants have made up around half of those Asian migrants. They have included a variety of profiles, but a significant proportion of students. On the demand side of global migration flows, Barker also highlights the rise of the old-age dependency ratio in developed countries. The ratio of dependent seniors to active people was multiplied by two in OECD countries between 1960 and 2018—from 13.6% to 26.3%. In core continental European countries—including Germany, France, Italy, and the Benelux countries—this ratio reaches or exceeds 30%. This imbalance creates a demand for young active immigrants in order to fund the old-age care system and restore the equilibrium of pension systems. On the regulatory side, the chapter by Andri Chassambouli in this volume highlights how US immigration rules have involuntarily encouraged some chain migration, by resorting for admission to referrals through job offers. This has made networks of co-ethnics instrumental in the expansion of migration flows to the United States. To sum up, economic development in Asia and China in particular, the growth of the old-age dependency ratio in developed countries, and the dynamics of chain migration have constituted long-term trends underpinning recent migratory globalisation. These are fascinating new research questions for economic historians of migratory globalisation.

Last but not least, the macroeconomics of migration is useful for economic historians to connect migration trends and business cycles. The chapter by Matija Lozej in this volume includes a graph of migration flows over the business cycle in selected European countries. Such graph could inspire economic historians of migration in any period. It depicts the positive or negative net migration ratio over time, that is the level of net migration over the total population. The variations in this ratio can be associated with business cycles. In the context of the recent Great Recession, followed by the sovereign debt crises in various European countries, the graph highlights major fluctuations in the net migration ratios in Ireland, Spain, and Cyprus. From a positive net migration ratio of nearly 1.5% in 2006, Ireland registered a negative net migration ratio close to −1% three years later. From 0.75% in 2007, Spain's net migration ratio reversed to −0.75% in 2013. The largest variation occurred in Cyprus, where a positive net migration ratio of 1.25% in 2011 was followed by a negative net migration ratio below −2% in 2014. Such results are particularly useful to connect migration history with other historical developments, including macroeconomic shocks, but also other kinds of upheavals such as wars or revolutions.

This leads us to the second field where historians could learn from macroeconomists: the history of the European Union. In that case too, familiarity with macroeconomic research may serve to open up new important avenues for historiographical research. The essays collected in this volume testify to the important role that migration flows inside the European Union played in the context of the Great Recession. The chapter by Bandeira, Caballé, and Vella reports the magnitude of emigration from the country that was the most hardly hit by the recession. Half a million of working age residents in Greece—7% of the active population—emigrated between 2010 and 2015 in search of better economic opportunities. 400,000 also left Spain annually between 2010 and 2014—the highest level of emigration in Spanish history (Izquierdo et al. 2016, pp. 5–6). Most of those emigrants headed for other countries inside the European Union, using the free movement rights of European citizens. Germany and the United Kingdom received more than half of the emigrants from Greece after 2010 (Labrianidis and Pratsinakis 2016). 40% of the outflow from Spain was directed to the rest of the European

Union (Izquierdo et al. 2016). Despite a number of studies in economics and political science, migration flows inside the European Union during the Great Recession could be better known. More historical research could help reach conclusions regarding the extent to which those migration flows played a role of social stabilisation in origin countries. For instance, the chapter by Barker in this volume highlights the risk of brain waste, with skilled emigrants suffering from a lack of recognition of their qualifications in other countries. This may suggest that emigration played only a limited role of social stabilisation. Conversely, more research could better highlight the politically destabilising role of those flows in destination countries, such as the United Kingdom or Germany. This review of recent macroeconomic works thus opens up a variety of historical research projects, including more qualitative studies on individual migrants' trajectories between European countries in the context of the Great Recession.

One of the most interesting ideas in this volume relates to the interaction between those migration flows within the European Union and the austerity policies conducted in the wake of the public debt crisis in Southern Europe. Bandeira, Caballé, and Vella argue that austerity policies in recession-hit countries of Southern Europe further contributed to emigration. Workers left their countries with high taxes for other European countries with more favourable tax levels. By doing so, they reinforced "the fall in internal demand and employment" in their countries of origin. The erosion of the tax base due to emigration required higher tax increases for a longer period to return to a balanced budget and reduce the public debt. Those authors consider that the Greek GDP, which fell by 25% in the Great Recession, may have fallen by 20% in the absence of emigration. The debate over the causes of the Eurozone crisis will certainly be one of the main debates that historians of the European Union will have to address in the following years and decades. Those historians will have to reflect on the suggestions of those three macroeconomists, who thus underline inherent flaws—or, at least, punitive features—in the working of the European monetary union.

Besides the economic history of migratory globalisation and the history of the European Union, the third historiographical field where macroeconomic research can provide useful input is the history of the disputes surrounding immigration in developed countries. Here, macroeconomics offers intellectual tools to address the question of the impact of immigration on local workers' wages and employment level. Migration historians have approached the disputes surrounding immigration in developed countries mostly by investigating questions of identity and racism (Chin 2017). They have not yet highlighted those disputes by investigating whether immigration could reduce natives' wages and whether this has been a significant factor in restrictive immigration policies. Insights from macroeconomics can help historians move away from a cultural focus and investigate the economic dimension of disputes. The question of the impact of immigration on local workers' wages and employment level has generated large literature in macroeconomics and is a key thread in this collection of essays. Even though historians are reluctant to engage with theoretical literature, it may be worthwhile understanding certain key macroeconomic mechanisms in order to select relevant empirical material. The essays in this volume report such mechanisms. As Llull emphasises, an increase in labour supply not compensated by a large enough increase in the supply of capital is likely to increase labour market competition and create downwards pressure on wages. As Lozej points out, even in the case of a productivity increase, immigration increases the number of searching workers with the effect of decreasing labour market tightness and preventing upwards wage pressure. Figures 8.2 and 8.3 in Lozej's chapter detail the theoretical impact of a productivity shock, with and without migration. The results show that immigration deteriorates native workers' conditions as far as unemployment, number of searching natives, and wages are concerned. Any explanation of the disputes that have surrounded immigration in developed countries since half a century has to address the role of such factors.

The essays in this volume also report empirical validation of those theoretical mechanisms. Several figures highlight that immigrants receive on average lower wages than natives, even after controlling for education and language. In 2000, in the United States, there was a 20% wage gap between immigrants and natives. In Germany, Bandeira, Caballé, and Vella report in their chapter a moderate negative effect on the welfare of low skill workers in manufacturing, following the 25% increase in immigration between 2012 and 2016 (Iftikhar and Zaharieva 2019). In

Canada, data from the 2016 census show that immigrants with foreign degrees at Bachelor level or above earned 20–25% less than natives with similar Canadian degrees. Immigrants accepting wages significantly lower than those of natives is a factor creating general downwards pressure on wages in destination countries. These findings are key for historians trying to better describe the disputes surrounding immigration in developed countries since half a century.

To sum up, in writing the economic history of migratory globalisation, the history of the European Union, and the history of the disputes surrounding immigration in developed countries, historians can learn from the macroeconomic literature. The interaction between historians and macroeconomists can also run in the other direction, as we will now turn to explain.

9.2.2 What Macroeconomists Can Learn from Historical Research

Macroeconomists too can learn from historical works and the historical approach. In the first place, historical research can help macroeconomists integrate in their models the diversity of labour market institutions. There is some divergence between theoretical expectations and empirical findings in the macroeconomic literature about migration. Results often diverge among studies. Even in this volume, Chap. 3 considers that immigration has a positive effect on most macroeconomic variables, whereas Chap. 2 takes the opposite view. D'Albis and Boubtane consider the "positive effect … linked to the human capital contribution of recent migration flows," with reference to data from 22 OECD countries covering the years 1987–2006 (Boubtane et al. 2016). According to the authors, immigrants in France "are likely to occupy jobs that are rather complementary to those of resident workers", with therefore no negative impact on the welfare of the latter. Yet, according to Llull, "a one-percentage-point increase in the share of immigrants reduces GDP per capita by 2%, employment rate by 0.89 point, … whereas it increases unemployment rate by 0.55 point." It is a common thread in this collection of essays that academic research on the effect of immigration on major labour market variables has not yet reached a consensus. As these essays report, the controversy dates back at least to the 1990 article by David Card on the impact of the Mariel Boatlift on the Miami labour market (Card 1990). George Borjas criticised Card's results in a 2003 article in which he suggested to better consider the mobility of workers inside the United States (Borjas 2003). Based on an analysis by skill group at the US level, Borjas showed that immigration in certain skill groups was correlated with lower wages. Economists have thus not agreed on the best method to measure empirically the impact of immigration on wages. Yet, from the historian's point of view, it seems that macroeconomic studies could also better consider the nature of labour market regulations.

There seems to be little focus on labour market regulations in macroeconomic research about migration. A potential explanation is the prevalence of research from the United States, where labour markets are less regulated than in Europe. Yet, when conducting empirical studies, macroeconomists could better take into consideration how the pool of immigrants that they study are already constructed by immigration policies and labour market policies. Because only certain immigrants are allowed to come and their jobs must respect certain regulations, the effect on variables such as unemployment, wages, public revenues, and expenditures may be affected. With rigid wages, immigration is unlikely to affect wages negatively. Wage rigidity may be the result of specific labour market regulations, including high minimum wages or collective agreement standards. The debates macroeconomists are grappling with are thus unlikely to find universal solutions. The impact of immigration on wages, on the size of the informal economy, or on unemployment are likely to depend on the specificity of labour market institutions in each country, including minimum wages, wage-bargaining institutions, or lack of state control. Empirical debates may end with more consensus if macroeconomists could situate their findings in historically constructed labour markets. It would mean more methodological complexity, but it would not prevent mathematical reasoning and may serve to clarify the inconclusive nature of results among studies on the macroeconomic impact of migration. Admittedly, there have already been works trying to integrate the lack of flexibility of the labour market when measuring the effect of immigration on employment and the essays in this volume refer to them

(Angrist and Kugler 2003). Yet, further work should take into account, for instance, minimum wages—major labour market institutions, likely to affect the impact immigration can have on natives' wages and employment.

If labour market institutions are likely to affect the impact of immigration on natives' wages and employment level, then macroeconomists could find out which types of potential market biases exist in selected countries by reviewing appropriate historical literature. It is likely that in a number of European countries, labour market institutions were transformed from the late 1960s onwards, with the effect of preventing immigration from creating downwards pressure on the wages of local low-skilled workers (Comte 2014, 2015). A lack of universal results on the negative impact of immigration on wages would therefore reflect less theoretical uncertainty than the variety of regulatory devices insulating local low-skilled workers from downwards market pressure. However, macroeconomists' lack of interest in the historical literature on this matter is partly justified given that the historiography on the political construction of labour market institutions remains little developed. Existing works on the development of labour laws also often exclusively focus on the struggle between labour and capital to explain labour market institutions. Alternative factors related to the increase in labour supply and the competition between immigrants and natives remain little considered to explain labour market institutions in developed countries (Penninx and Roosblad 2000; Didry 2016).

Besides the historical construction of labour markets, a second and already more developed field of historiographical research could help macroeconomists investigate more precise questions related to the impact of immigration in destination countries. Historical research can help macroeconomists find major questions that governments address about migration but are not salient in public debates. For instance, outside publicised debates, archival research shows that social security experts have generally had little interest in determining whether immigrants contribute *in general* more or less than they cost to host countries' social security systems. The questions that are more relevant to their concerns are more specific. They include, for example, whether the export of family or unemployment benefits can reduce the immigration of non-dependent, favour the emigration of unemployed immigrants, and be a profitable policy for destination countries' social security institutions (Comte 2018; Stokes 2019). More broadly, familiarity with historical literature could help macroeconomists choose their research questions in line with governments' major concerns, when they deal with or negotiate about migration.

To sum up, there are some blind spots and missed opportunities between macroeconomics and history. A range of new research questions and methods could emerge in both disciplines if scientific transfers between them became more intense. Similar considerations arise in the interaction between macroeconomics and political science, as we will now turn to explain.

9.3 Migration at the Crossroads of Political Science and Macroeconomics

Interdisciplinary integration between political science and economics has already been more substantive in terms of concepts, theories, and methods than between history and economics (Boswell and Mueser 2008). Yet, more synergy between political science and economics is crucial for "economic models of migration devoid of political dimensions and political models that fail to credit the economic underpinnings of the migration process risk being naïve and incomplete" (Freeman and Kessler 2008, p. 656). The remainder of this chapter will highlight the way the findings of this volume can be linked to the on-going political science debates about migration. It will also offer some ideas about possibilities to expand the interdisciplinary research agenda, given the changing nature of international migration in a globalising world.

9.3.1 A Short Overview of Political Science Approaches to Macroeconomics in the Field of Migration

Looking back at the evolution of the study of migration in social science, some of the earliest foundational insights regarding the regularities of international migration originate in economics, namely push-and-pull models based on neoclassical economics (King 2012, p. 13). These first systematic attempts to make sense of human mobility were focused on the unequal spatial distribution of labour and capital: in some regions labour was plentiful, capital scarce, and wages low, while in other regions the opposite was true—hence the resulting flow of workers from the former to the latter (influential works include Lewis 1954 and Kindleberger 1967). Yet, these models were criticised for being far removed from and even contradicting empirical reality, for example, by failing to explain why so few people migrated, and why comparable economies exhibited quite different rates of migration (Arango 2004). More importantly, by implying that labour migration from poor to rich countries met ostensibly mutual needs, these economic models obscured the badly balanced costs and benefits undergirding human mobility.

By contrast, political economists theorised migration as primarily demand-driven and more specifically motivated by the uneven distribution of power on a global scale—largely reflecting the persisting legacies of colonialism—which was producing and sustaining dependency and unequal development between the global "centre" and "periphery" (Sassen 1988; Wallerstein 1974). Piore (1979) further argued that specific sectors of high-income economies attracted the bulk of international labour migration. Foreign workers were allocated in the secondary tier of segmented labour markets, where the most unpleasant low-skilled, low-wage jobs concentrated, which were the least attractive to native workers.

Gradually, scholars directed more attention to the broader context of migration, stressing individuals' embeddedness in the social world (Granovetter 1985). Network theories of migration, in particular, began to highlight the role of webs of relationships and interpersonal ties in facilitating migration. Networks, it was argued, were instrumental in diffusing information and reducing transaction costs, which facilitated migration, making it a self-perpetuating process. Drawing on the work of Pierre Bourdieu, Massey et al. (1990) pioneered an understanding of migration networks as a form of social capital, convertible to other forms of capital (van Hear 2014). From a different angle but in a similar spirit, the "new economics of migration" also shifted the analytical focus from the individual towards larger social entities (households or local communities) as the relevant units of analysis. The argument was that people took migration decisions as members of a specific group rather than as isolated individuals, with the aim of not simply improving their own material circumstances, but as part of a collective strategy to diversify the sources of income and to thwart potential risk (Stark and Bloom 1985).

From the 1990s onwards, sociology, anthropology, human geography, and cultural studies began to exert profound influence on the study of migration. Employing qualitative methodology, this research focused on migrancy as a lived experience (King 2012). Building on network theories, new research also increasingly challenged the conceptualisation of migration as a unidirectional movement from A to B. The term "transmigrant" was introduced to describe the growing number of individuals, whose "lives cut across national boundaries and bring two societies into a single social field" (Glick Schiller et al. 1992, p. 1). Since these first formulations the view of mobility has further diversified to include a variety of unceasing flows of people, money, and ideas (Mau 2010).

As far as political science is concerned, it was relatively slow to show an interest in migration. The politicisation of immigration in high-income industrial societies from the 1990s onwards (Castles 2013, p. 131) directed political scientists' attention to this topic. On the one hand, it was argued that stances towards globalisation—including the particularly salient and polarising issue of immigration—were reshaping political competition in Western Europe, by leading to the formation of a new structural conflict between globalisation's "winners" and "losers" (Kriesi et al. 2006, p. 950). On the other hand, it was understood that managing the flow of people across borders had become a central element to contemporary state policy more generally. To capture this process, James Hollifield coined the term "migration state" claiming that "regulation of international migration is as important as providing for the security of the state and the economic well-being of the citizenry" (2004, p. 885). Likewise, Hein De Haas (2010, p. 227) has influentially asserted the "vital role of states" to explain the heterogeneity of migration impacts on development.

Today there exists a burgeoning literature examining the intersection of migration and politics: from the determinants of public attitudes towards migration (Hainmueller and Hiscox 2010) to voting for anti-immigrant political parties (Van Der Brug et al. 2000); from managing immigration and extending rights to immigrants (Koopmans and Michalowski 2017) to constructing diasporas and tying them to sending states (Gamlen 2006). Gradually, political scientists also incorporated migrant political agency into their research agenda, in terms of immigrants' political mobilisation and participation in receiving societies (Koopmans et al. 2005) as well as emigrants' engagement in the politics of sending states (Østergaard-Nielsen 2003).

9.3.2 International Migration: Between Markets and Politics

While the political science literature is wide-ranging and multifaceted, it is founded on a general understanding of international migration as a challenge in a globalising world made up of nation states—a challenge stemming from the profound contradiction "between market forces demanding free movement and […] political forces demanding control" (Castles 2013, p. 131; Hollifield 2004, p. 885). It is exactly this intersection between markets and politics that provides the most fertile ground for synergy between the discipline of economics and political science.

The most obvious interconnection is the common interest of the two fields in the economic and redistributive consequences of migration. Does migration impose downwards pressure on wages? Does it increase job competition? Do migrants consume more in public services than they pay in taxes? These are among the most pressing questions in many societies with high rates of net immigration. While economists have significantly improved our understanding of the impact of migration on the economic and public finances of host countries (and, more recently, also sending countries), the existing literature remains inconclusive as to the precise direction and size of these effects. Chapters 2 and 3 in this volume eloquently discuss the state of the debate and provide insights into what may explain radically different results.

The magnitude and distribution of the costs and benefits of migration matter. The perception that newcomers adversely impact domestic workers' position in receiving states' labour markets and/or that they exacerbate the erosion of welfare states by taking out more than they contribute are among the most often cited justifications for closure and protectionism. Scientific evidence can therefore provide crucial input for policy-making. At the same time, labour market competition between natives and migrants as well as the ostensible fiscal burden imposed by migrants are thought to influence migration-related attitudes, too, which is the research focus of a sizeable political economy literature. Evidence on this front, however, is as yet inconclusive. The established wisdom to date is that economic self-interest appears to have less explanatory power than social-psychological factors in explaining public attitudes towards immigration (Hainmueller and Hopkins 2014), but more research is needed to ascertain both the precise effects and the underlying causal mechanisms.

Another question is whether it makes sense to speak about the costs and benefits of migration independently of its broader context in the first place. Migration does not occur in isolation from the large-scale global structural changes in the economy but is one part of a complex puzzle. For example, trade liberalisation, automation, and the transition to a service economy can also lead to adjustment costs and the loss of jobs. Then the question that we have to ask is not only what the economic effects of migration are, but also how these effects compare to other facets of a transforming economy—in other words, what is the relative impact of migration? A research agenda combining the insights of political science and economics would be ideally placed to assess labour migration in the context of the distribution of national income and wealth, examining migration policy in tandem with other fields, most obviously, but not only, labour market policy.

A different way to achieve a similar goal, that is to ground economic analyses of migration more firmly in the socio-political context, would be to examine migration as part of broader "population politics" (Abernethy and Hardin 2000) along the lines of Chap. 3 in this volume. D'Albis and Boubtane consider that the OECD host countries they study are net beneficiaries of international migration. The reason is that working-age migrants enter ageing societies, with large intergenerational transfers. Further research could usefully integrate the analysis of patterns of fertility, internal population movements, demographic characteristics of racial and ethnic minority groups, immigration as well as emigration rates. While these aspects are often (and justifiably) examined in isolation from one another, when they enter the political sphere, they seem to raise the same compositional concerns—with regard to the categories of race and ethnicity—and the same longing for a patriarchal value-system—with regard to the category of gender (Inglehart and Norris 2016). The effort in Chap. 8 to analyse in a single framework immigration as well as emigration offers another great example of the insights such an integrated, relational approach can generate.

In Chap. 7, Bandeira, Caballé, and Vella take the point of view of the economies that are left behind. This is an important corrective to the tendency in both economics and political science to focus predominantly on the issues raised by migration in receiving states. Yet, as Alejandro Portes rightly observes: "Whether positive or negative, migration-induced social change in sending countries and regions tends to be more far-reaching than in receiving societies" (2010, p. 1555). Focusing on cases when emigration yields unfavourable effects, Gunnar Myrdal has influentially theorised the principle of cumulative causation. Emigration, in this reading, is a self-reinforcing mechanism that deprives less developed societies of precious labour force. They become increasingly dependent on and dominated by the developed ones, which perpetuate further emigration (King 2012, p. 17).

Indeed, large-scale emigration (often in combination with adverse demography) is increasingly recognised as a problem even in places where freedom of movement was celebrated before, like in Southern and Eastern European Union member states. Mirroring the literature on the politicisation of immigration, there is now increased scholarly interest in the politicisation of *emigration* in sending states. While advanced academic research on this topic is scarce, a recent public opinion survey conducted in 14 European countries shows that people in Romania, Hungary, Spain,

Italy, Poland, and Greece worry about emigration more than about immigration; in some countries, a majority of respondents would even support the introduction of emigration controls (Rice-Oxley and Rankin 2019). Governments have begun to react to public pressure, for instance, by devising policy proposals that incentivise return, such as Portugal's "Regressar" programme, which promises to cut in half returnees' income tax bills for five years following repatriation, as well as covering (part of) relocation costs and helping to (re-)register professional qualifications (The Economist 2019).

The recent academic interest in what happens to the immobile mirrors a broader shift in emphasis within the study of migration. As Nicholas van Hear remarks, part of the existing literature "perhaps celebrated mobility uncritically, to the neglect of immobility as its counterpart" (2014, p. 109). Focusing on the European Union in particular it has been argued that EU-citizenship, by empowering "a relatively small constituency of mobile citizens, at the (perceived) expenses of large majorities of non-mobile natives" produces political asymmetries (Ferrera 2019, p. 186). Indicating the political relevance of immobility, an analysis published in the *Financial Times* regarding the British referendum to exit the EU found a surprisingly strong correlation between the "Leave" vote and not having a passport, the third most important characteristic after education and occupation (Burn-Murdoch 2016).

At the same time, focusing on native populations' reactions to immigration-related change—such as the transformation of labour markets or cultural and demographic shifts—should not obscure the considerable costs borne by migrants and their families (Meardi et al. 2012). Doubtlessly, migration can significantly improve people's life chances, but migrants can face the stigma associated with working in the secondary tiers of dual labour markets; even the high-skilled experience the depreciation of their qualifications (Chap. 4 in this volume analysing brain waste is a case in point).

Moreover, migrants are often pushed into the informal economy for lack of legal status. Migrant "illegality" is among the most vociferously argued political issues, and immigration is often linked to criminality in the political discourse, cast as a danger to public order, and even as an existential threat (Huysmans 2000). As Kyrkopoulou and Palivos show, outcomes depend on political decisions: state policy emerges as a key variable, with amnesty reducing the size of the informal sector as well as the overall unemployment rate according to the authors. But the role of state policy does not stop there; it includes forms of influence that disfigure labour markets in ways that are concealed from the larger public. For example, Portuguese policy towards the labour market and immigration in the 1990s and early 2000s followed a "covert expansive approach towards irregular immigration that enhanced the fulfilment of the demand for unskilled labour" (Carvalho 2018, p. 507). The appreciation of such hidden agendas or, for that matter, policy implementation gaps and failures, constitutes another fruitful avenue for collaboration between political scientists and economists.

9.3.3 A Future Interdisciplinary Research Agenda on Migration

The free movement of goods, services, and capital in the global economy inevitably implicates the physical movement of persons across international borders. Economics is uniquely positioned in rendering these processes and their effects measurable, while political science can, in turn, elucidate the power dynamics that underlie them. That being said, both disciplines will have to adapt to the changing context of human mobility, including such broad and complex transformations as a transition to post-Fordist production, increasing social inequality, and climate change (Delgado Wise and Márquez Covarrubias 2012, p. 96).

What should an interdisciplinary research agenda examining twenty-first century migration look like? First, it should be global in its reach, drawing its cases from all the world regions. The tendency to focus on high-income economies that are mainly situated on the receiving end of international migration is still with us, and this volume is no exception, with its exclusive focus on OECD countries.

Second, migration could be fruitfully recast as a matter not only of *mobility* but also *immobility*. The realisation that the vast majority of people do not migrate, even when they would have incentives to do so, is not new (Malmberg 1997). However, in an age of ever-increasing physical (and virtual) mobility, it does make sense to ask whether norms in some places are beginning to shift and whether sedentarism is increasingly becoming the exception rather than the rule. If this is so, how may this reconfiguration impact the economy, politics and society?

Third, we need more sophisticated ways to understand radically new mobility forms. The borders of nation-states become progressively more porous and people's movements more complex in a way that the conventional definition of international migration cannot fully capture. The European single market, for example, is unique in that it has curtailed the prerogative of nation-states to categorise intra-EU movers as international migrants in the conventional sense (Favell 2007). The increasing porousness of borders urges researchers to reflect on and question, more broadly, whether the nation-state constitutes the appropriate spatial unit of analysis in the first place. The tendency to assume that "the nation/state/society is the natural social and political form of the modern world" (Wimmer and Glick Schiller 2003, p. 301) has persisted across many disciplinary fields despite long-standing criticism. To be sure, as Rogers Brubaker warns, "the nation-state remains the decisive locus of membership even in a globalizing world; struggles over belonging in and to the nation-state remain the most consequential forms of membership politics" (2010, p. 77). Nonetheless, nation-states are, in the end, political constructions and so there is still merit in carefully exploring the relevance of different scales of analysis.

Lastly, an interdisciplinary agenda tackling contemporary international migration should strive to transcend not only disciplinary boundaries but also the relative isolation of academic knowledge-production from both public policy and public discourse. Regardless of academic sub-discipline, we all need to find ways to communicate advances in migration research effectively and constructively.

9.4 Conclusion

In this chapter, we hope to have provided macroeconomists, historians, and political scientists with some ideas as to how to benefit from interdisciplinary transfers. These include transfers of information and of methodological instruments, but also insights into the design of research questions. We remain convinced that social scientists in the field of migration will find their most innovative ideas to highlight current challenges at the crossroads of different disciplines.

References

Abernethy, Virginia, and Garrett Hardin. 2000. *Population Politics*. New York: Routledge.

Albis, Hippolyte (d'), Ekrame Boubtane, and Dramane Coulibaly. 2019. "Immigration and Public Finances in OECD Countries," *Journal of Economic Dynamics and Control* 99: 116–151.

Angrist, Joshua D., and Adriana Kugler. 2003. "Protective or Counter-Productive? Labour Market Institutions and the Effect of Immigration on EU Natives." *Economic Journal*, 113: 302–331.

Arango, Joaquin. 2004. "Theories of International Migration." In *International Migration and the New Millennium: Global Movement and Settlement*. Edited by Danièle Joly, 15–36. Aldershot: Ashgate.

Borjas, George J. 2003. "The Labor Demand Curve Is Downward Sloping: Reexamining the Impact of Immigration on the Labor Market." *The Quarterly Journal of Economics* 118(4): 1335–74.

Boswell, Christina, and Peter R. Mueser. 2008. "Introduction: Economics and Interdisciplinary Approaches in Migration Research." *Journal of Ethnic and Migration Studies* 34(4): 519–529.

Boubtane, Ekrame, Jean-Christophe Dumont, and Christophe Rault. 2016. "Immigration and economic growth in the OECD countries 1986–2006," *Oxford Economic Papers* 62: 340–360.

Brubaker, Rogers. 2010. "Migration, Membership, and the Modern Nation-State: Internal and External Dimensions of the Politics of Belonging." *Journal of Interdisciplinary History* 41(1):61–78.

Burn-Murdoch, John. 2016. "Brexit: voter turnout by age." *Financial Times*, June 24. https://www.ft.com/content/1ce1a720-ce94-3c32-a689-8d2356388a1f. Accessed on 10 December 2019.

Card, David E. 1990. "The Impact of the Mariel Boatlift on the Miami Labor Market." *Industrial and Labor Relations Review*, 43: 245–257.

Carvalho, João. 2018. "'Bringing the state back in': A political economy analysis of Portuguese immigration policy." *Mediterranean Politics* 23(4):501–521.

Castles, Stephen. 2013. “The Forces Driving Global Migration.” *Journal of Intercultural Studies* 34(2):122–140.
Chin, Rita. 2017. *The Crisis of Multiculturalism in Europe: A History*. Princeton, NJ: Princeton University Press.
Comte, Emmanuel (ed.) 2014. Les Régimes de l’emploi en Europe méditerranéenne depuis les années 1960. *Les Cahiers Sirice* (11).
Comte, Emmanuel. 2015. “The Origins of the May 1968 Labour Crisis in France.” *Max Weber Programme Red Number Series*. San Domenico di Fiesole: European University Institute.
Comte, Emmanuel. 2018. *The History of the European Migration Regime: Germany’s Strategic Hegemony*. Abingdon, Oxon, OX; New York, NY: Routledge.
De Haas, Hein. 2010. “Migration and Development: A Theoretical Perspective.” *International Migration Review* 44:227–264.
Delgado Wise, Raúl, and Humberto Márquez Covarrubias. 2012. “Contemporary migration seen from the perspective of political economy: theoretical and methodological elements.” In *Handbook of Research Methods in Migration*, edited by Carlos Vargas-Silva, 92–116. Cheltenham; Northampton: Edward Elgar.
Didry, Claude. 2016. *L’Institution du travail: Droit et salariat dans l’histoire*. Paris: La Dispute.
Favell, Adrian. 2007. “Rebooting migration theory: Interdisciplinarity, globality and postdisciplinarity in migration studies.” In *Migration Theory: Talking Across Disciplines* (2nd ed.), edited by Caroline Brettell and James Hollifield, 259–27. London: Routledge.
Ferrera, Maurizio. 2019. “EU Citizenship Needs a Stronger Social Dimension and Soft Duties.” In *Debating European Citizenship*, edited by Rainer Bauböck, 181–198. Cham: Springer.
Freeman, Gary P., and Alan K. Kessler. 2008. “Political Economy and Migration Policy.” *Journal of Ethnic and Migration Studies* 34(4): 655–678.
Gamlen, Alen. 2006. “Diaspora Engagement Policies: What are they, and what kinds of states use them?” *Working Paper No. 32*, University of Oxford, 1–31.
Glick Schiller, Nina, Linda Basch, and Cristina Blanc-Szanton. 1992. “Transnationalism: A New Analytic Framework for Understanding Migration.” *Annals of the New York Academy of Sciences*, 645(1):1–24.
Granovetter, Mark. 1985. “Economic Action and Social Structure: The Problem of Embeddedness.” *American Journal of Sociology* 91:481–510.

Hainmueller, Jens, and Michael Hiscox. 2010. "Attitudes toward Highly Skilled and Low-skilled Immigration: Evidence from a Survey Experiment." *American Political Science Review* 104(1):61–84.

Hainmueller, Jens, and Daniel J. Hopkins. 2014. "Public Attitudes Toward Immigration." *Annual Review of Political Science* 17:225–49.

Hollifield, James F. 2004. "The Emerging Migration State." *International Migration Review* 38(3): 885–912.

Huysmans, Jef. 2000. "The European Union and the Securitization of Migration." *Journal of Common Market Studies* 38: 751–777.

Iftikhar, Zainab, and Anna Zaharieva. 2019. "General equilibrium effects of immigration in Germany: Search and matching approach," *Review of Economic Dynamics* 31: 245–276.

Inglehart, Ronald F., and Pippa Norris. 2016. "Trump, Brexit, and the Rise of Populism: Economic Have-Nots and Cultural Backlash." *Working Paper Series 16–026*, Harvard University, John F. Kennedy School of Government.

Izquierdo, Mario, Juan Jimeno, and Aitor Lacuesta. 2016. "Spain: from massive immigration to vast emigration?" *IZA Journal of Migration* 5(10).

Kindleberger, Charles Poor. 1967. *Europe's Postwar Growth: The Role of Labor Supply*. Cambridge: Harvard University Press; London: Oxford University Press.

King, Russel. 2012. "Theories and Typologies of Migration: An Overview and A Primer." *Willy Brandt Series of Working Papers in International Migration and Ethnic Relations 3/12*, Malmö Institute for Studies of Migration, Diversity and Welfare, Malmö University.

Koopmans, Ruud, and Ines Michalowski. 2017. "Why Do States Extend Rights to Immigrants? Institutional Settings and Historical Legacies Across 44 Countries Worldwide." *Comparative Political Studies 50*(1): 41–74.

Koopmans, Ruud, Paul Statham, Marco Giugni, and Florence Passy. 2005. *Contested Citizenship: Immigration and Cultural Diversity in Europe*. Minneapolis: University of Minnesota Press.

Kriesi, Hanspeter, Edgar Grande, Romain Lachat, Martin Dolezal, Simon Bornschier, and Timotheos Frey. 2006. "Globalization and the transformation of the national political space: Six European countries compared." *European Journal of Political Research* 45: 921–956.

Labrianidis, Lois, and Manolis Pratsinakis. 2016. *Greece's new emigration at times of crisis*. Technical report, Hellenic Observatory, LSE.

Lewis, W. Arthur. 1954. "Economic Development with Unlimited Supplies of Labour." *Manchester School of Economic and Social Studies* 22:139–191.

Malmberg, Gunnar, 1997. "Time and Space in International Migration." In *International Migration, Immobility and Development. A Multidisciplinary View*, edited by Tomas Hammar, Grete Brochmann, Kristof Tamas, and Thomas Faist, 21–48. Oxford: Berg Publishers.

Massey, Douglas S., Rafael Alarcon, Jorge Durand, and Humberto González (1990), *Return to the Aztlan: The Social Process of International Migration from Western Mexico*. Berkeley, CA: University of California Press.

Mau, Steffen. 2010. *Social Transnationalism. Lifeworlds Beyond the Nation-State*. London: Routledge.

Meardi, Guglielmo, Antonio Martín and Mariona Lozano Riera. 2012. "Constructing Uncertainty: Unions and Migrant Labour in Construction in Spain and the UK." *Journal of Industrial Relations* 54(1): 5–21.

Østergaard-Nielsen, Eva. 2003. "The Politics of Migrants' Transnational Political Practices." *International Migration Review* 37:760–786.

Piore, Michael. 1979. *Birds of Passage: Migrant Labor and Industrial Societies*. Cambridge; New York: Cambridge University Press.

Portes, Alejandro. 2010. "Migration and Social Change: Some Conceptual Reflections." *Journal of Ethnic and Migration Studies* 36(10):1537–1563.

Radu, Dragos. 2008. "Social Interactions in Economic Models of Migration: A Review and Appraisal." *Journal of Ethnic and Migration Studies* 34(4):531–548.

Rice-Oxley, Mark and Jennifer Rankin. 2019. "Europe's south and east worry more about emigration than immigration – poll." *The Guardian*, April 1. https://www.theguardian.com/world/2019/apr/01/europe-south-and-east-worry-more-about-emigration-than-immigration-poll. Accessed on 10 December 2019.

Sassen, Saskia. 1988. *The Mobility of Labor and Capital*. New York: Cambridge University Press.

Schneider, Friedrich, Andreas Buehn, and Claudio Montenegro. 2010. "New Estimates for the Shadow Economies all over the World." *International Economic Journal* 24(4): 443–461.

Stark, Oded, and David E. Bloom. 1985. "The New Economics of Labour Migration." *American Economic Review* 75(2):173–178.

Stokes, Lauren. 2019. "'An Invasion of Guest Worker Children': Welfare Reform and the Stigmatisation of Family Migration in West Germany." *Contemporary European History* 28(3): 372–389.

The Economist. 2019. "Portugal tries to lure emigrants back," 1 August, https://www.economist.com/finance-and-economics/2019/08/01/portugal-tries-to-lure-emigrants-back. Accessed on 10 December 2019.

Trade Unions, Immigration, and Immigrants in Europe, 1960–1993: A Comparative Study of the Attitudes and Actions of Trade Unions in Seven West European Countries, edited by Rinus Penninx and Judith Roosblad. 2000. New York; Oxford: Berghahn Books.

United Nations, Department of Economic and Social Affairs, Population Division. 2017. International Migrant Stock: The 2017 Revision, https://www.un.org/en/development/desa/population/migration/data/estimates2017/estimates17.asp. Accessed on 30 May 2019.

Van Der Brug, Wouter, Meindert Fennema, and Jean Tillie. 2000. "Anti-immigrant Parties in Europe: Ideological or Protest Vote?" *European Journal of Political Research* 37: 77–102.

Van Hear, Nicholas. 2014. "Reconsidering Migration and Class." *International Migration Review* 48: 100–121.

Wallerstein, Immanuel. 1974. *The Modern World-System: Capitalist Agriculture and the Origins of the European World-Economy in the Sixteenth Century*. New York: Academic Press.

Wimmer, Adreas, and Nina Glick Schiller. 2003. "Methodological Nationalism, the Social Sciences, and the Study of Migration: An Essay in Historical Epistemology." *The International Migration Review* 37(3): 576–610.

Index[1]

A

B

C

[1] Note: Page numbers followed by 'n' refer to notes.

E. Vella et al. (eds.), *Understanding Migration with Macroeconomics*,
https://doi.org/10.1007/978-3-030-40981-4

The manufacturer's authorised representative in the EU is Springer
Nature Customer Service Centre GmbH, Europaplatz 3, 69115 Heidelberg,
Germany. If you have any concerns regarding our products, please
contact ProductSafety@springernature.com

Printed and bound by CPI Group (UK) Ltd, Croydon, CR0 4YY
30/09/2026
02225645-0007